ELEMENTS OF

Literature

THIRD COURSE

LANGUAGE AND WRITING
SKILLS WORKSHEETS

HOLT, RINEHART AND WINSTON
Harcourt Brace & Company

Austin • New York • Orlando • Atlanta • San Francisco • Boston • Dallas • Toronto • London

To the Teacher

The worksheets in this booklet cover a comprehensive range of writing skills instruction and practice. Each chapter of the booklet culminates in a review activity. Worksheets fall into the following categories:

- *Writer's Quick Reference*—These worksheets provide explanations of common usage problems, followed by practice items.
- *Grammar and Usage*—This section is subdivided into chapters on parts of speech; agreement; and verb, pronoun, and modifier usage. The worksheets provide explanation, examples, and activities on key grammar concepts.
- *Phrases, Clauses, Sentences*—The worksheets in this section provide instruction and practice in topics ranging from uses of phrases to effective sentence writing.
- *Mechanics*—These worksheets provide explanations, examples, and practice items on capital letters, punctuation, and spelling and vocabulary.
- *Composition*—The worksheets in this section reinforce students' understanding of the writing process. One chapter focuses on skills related to paragraph and composition structure. Another helps students develop the skills necessary to create a research paper.
- *Resources*—This section of the booklet provides lessons in the use of media resources—including reference materials, newspapers, and dictionaries—and in the conventions of letter writing and manuscript preparation.

To facilitate the integration of language and literature instruction, these **Language and Writing Skills Worksheets** are cross-referenced in the *Annotated Teacher's Edition* of **Elements of Literature: Third Course.**

1997 Reprint by Holt, Rinehart and Winston, Inc.
Copyright © 1995 by Holt, Rinehart and Winston, Inc.

Portions of this work were published in previous editions.

Printed in the United States of America

ISBN 0-03-095730-3

2 3 4 5 6 082 99 98 97 96

Table of Contents

WRITER'S QUICK REFERENCE

GRAMMAR AND USAGE

CHAPTER 1   THE PARTS OF SPEECH

CHAPTER 2   AGREEMENT

CHAPTER 3 USING VERBS CORRECTLY

CHAPTER 4 USING PRONOUNS

CHAPTER 5 USING MODIFIERS

PHRASES, CLAUSES, SENTENCES

CHAPTER 6 PHRASES

CHAPTER 7 CLAUSES

CHAPTER 8 SENTENCE STRUCTURE

CHAPTER 9 WRITING COMPLETE SENTENCES

CHAPTER 10 WRITING EFFECTIVE SENTENCES

Mechanics

CHAPTER 11 CAPITALIZATION

CHAPTER 12 PUNCTUATION

CHAPTER 13 PUNCTUATION

CHAPTER 14 PUNCTUATION

CHAPTER 15 SPELLING AND VOCABULARY

COMPOSITION

CHAPTER 16 THE WRITING PROCESS

CHAPTER 17 PARAGRAPH AND COMPOSITION STRUCTURE

CHAPTER 18 THE RESEARCH PAPER

RESOURCES

Name _____ Date _____ Class _____

Common Usage Problems A

The following guidelines will help you avoid errors in usage.

accept, except   *Accept* is a verb meaning "to receive." *Except* may be either a verb meaning "to leave out" or a preposition meaning "excluding."

advice, advise   *Advice* is a noun meaning "suggestion about what to do." *Advise* is a verb meaning "to offer a suggestion, to recommend."

affect, effect   *Affect* is a verb meaning "to influence." As a verb, *effect* means "to accomplish." As a noun, *effect* means "the result [of an action]."

ain't   Avoid this word in formal speaking and in all writing other than dialogue; it is nonstandard English.

all ready, already   *All ready* means "all prepared." *Already* is an adverb meaning "by a certain time" or "even now."

all together, altogether   *All together* means "everyone in the same place." *Altogether* is an adverb meaning "entirely."

Exercise   Underline the word or expression in parentheses that is correct according to standard usage.

> EXAMPLE: 1. Everyone seemed greatly (<u>affected</u>, effected) by her speech on animal rights.

1. The (affects, effects) of lasers on surgical procedures have been remarkable.

2. Ms. Yu (accepted, excepted) my excuse for being late.

3. This weather (ain't, isn't) ordinary.

4. A lawyer can (advice, advise) you of your rights.

5. Are you (all ready, already) to go to the theater?

6. Sarah can probably give you some good (advice, advise) about what to wear to the interview.

7. The luau has (all ready, already) started, but we can still get seats.

8. The house is completed (accept, except) for interior painting.

9. If we are finally (all together, altogether), we can go.

10. There is much discussion about whether the full moon (affects, effects) human behavior.

Writer's Quick Reference

 **WORKSHEET 2** ## Common Usage Problems B

The following guidelines will help you avoid errors in usage.

and etc.   The abbreviation for the Latin phrase *et cetera,* meaning "and other things," is *etc.* Thus, do not use *and* with *etc.*

anyways, anywheres   Use these words (and others like them, such as *everywheres, nowheres,* and *somewheres*) without the final *s.*

at   Do not use *at* after *where.*

bad, badly   *Bad* is an adjective. *Badly* is an adverb. In standard English, only the adjective form, *bad,* should follow a linking verb (such as *feel, see, hear, taste,* or *smell*) or a form of the verb *be.*

being as, being that   Use *since* or *because* instead of these expressions.

beside, besides   *Beside* is a preposition that means "by the side of" or "next to." As a preposition, *besides* means "in addition to" or "other than." As an adverb, *besides* means "moreover."

between, among   Use *between* when referring to two things at a time, even though they may be part of a group consisting of more than two. (*There are no gas stations* between *here and Pottsville.*) Use *among* when referring to all members of a group rather than to separate individuals in a group. (*A debate broke out* among *the class members.*)

Exercise   Circle the ten errors in standard English usage in the following paragraph.

> EXAMPLE: [1] (Being as) you like dinosaurs, let me tell you about Paul Sereno.

[1] The area around San Juan, Argentina, is one of the best places anywheres to find dinosaur fossils. [2] In 1988, Paul Sereno's discovery there broke a previous record between fossil hunters for the oldest dinosaur remains. [3] On an expedition from the University of Chicago, where he was a biologist at, Sereno found the oldest dinosaur fossils ever unearthed up to that time. [4] Beside being extremely old, the 230-million-year-old skeleton was amazingly complete except for the hind limbs. [5] The skeleton may look badly to us, but it sure looks great to dinosaur experts. [6] Sereno and his herrerasaurus have affected the work of biologists and dinosaur-lovers everywheres. [7] Being that you have studied about dinosaur discoveries in magazines, newspapers, books, and etc., you will know that Sereno's find is unusual. [8] Wouldn't you have liked to be standing besides Sereno during his big discovery? [9] Between all the people I know, you would most appreciate Sereno's work.

Name _____ Date _____ Class _____

Common Usage Problems C

The following guidelines will help you avoid errors in usage.

borrow, lend   *Borrow* means "to take [something] temporarily." *Lend* means "to give [something] temporarily."

bring, take   *Bring* means "to come carrying something." *Take* means "to go carrying something."

bust, busted   Avoid using these words as verbs. Use a form of either *burst* or *break*, depending on the meaning.

capital, capitol   As a noun, *capital* means "center of government" or "wealth." As an adjective, it means "punishable by death," "of major importance," or "uppercase." *Capitol* is a noun meaning "a building in which a legislature meets" (capitalized when referring to a building for a national legislature).

coarse, course   *Coarse* is an adjective meaning "rough" or "crude." *Course* is a noun meaning "a path of action," "a unit of study," "a track or way," or "one part of a meal." With *of, course* means "naturally" or "certainly."

complement, compliment   As a noun, *complement* means "something that makes whole or complete." As a verb, it means "to make whole or complete." As a noun, *compliment* means "praise." As a verb, it means "to express praise."

Exercise   Underline the word in parentheses that is correct according to standard usage.

EXAMPLE: 1. The hot-water boiler (busted, <u>burst</u>) and flooded the cellar.

1. Liza promised to (bring, take) me the new CD.

2. I think that fresh fruit would (complement, compliment) the dinner nicely.

3. Will you (borrow, lend) me your new Mozart CD?

4. That (coarse, course) in African art history is extremely interesting.

5. My parents need more (capital, capitol) to buy the forty acres.

6. What is the (capital, capitol) of Wyoming?

7. Please (bring, take) this note to the manager's office.

8. While in Austin, we toured the inside of the (capital, capitol).

9. Gloria received many (complements, compliments) on her singing.

10. Did the piñata (bust, burst) when it hit the floor?

Name _____ Date _____ Class _____

WORKSHEET 4   *Common Usage Problems D*

The following guidelines will help you avoid errors in usage.

consul, council, counsel   *Consul* is a noun meaning "a representative of a foreign country." *Council* is a noun meaning "a group called together to accomplish a job." As a noun, *counsel* means "advice." As a verb, it means "to give advice."

councilor, counselor   A *councilor* is a member of a council. A *counselor* is a person who gives advice.

des´ert, desert´, dessert´   *Des´ert* is a noun meaning "a dry region." *Desert´* is a verb meaning "to leave or abandon." *Dessert´* is a noun meaning "the final course of a meal."

discover, invent   *Discover* means "to be the first to find, see, or learn about something that already exists." *Invent* means "to be the first to do or make something."

done   *Done* is the past participle of *do*. Avoid using *done* for *did*, which is the past form of *do* and which does not require an auxiliary verb. When *done* is used as an adjective, it does not require an auxiliary verb.

don't, doesn't   *Don't* is the contraction of *do not*. *Doesn't* is the contraction of *does not*. Use *doesn't*, not *don't*, with *he, she, it, this,* and singular nouns.

Exercise   Underline the word in parentheses that is correct according to standard usage.

      EXAMPLE: 1. (Don't, <u>Doesn't</u>) Otis know that we're planning to leave?

1. Whoever (discovered, invented) the escalator must have been ingenious.

2. When the meeting was over, one (councilor, counselor) volunteered to write up the council's report.

3. Any car that crosses the (dessert, desert) should carry extra water.

4. The guide identified the man as the Italian (counsel, consul).

5. Our teacher (doesn't, don't) require us to type our reports.

6. Who (discovered, invented) what makes fireflies glow?

7. Years after the war ended, a soldier who had refused to (desert, dessert) his post was discovered.

8. The children (done, did) their chores and then went out to play.

9. I asked the guidance (councilor, counselor) to help me choose courses.

10. We make a frozen (dessert, desert) with bananas and cherry juice.

Name _____ Date _____ Class _____

Common Usage Problems E

The following guidelines will help you avoid errors in usage.

double negative A double negative is the use of two negative words when one is enough. Common negative words include *hardly, neither, never, no, none, no one, not, nothing, nowhere,* and *scarcely.*

That answer doesn't make any [*not* no] sense.

I can [*not* can't] hardly turn the key in the lock.

double subject Do not use an unnecessary pronoun (*he, she, it, they*) after the subject of a clause or a sentence. This error is called the double subject.

emigrate, immigrate *Emigrate* means "to leave a country or a region to settle elsewhere." *Immigrate* means "to come into a country or a region to settle there."

fewer, less *Fewer* tells "how many"; it is used with plural nouns. *Less* tells "how much"; it is used with singular nouns.

formally, formerly *Formally* means "properly; according to strict rules." *Formerly* means "previously" or "in the past."

Exercise A: Revising Rewrite each sentence correctly on the line provided.

EXAMPLE: 1. What you're saying doesn't make no sense to me.
What you're saying doesn't make any sense to me.

1. Rachel didn't say nothing to him.

   _____

2. There wasn't scarcely enough water in the pond to keep the fish alive.

   _____

3. I haven't borrowed no books from the library this week.

   _____

4. Laura couldn't hardly make herself heard.

   _____

5. Hasn't no one in the class read *And Now Miguel*?

   _____

Exercise B Underline the correct word in each sentence below.

1. Must we dress (formally, formerly) for the awards dinner?

2. Sean's family (emigrated, immigrated) to this country from Ireland.

3. Americans today are using (fewer, less) salt than they did years ago.

4. (Mr. Evans, Mr. Evans he) said I should take French next year.

QUICK REFERENCE

Writer's Quick Reference

WORKSHEET 6   *Common Usage Problems F*

The following guidelines will help you avoid errors in usage.

good, well   *Good* is an adjective. *Well* may be used as an adjective or an adverb. Never use *good* to modify a verb; instead, use *well* as an adverb meaning "capably" or "satisfactorily."

had ought, hadn't ought   Unlike other verbs, *ought* is not used with *had*.

hisself, theirselves   In formal situations, do not use these words for *himself* and *themselves*.

imply, infer   *Imply* means "to suggest indirectly." *Infer* means "to interpret" or "to draw a conclusion [from a remark or an action]."

its, it's   *Its* is the possessive form of *it*. *It's* is the contraction of *it is* or *it has*.

kind of, sort of   Avoid using these terms in formal situations. Instead, use *somewhat* or *rather*.

kind of a, sort of a   In formal situations, omit the *a*.

Exercise   Underline the word or expression in parentheses that is correct according to standard usage.

> EXAMPLE: 1. North Carolina and (it's, <u>its</u>) neighbor, South Carolina, were among the thirteen original states.

1. Former Senator S. I. Hayakawa of California plays several instruments (good, well).

2. I did not mean to (imply, infer) that your speech was ineffective.

3. What (kind of a, kind of) notebook do you like to use?

4. The sparrow flew back to (it's, its) nest.

5. My parents were (sort of, somewhat) upset about our party plans.

6. From John's report, I (implied, inferred) that he liked the book.

7. Damon cut (hisself, himself) when he sharpened the kitchen knives.

8. (It's, Its) a beautiful day for a hike, don't you think?

9. I usually do (good, well) on that kind of test.

10. I think Greta (had ought, ought) to let me have those jeans.

Writer's Quick Reference

Common Usage Problems G

The following guidelines will help you avoid errors in usage.

kind(s), sort(s), type(s) Use *this* or *that* with the singular form of each of these nouns. Use *these* or *those* with the plural form.

learn, teach *Learn* means "to acquire knowledge." *Teach* means "to instruct" or "to show how."

leave, let *Leave* means "to go away" or "to depart from." *Let* means "to allow" or "to permit." Avoid using *leave* for *let*.

like, as In formal English, use *like* to introduce a prepositional phrase, and use *as* to introduce a subordinate clause.

of *Of* is a preposition. Do not use *of* in place of *have* after verbs such as *could*, *should*, *would*, *might*, *must*, and *ought* [*to*]. Do not use *had of* for *had*. Do not use *of* after prepositions such as *inside*, *off*, or *outside*.

principal, principle As a noun, *principal* means "the head of a school." As an adjective, it means "main or most important." *Principle* is a noun meaning "a rule of conduct" or "a general truth."

Exercise In each sentence of the following paragraph, underline the correct word or words in parentheses.

> EXAMPLE: [1] The (<u>principal</u>, principle) suggested that I write my report on the Chinese inventions of paper and printing.

[1] (Leave, Let) me tell you that the (principal, principle) part of my report will be on papermaking. [2] Ms. Franks (learned, taught) me that the Chinese invented paper as we know it early in the second century A.D.; I would have been amazed if I (had of, had) seen them make paper by soaking, drying, and flattening mulberry bark. [3] By A.D. 200, the Chinese were using paper for writing and painting, (like, as) they do today. [4] The Chinese also used paper for (this, these) kinds of things: umbrellas, fans, and lanterns. [5] You could have knocked me (off of, off) my chair when I learned that the Chinese were printing by A.D. 600—some eight hundred years before the invention of modern printing in Germany.

QUICK REFERENCE

Writer's Quick Reference

WORKSHEET 8   *Common Usage Problems H*

The following guidelines will help you avoid errors in usage.

quiet, quit, quite   *Quiet* is an adjective meaning "silent; still." *Quit* is a verb meaning "to stop." *Quite* is an adverb meaning "completely; rather; very."

slow, slowly   *Slow* is an adjective. *Slowly* is an adverb.

some, somewhat   In formal situations, do not use *some* to mean "to some extent." Instead, use *somewhat*.

stationary, stationery   *Stationary* is an adjective meaning "in a fixed position." *Stationery* is a noun meaning "writing paper."

than, then   *Than* is a conjunction used in comparisons. *Then* is an adverb meaning "at that time" or "next."

their, there, they're   *Their* is a possessive form of the pronoun *they*. As an adverb, *there* means "at that place." As an expletive, it is used to begin a sentence. *They're* is the contraction of *they are*.

theirs, there's   *Theirs* is a possessive form of the pronoun *they*. *There's* is the contraction for *there is*.

Exercise   In each sentence of the following paragraph, underline the correct word or contraction in parentheses.

> EXAMPLE: [1] Some writers are (quiet, <u>quite</u>) talented in nonliterary ways.

[1] Dorothy Sayers, John Dos Passos, and Vladimir Nabokov are best known for (their, they're) novels. [2] (Theirs, There's) no doubt that they were talented writers. [3] However, these authors had more (than, then) one talent. [4] Sayers, whose detective stories feature Lord Peter Wimsey, a character who is (quiet, quite) sophisticated, was an expert on medieval history. [5] Dos Passos wrote many novels in the early and mid-1900s, and his work was popular (then, than). [6] However, interest in his work has decreased (some, somewhat). [7] Many modern readers may think his novels are (slow, slowly). [8] (There, They're) is something I've heard about Dos Passos that I find intriguing—he once invented a bubble-blowing toy gun. [9] Nabokov was a writer of serious novels, but he also was (quit, quite) an authority on butterflies. [10] He published numerous articles on these busy but (quite, quiet) insects.

Writer's Quick Reference

 **Common Usage Problems I**

The following guidelines will help you avoid errors in usage.

them   *Them* should not be used as an adjective. Use *those*.

this here, that there   The words *here* and *there* are unnecessary after *this* and *that*.

to, too, two   *To* is used as a preposition or as the sign of the infinitive form of a verb. *Too* is an adverb meaning "also" or "overly." As an adjective, *two* means "totaling one plus one." As a noun, it means "the number between one and three."

try and   Use *try to,* not *try and*.

way, ways   Use *way,* not *ways,* in referring to a distance.

weak, week   *Weak* is an adjective meaning "feeble" or "lacking force; not strong." *Week* is a noun meaning "seven days."

weather, whether   *Weather* is a noun meaning "climate conditions outdoors." *Whether* is a conjunction used (with *or*) to introduce alternatives. *Whether* is also used (with or without *or*) in indirect questions and in expressions of doubt.

Exercise   Underline the word or expression in parentheses that is correct according to standard usage.

EXAMPLE: 1. (Them, <u>Those</u>) dogs have impressive pedigrees.

1. It is only a short (way, ways) to the video store.

2. I wish that (this, this here) radio would work.

3. Why don't you (try and, try to) fix it for me?

4. The (whether, weather) in the Caribbean does not change as dramatically as it does in New England.

5. Quick, give me (them, those) papers!

6. Last year I spent an entire (weak, week) in San Juan.

7. Most days, we walked (too, to) the old, historic part of the city.

8. My legs feel very (week, weak) after an afternoon of scuba diving.

9. (That, That there) motorbike belongs to my cousin.

10. We saw (two, too) famous major-league baseball players outside the stadium in Baltimore.

QUICK REFERENCE

Writer's Quick Reference

WORKSHEET 10   *Common Usage Problems J*

The following guidelines will help you avoid errors in usage.

what   Use *that*, not *what*, to introduce an adjective clause.

when, where   Do not use *when* or *where* to begin a definition.

where, when   Do not use *where* or *when* for *that*.

who, which, that   The relative pronoun *who* refers to persons only; *which* refers to things only; *that* may refer to either persons or things.

who's, whose   *Who's* is the contraction of *who is* or *who has*. *Whose* is the possessive form of *who*.

without, unless   Do not use the preposition *without* in place of the conjunction *unless*.

your, you're   *Your* is a possessive form of *you*. *You're* is the contraction of *you are*.

Exercise   Underline the word or expression in parentheses that is correct according to standard usage.

> EXAMPLE: 1. (<u>Whose</u>, Who's) idea was it to visit El Yunque rain forest?

1. On the news, I heard (where, that) the game was called off because of rain.

2. Is she the player (who, which) is favored to win at Wimbledon this year?

3. Eat some of this mango paste with (you're, your) toast.

4. *A River Runs Through It* is one movie (that, what) I want you to see.

5. Our school has one bus (who, that) is always half full.

6. A logjam (is where you have, is) a deadlock.

7. Call me if (you're, your) going to the meeting about the recycling program.

8. I'd like to know (whose, who's) bicycle is blocking the driveway.

9. Can you tell me (whose, who's) going on the field trip?

10. He would not have released the report (without, unless) he had first verified his sources.

Writer's Quick Reference

WORKSHEET 11 *Review*

Exercise A   In each of the following sets of expressions, one expression contains an error in usage. First, write the letter of each incorrect expression on the line provided. Then write the correct expression.

EXAMPLE: 1. a. between the two of us
　　　　　　 b. not going anywheres
　　　　　　 c. the woman whom I saw
　　　　　b. not going anywhere

1. a. quit his job
　 b. where he lives at
　 c. a capital idea

_____

2. a. will effect her health
　 b. to borrow a pencil from you
　 c. emigrated from Cuba

_____

3. a. traveled a long ways
　 b. try to succeed
　 c. a sincere compliment

_____

4. a. that type of wrench
　 b. the tribal council
　 c. learned him how to swim

_____

5. a. busted a jar
　 b. kind of bear
　 c. haven't any

_____

6. a. a look at them animals
　 b. improved somewhat
　 c. formerly of San Antonio

_____

7. a. sings like a bird
　 b. without I say so
　 c. the stationary bicycle

_____

8. a. all students except her
　 b. a person that I trust
　 c. read in the newspaper where

_____

9. a. the principle involved
　 b. bigger then a breadbox
　 c. fell off the wall

_____

10. a. these kind of shoes
　 b. ought to wait his turn
　 c. did her assignment

_____

Exercise B   Underline the word or expression in parentheses that is correct according to standard usage.

EXAMPLE: Alvin Ailey has significantly [1] (<u>affected</u>, effected) modern dance in America.

Alvin Ailey [1] (could of, could have) just dreamed of being a famous choreographer; instead, he formed an interracial dance company [2] (what, that) is known all over the world. Ailey started his dance company with [3] (less, fewer) than ten dancers in New York City in 1958. Today, the Alvin Ailey American Dance Theater has a very [4] (good, well) reputation [5] (between, among) modern-dance lovers [6] (everywhere, everywheres). Ailey also ran a dance school and [7] (discovered, invented) many fine young dancers there. [8] (Beside, Besides) teaching, he choreographed operas, television specials, and numerous ballets, including *Survivors* (1987), an energetic celebration of the anti-apartheid movement in South Africa. Ailey and his company have [9] (accepted, excepted) much praise, countless compliments, numerous rave reviews, [10] (and etc., etc.), for their creativity.

Exercise C   Underline the word or expression in parentheses that is correct according to standard usage.

EXAMPLE: 1. Why won't you (<u>accept</u>, except) my help?

1. (Don't, Doesn't) anyone know when this game will start?

2. (It's, Its) the (weather, whether) that is giving me a headache.

3. What (advice, advise) did the coach give you about your tennis serves?

4. Did you (bring, take) flowers to your aunt when you went to visit her in her new home?

5. Jason was (kind of, somewhat) surprised to see us at the train station.

6. (This here, This) skateboard is Manuel's favorite.

7. Optimism is (when a person always looks on the bright side, always looking on the bright side).

8. The tire came (off, off of) the truck and rolled into the (desert, dessert).

9. (My parents they, My parents) refuse to (leave, let) me stay out past ten o'clock.

10. Betty has (all ready, already) handed in her paper.

11. (Being as, Since) you are going to the store tomorrow, I will wait and go then.

12. They were (all together, altogether) at dinner.

13. His (coarse, course) manners offended everyone.

14. Miss Jee is the (councilor, counselor) for our camp group.

15. Next (weak, week) the Bears will play the Packers.

16. My brother Jorge and I rode our bikes four miles (to, too) the beach.

17. The treasure hunters (could hardly, couldn't hardly) believe (their, there) eyes when they opened the chest and saw a pile of glittering coins.

18. Let's walk (slow, slowly) so Janice can catch up with us.

19. Did you mean to (imply, infer) that she does not deserve the award?

20. (Whose, Who's) bat is this?

Name _____ Date _____ Class _____

Types of Nouns A

A **noun** is a word used to name a person, place, thing, or idea. A **proper noun** names a particular person, place, thing, or idea and is always capitalized. A **common noun** is a general name for a person, place, thing, or idea. A common noun is not capitalized unless it begins a sentence or is part of a title.

COMMON NOUNS: scientist, eraser   PROPER NOUNS: George Washington Carver, Japan

A **concrete noun** names an object that can be perceived by the senses. An **abstract noun** names an idea, a feeling, a quality, or a characteristic.

CONCRETE NOUNS: apple, desk   ABSTRACT NOUNS: love, perfection

Exercise A   On the line provided, identify each of the following nouns as *common* or *proper*. If the noun is proper, name a corresponding common noun.

EXAMPLE: 1. Detroit *proper—city*

1. man   _____
2. Virginia   _____
3. gumbo   _____
4. movie   _____
5. airport   _____

6. ocean   _____
7. Australia   _____
8. Bunker Hill   _____
9. Alice Walker   _____
10. automobile   _____

Exercise B   In the following sentences, classify each italicized noun as proper or common and as concrete or abstract. On the line provided, write *C* if the noun is common or *P* if the noun is proper. Then write *CON* if the noun is concrete or *AB* if the noun is abstract.

EXAMPLE: 1. All of Sarah's *notebooks* _C/CON_ are new.

1. *Sarah* _____ begins *classes* _____ at a new school on Friday.

2. She was impressed with the *friendliness* _____ of the *faculty* _____ at registration.

3. Sarah will encounter many unfamiliar *faces* _____ on her first day at *school* _____.

4. I have heard that the *principal* _____ of the high school in *Westlake* _____ is a fair and understanding woman.

5. She is sympathetic to the *needs* _____ and *fears* _____ of new students.

GRAMMAR/USAGE

Chapter 1: The Parts of Speech

WORKSHEET 2 *Types of Nouns B*

A **collective noun** names a group of persons or things.

   family   class   team   herd   band   council

A **compound noun** consists of two or more words used together as a single noun. The parts of a compound noun may be written as one word, as two or more words, or as a hyphenated word.

   wheelchair   Lake Erie   Dr. Charles Drew   sister-in-law   Leslie Marmon Silko

Exercise A   In each of the following sentences, decide if the italicized words are collective nouns or compound nouns. On the line provided, write *collective* or *compound*.

          EXAMPLE: 1. The *committee* voted to sponsor a classic film series.

                  collective

1. Each *group* will give a report on a different classic movie. _____

2. Have you ever seen the film *Dr. Zhivago*? _____

3. My *stepmother* has seen that movie twenty times. _____

4. I always like to see movies in theaters so that I can observe the reactions of the *audience*. _____

5. In West Virginia, my *family* saw many old movies at a bargain theater. _____

Exercise B   Each of the following sentences contains at least one compound noun. Circle the compound noun(s) in each sentence.

          EXAMPLE: 1. The (vice-president) will speak here on (Labor Day.)

1. I use a word processor or a typewriter in class.

2. We went swimming in the Gulf of Mexico.

3. My brother-in-law lives in Council Bluffs, Iowa.

4. My Old English sheepdog is still a puppy.

5. The almanac that Benjamin Banneker created gave exact times for sunrises and sunsets.

6. We used to play hide-and-seek in the old barn.

7. Sitting Bull was the chief who masterminded the Sioux victory at the Battle of the Little Bighorn.

8. Meet me at the bowling alley near the post office.

9. The fountain pen is not as popular as the ballpoint.

10. Luis Valdez is a dramatist, actor, and director.

Name _____ Date _____ Class _____

WORSHEET 3

Pronouns and Antecedents; Personal Pronouns

A **pronoun** is a word used in place of one or more nouns. The noun that the pronoun replaces is called the **antecedent** of the pronoun. In the following example, the arrows point from the pronouns to their antecedents.

Shelley brought **her books** and put **them** on the table.

The most commonly used pronouns are **personal pronouns**.

FIRST PERSON: I, my, mine, me, we, our, ours, us

SECOND PERSON: you, your, yours

THIRD PERSON: he, his, him, she, her, hers, it, its, they, their, theirs, them

I heard Alvin ask Beth if **he** could borrow **your** tape.

Exercise A Underline each personal pronoun in the following paragraph. Then draw an arrow to each pronoun's antecedent or antecedents. [Note: Not every sentence contains a personal pronoun. Some antecedents may occur in a previous sentence.]

EXAMPLE: [1] In about A.D. 1150, a historian wrote down a strange tale
English villagers had told him.

[1] Since many people told the same story, the historian believed it. [2] Supposedly, a young boy and girl with bright green skin had been found wandering in the fields. [3] They spoke a foreign language and wore clothing made of an unknown material. [4] At first, the two children would eat only green beans; later, when they learned to eat bread, their skin gradually lost its greenness. [5] After learning English, the girl said she and her brother had come from a land called Saint Martin. [6] This story sounds like science fiction, doesn't it? [7] Perhaps the villagers invented it to amuse their friends and to fool historians.

Exercise B Underline the personal pronouns in the following sentences. Then draw an arrow to each pronoun's antecedent. [Note: Not every pronoun will have an antecedent.]

EXAMPLE: 1. Your sister asked me if she could borrow a coat.

1. Kito's teacher gave him a second chance to complete the math problem.

2. Did you see the painting that Julian did for the art fair at his school?

3. Seema's father reminded her that she had not fed the bird all day and that it was probably hungry.

4. Cynthia and Julia took our books by mistake, and Diego and I have theirs.

5. Louie asked her to help him carry in the groceries from the car.

GRAMMAR/USAGE

Name _____ Date _____ Class _____

 **WORKSHEET 4** *Types of Pronouns*

A **reflexive pronoun** refers to the subject and directs the action of the verb back to the subject. An **intensive pronoun** emphasizes a noun or another pronoun. Reflexive and intensive pronouns are *myself, yourself, himself, herself, itself, ourselves, yourselves,* and *themselves.*

REFLEXIVE: The guests can serve **themselves**.

INTENSIVE: Anthony made the biscuits **himself**.

A **relative pronoun** *(who, whom, whose, which, that)* introduces a subordinate clause.

I wonder **who** will win the game.

An **interrogative pronoun** *(who, whom, whose, which, what)* introduces a question.

Which is the right answer?

A **demonstrative pronoun** *(this, that, these, those)* points out a person, a place, a thing, or an idea.

These are beautiful flowers.

An **indefinite pronoun** such as *all, each, either, everyone, several, nobody,* or *someone* refers to a person, a place, or a thing that is not specifically named.

Everyone is responsible for the environment.

Exercise Each of the following sentences contains an italicized reflexive, intensive, relative, interrogative, demonstrative, or indefinite pronoun. Identify the type of pronoun on the line provided.

EXAMPLE: 1. *Both* of my parents enjoy exotic foods. <u>*indefinite*</u>

1. *Who* is the tennis player wearing the blue shorts? _____

2. Ms. Gates told Darla to collect the tests *herself*. _____

3. Are *these* the exhibits for the science fair? _____

4. *Everybody* thought our ecology project was unusual. _____

5. I accidentally locked *myself* out of the house. _____

6. The book *that* I bought yesterday is missing some pages. _____

7. *Whom* did the judges choose? _____

8. Mrs. Lancaster is the counselor *who* will help you the most. _____

9. We will try to fix the flat tire *ourselves*. _____

10. I would not choose *either* of the candidates. _____

Name _____ Date _____ Class _____

Nouns, Pronouns, and Adjectives

A **noun** names a person, place, thing, or idea. A **pronoun** is a word used in place of one or more nouns.

    I gave **it my** best **shot.** [*I, it,* and *my* are pronouns. *Shot* is a noun.]

An **adjective** is a word used to modify a noun or pronoun. The most frequently used adjectives—*a, an,* and *the*—are called **articles.** *The* is the **definite article;** *a* and *an* are **indefinite articles.**

    A fierce wind whipped **the purple** bandanna on **the** clothesline.

Some words may be used either as adjectives or as pronouns.

            ADJECTIVE: **That** tree is a hickory.   PRONOUN: **That** is a hickory tree.

Some nouns may be used as adjectives.

        COMMON NOUN: summer   ADJECTIVE: **summer** holiday

        PROPER NOUN: Florida   PROPER ADJECTIVE: **Florida** sunshine

In some cases, adjectives follow the words they modify.

    The gardener, **tired** and **dirty,** finished planting the roses.

Exercise A Underline the adjectives, not including articles, in the following sentences.

        EXAMPLE: 1. Tell me about a <u>popular</u> movie.

1. *Dances with Wolves* is a movie about a Civil War veteran named John J. Dunbar.

2. In the movie, Dunbar, a Union Army lieutenant, learns to live with Native Americans.

3. Kevin Costner, the director, wanted an accurate depiction of the Lakota people.

4. The actors spoke Lakota, and authentic clothing was reproduced.

5. The talented actors Graham Greene and Floyd Red Crow Westerman were two Native Americans selected for key parts in the acclaimed movie.

Exercise B On the lines provided, identify each italicized word in the following sentences as an adjective *(ADJ)*, a pronoun *(PRO)*, or a noun *(N)*.

        EXAMPLE: 1. *Many* <u> ADJ </u> *people* <u> N </u> do not like to watch a movie
                that <u> PRO </u> is very long.

1. However, the *three-hour* _____ movie was a *box-office* _____ *success* _____ .

2. *Hollywood* _____ *critics* _____ expected the movie to bomb.

3. *Many* _____ appreciated Costner's *sensitive* _____ depiction of the *Lakota* _____ .

4. Mary McDonnell, *entertaining* _____ and *dramatic* _____ , earned an *Oscar* _____ nomination for her portrayal of a character named Stands with a Fist.

5. *She* _____ was a newcomer to the *film* _____ industry.

GRAMMAR/USAGE

Chapter 1: The Parts of Speech

WORKSHEET 6 | Action Verbs and Linking Verbs

A **verb** is a word used to express an action or a state of being. An **action verb** expresses activity, whether physical or mental.

PHYSICAL ACTIVITIES: pay   jump   work   walk   bake   shuffle

MENTAL ACTIVITIES: think   love   hope   consider   admire   worry

An action verb can be transitive or intransitive. A **transitive verb** expresses an action directed toward a person or a thing. Words that receive the action of transitive verbs are called **objects**. An **intransitive verb** expresses action (or tells something about the subject) without reference to an object. Some verbs can be transitive or intransitive.

TRANSITIVE VERB: The Puritans **left** England.

INTRANSITIVE VERB: They **left** for religious reasons.

A **linking verb** links the subject with a noun, a pronoun, or an adjective. Some common linking verbs are forms of the verbs *be, appear, become, feel, look, seem, taste,* and *sound.* The noun, pronoun, or adjective following a linking verb completes the meaning of the verb and refers to the subject. Some linking verbs can be used as action verbs.

LINKING VERB: That song **sounded** familar.

ACTION VERB: The fire warden **sounded** the alarm.

Exercise A   Underline the verb in each of the following sentences, and identify it as transitive or intransitive. On the line provided, write the verb and *T* if it is transitive or *I* if it is intransitive.

EXAMPLE: 1. Colonial America <u>offered</u> freedom to a variety of people.
         offered, T

1. Victims of religious intolerance sought a new life.   _____

2. Indentured servants also sailed to American shores.   _____

3. The poor of England desired economic freedom here.   _____

4. They worked in America as payment for their passage.   _____

5. Many remained in America after settling their debts.   _____

Exercise B   On the line provided, identify the linking verb in each of the following sentences. Then list the words that are linked by the verb.

EXAMPLE: 1. Dixie is usually a very obedient dog. *is—Dixie, dog*

1. He felt foolish when his car ran out of gas.   _____

2. Everything that you cook tastes wonderful.   _____

3. The plot of that novel seems childish.   _____

4. I am happy that you won the chess match.   _____

5. Stef's band sounded great in the concert.   _____

Chapter 1: The Parts of Speech

The Verb Phrase

A **verb phrase** consists of a main verb preceded by at least one **helping verb** (also called an **auxiliary verb**). Some commonly used helping verbs are forms of the verbs *be*, *have*, and *do* and other words such as *may*, *might*, *must*, *can*, *shall*, *will*, *could*, *should*, and *would*.

Our class **has been reading** a story by Nicholasa Mohr.

Sometimes the parts of a verb phrase are interrupted by other parts of speech. The word *not* and its contraction, *–n't*, are never part of a verb phrase; they are adverbs.

Exercise A On the lines provided, identify all the verbs and verb phrases in the following sentences. Include all helping verbs, even if the parts of a verb phrase are separated by other words.

> EXAMPLE: 1. We will probably go to the movie if we can finish our assignment. *will go, can finish*

1. Mr. Jensen always sweeps the floor first. _____

2. Then he washes the chalkboards. _____

3. He works slowly but steadily. _____

4. The weather forecaster had not predicted rain. _____

5. All morning the barometer was dropping rapidly. _____

6. The storm was slowly moving in. _____

7. Your dog will become fat if you feed it too much. _____

8. Dogs will usually eat everything you give them. _____

9. Most cats will stop when they have had enough. _____

10. After our team has had more practice, we will win. _____

Exercise B Underline the four verb phrases that appear in the following paragraph.

After World War II many Puerto Ricans were able to buy inexpensive, one-way tickets to the mainland of the United States. Because of the language difference, Puerto Ricans may have felt like strangers in their own country. Feeling like foreigners couldn't have been easy for them. Spanish-speaking communities in New York City offered support for new arrivals. By the end of World War II, a large Puerto Rican community had already settled in El Barrio, in Spanish Harlem. Many of the new wave of Puerto Ricans settled in the South Bronx. In fact, the South Bronx was soon known to Puerto Ricans who lived there as *El Bronx*. Today, Puerto Ricans live all over New York City, but strong Puerto Rican communities still exist in the Bronx and Harlem.

GRAMMAR/USAGE

Name _____ Date _____ Class _____

The Adverb

An **adverb** is a word used to modify a verb, an adjective, or another adverb. An adverb modifies by telling *where, when, how,* or *to what extent (how often* or *how much).*

The boy ran **upstairs**. [The adverb *upstairs* modifies the verb *ran* and tells *where*.]

Jean ran **unusually** fast yesterday. [The adverb *unusually* modifies the adverb *fast*, telling *how* fast.]

Raccoons raid our trash cans **nightly**. [The adverb *nightly* modifies the verb *raid*, telling *how often*.]

Exercise A   Complete each of the following sentences by supplying an appropriate adverb on the line provided. The word in parentheses tells you what information the adverb should give about the action. On the line following each sentence, write the verb, adjective, or adverb that the adverb modifies.

EXAMPLE: 1. He moved his hand *gracefully* (how). *moved*

1. The soldiers must move _____ (how).   _____

2. You will probably sleep well _____ (when).   _____

3. Tonya took a deep breath and jumped _____
    (where).   _____

4. My uncle Hans is _____ (to what extent) late.   _____

5. Did you study _____ (to what extent)?   _____

6. Handle the baby kittens _____ (how).   _____

7. Your taxi should be _____ (where) soon.   _____

8. I could _____ (to what extent) taste the tangy
    pasta sauce.   _____

9. _____ (when), you should paste the pictures on
    the poster.   _____

10. They whispered _____ (how) to Mr. Baldwin.   _____

Exercise B: Revising   On the lines provided, revise the following sentences by adding at least one appropriate adverb. Try not to use the adverbs *too, so,* and *very.*

EXAMPLE: 1. The hot weather sapped our energy.

The extremely hot weather rapidly sapped our energy.

1. Engineering degrees are popular because job opportunities in those fields are good.

    _____

2. I returned the book to Marcella, but she had planned her report without it.

    _____

Name _____ Date _____ Class _____

The Preposition and the Conjunction

A **preposition** is a word used to show the relationship of a noun or a pronoun to some other word in the sentence. A preposition introduces a prepositional phrase.

    I went **to** the card shop.   The cat is asleep **under** the table.

Prepositions consisting of more than one word are **compound prepositions**.

    You will find the thesaurus **next to** the dictionary.

A **conjunction** is a word used to join words or groups of words. **Coordinating conjunctions** and **correlative conjunctions** (pairs of conjunctions) connect sentence parts that are used in the same way.

COORDINATING CONJUNCTION: I called, **but** you weren't home.

CORRELATIVE CONJUNCTION: **Both** Ramon **and** Bill are coming with us.

Exercise A Underline the prepositions in the following sentences. Then on the line provided, use a different preposition to rewrite each sentence.

          EXAMPLE: 1. Mr. Corey will walk <u>with</u> me. *Mr. Corey will walk behind me.*

1. We walked toward the beach. _____

2. He arrived on a horse-drawn sled. _____

3. We will talk more about that meeting. _____

4. The eagle soared beyond the clouds. _____

5. Please sit near the windows. _____

Exercise B Underline the conjunctions in the following sentences. Then on the lines provided, identify them as *coordinating* or *correlative*.

          EXAMPLE: 1. Many people enjoy watching plays <u>and</u> dances.
                coordinating

1. Neither Jean nor I have ever seen a dance company performance. _____

2. I bought tickets for Jean and me to see an Alvin Ailey production.   _____

3. Ailey was born in Texas in 1931, but he later moved to New York. _____

4. He danced in Broadway shows, and in 1958, he formed the Alvin Ailey Dance Theater.   _____

5. Whether as a choreographer or as a director, he was much admired.   _____

GRAMMAR/USAGE

Chapter 1: The Parts of Speech

The Interjection; Determining Parts of Speech

An **interjection** is a word used to express emotion. It has no grammatical relation to the other words in the sentence. It is set off from the rest of the sentence by an exclamation point or a comma.

Wow! That is the most incredible news I've ever heard!

I like that shirt, but, **hey,** the color just isn't me.

The way a word is used in a sentence determines the word's part of speech. You can figure out what part of speech a word is from the word's **context**—the way the word is used in the sentence.

There is a huge ship unloading freight at the **dock** [noun].

The freighter will **dock** [verb] in the harbor.

Exercise A In the following dialogue, use appropriate interjections to fill in the numbered blanks. Be sure you punctuate each interjection correctly.

EXAMPLE: [1] " _Wow!_ You mean you actually got to go?" Michelle gasped.

[1] "_____ how was the concert?" asked Michelle. "Come on. Tell me all about it."

Jason shook his head. "The opening act was terrible. [2] _____ It seemed like they played forever!"

"But how was the rest of the show? [3] _____ Give me some details, Jason!"

"The drummer [4] _____ he acted like a wild man. He was all over the drums! But the best part was Stevie's twenty-minute guitar solo.

[5] _____ he really let loose. The crowd went crazy!"

Exercise B On the lines provided, identify the parts of speech of the italicized words.

EXAMPLE: 1a. The *electrical* storm was most unexpected. _adjective_

1a. Do not run *down* the stairs, please.   _____

 b. The child fell *down* and scraped her knee.   _____

2a. Mr. Gates told her to hand in her *test*.   _____

 b. I will *test* the water temperature first.   _____

3a. *These* are extremely tasty pears.   _____

 b. I prefer *these* flowers rather than those.   _____

4a. The *principal* will address the students this afternoon. _____

 b. Octavio has a *principal* part in the play.   _____

Name _____ Date _____ Class _____

 **Review**

WORKSHEET 11

Exercise A   On the line provided, identify the part of speech of each italicized word in the following sentences. Use the abbreviations *N* for noun, *P* for pronoun, and *ADJ* for adjective.

EXAMPLE: [1] Most high school *students* __N__ read at least *one* _ADJ_ play by William Shakespeare.

[1] *This* _____ article tells about Shakespeare's life. [2] *Shakespeare,* _____ perhaps the

most *famous* _____ playwright of all time, was born in Stratford-on-Avon in 1564. [3] He

was baptized in the *small* _____ church at Stratford shortly after *his* _____ birth. [4] In

1616, *he* _____ was buried in the *same* _____ church. [5] If you visit his grave, you can

find an *inscription* _____ placing a curse on *anyone* _____ who moves his bones. [6] Out

of *respect* _____ for his wish or because of fear of his curse, *nobody* _____ has disturbed

the grave. [7] This explains why his body was never moved to Westminster Abbey, where

many *other* _____ famous *English* _____ writers are buried. [8] Visitors to Stratford can

also see the house in *which* _____ Shakespeare was born. [9] At *one* _____ time, tourists

could visit the large house that Shakespeare bought for *himself* _____ and his family.

[10] *This* _____ was where they lived when he retired from the London *theater* _____ .

Exercise B   Each of the following sentences contains two verbs: an action verb and a linking verb. Underline the action verb once and the linking verb twice.

EXAMPLE: 1. When ice <u>covers</u> the tree branches, they <u>seem</u> fragile and glasslike.

1. I feel very disorganized whenever I misplace an important paper.

2. On summer vacations, I often swim all day and then become sleepy earlier than usual.

3. "A stitch in time saves nine" is one of my aunt's favorite sayings.

4. I am a clumsy piano player, even though I practice daily.

5. Before we reached the resort area, the weather became ugly.

6. My grandfather, a Texas rancher, loves dogs, and the porch of his ranch house always seems full of dogs of all shapes and sizes.

7. My grandmother is a lover of cats and always has several big Persian cats.

8. These cats feel happiest inside the house because the dogs chase any cat up a tree on sight.

9. In the tree, the cat looked angry and unhappy until a ranch hand finally came to the rescue with a ladder.

10. "Those dogs are a positive menace!" my grandmother tells my grandfather.

Exercise C   Underline all the helping verbs you find in each sentence in the following paragraph. [Note: Not all of the sentences have helping verbs.]

EXAMPLE: [1] I <u>am</u> writing my report on the artist Donald Evans.

[1] You may not have heard of him. [2] His four thousand tiny watercolors were painted to look like postage stamps. [3] First, he would invent a country and its geography, history, and customs. [4] One of his make-believe countries is called the Islands of the Deaf, or *Iles des Sourds* in French. [5] Its unit of money, the Pat, was named after a deaf friend of his. [6] He painted ten colorful stamps that cost from one Pat to ten Pats. [7] If he had been less imaginative, he might simply have used numerals on the stamps. [8] However, he also included a picture of the American Sign Language hand position and the French name for each number. [9] Have you ever seen any of his paintings? [10] *Tercentenary of the Island, Mountain of the Deaf* may be my favorite.

Exercise D   Decide what parts of speech the italicized words in the following sentences are. On the lines provided, write *V* for verb, *ADV* for adverb, *PREP* for preposition, *CON* for conjunction, or *I* for interjection.

EXAMPLE: ___V___ 1. I never *forget* a face, but I can't remember names.

_____ 1. *Not only* was Carl late *but* he *also* forgot his lunch.

_____ 2. Mother says, "Carl *would forget* his head if it weren't attached to his neck."

_____ 3. *Wow!* I wish I had a memory like Danielle has.

_____ 4. She *never* forgets anything.

_____ 5. Danielle can read something once *and* recall every single fact.

_____ 6. That *must be* an extremely valuable gift!

_____ 7. I have trouble remembering everything *except* my name and address.

_____ 8. Write things *down*, and you might have an easier time recalling them.

_____ 9. *In addition to* writing things down, you can use mnemonic devices, such as rhymes.

_____10. *Well*, that sounds like a good idea.

Exercise E   The following passage contains twenty numbered, italicized words. On the line provided, indicate which part of speech each of these words is. Use the following abbreviations:

N = noun	**ADV** = adverb
P = pronoun	**PREP** = preposition
ADJ = adjective	**CON** = conjunction
V = verb	**INTER** = interjection

EXAMPLE: Family discussions can be [1] *extremely* beneficial.
1. _ADV_

[1] *Every* night my [2] *family* has what we call a "talk time." We [3] *discuss* what we [4] *have done* [5] *during* the day. Sometimes it is hard for my [6] *little* brother to remember. Then Mom asks [7] *him* some questions.

"[8] *Oh,* I remember now," my brother eventually says. Then he tells about his morning [9] *or* afternoon adventures.

The things my brother says [10] *often* sound silly to me. I become impatient because I want to talk about my day [11] *at* school. School activities are [12] *most* important to me. I describe my daily [13] *trials* and tribulations. I start with tales [14] *of* the school-bus ride. Then [15] *I* tell about every class. I usually talk a lot about history and science, my [16] *favorite* classes. My brother [17] *generally* [18] *shouts,* "No more ancient-history stories!"

Then my parents grin [19] *and* ask, "Don't you want to hear about [20] *our* day?"

1. _____	11. _____
2. _____	12. _____
3. _____	13. _____
4. _____	14. _____
5. _____	15. _____
6. _____	16. _____
7. _____	17. _____
8. _____	18. _____
9. _____	19. _____
10. _____	20. _____

GRAMMAR/USAGE

Exercise F   On the line provided, write the part of speech of each italicized word in the following sentences. You may use abbreviations.

                        EXAMPLE: ___N___   1. The golfers enjoyed the newly mowed *green*.

_____ 1. Don't quit your *day* job!

_____ 2. I stayed up late last night and have been sleepy all *day*.

_____ 3. Teresa sang *well* during the recital.

_____ 4. *Well*, Nathan absolutely refuses to help me.

_____ 5. He played the same song *over* and over again until he got it right.

_____ 6. The frightened dog jumped *over* the chair.

_____ 7. "*So*, you're not going to the game, either, I hear!"

_____ 8. Darla was sick on Monday, *so* she missed her homework assignment.

_____ 9. Will you be around here on *Labor Day*?

_____ 10. He *labored* long over the math assignment.

Name _____ Date _____ Class _____

Number and Subject-Verb Agreement

When a word refers to one person or thing, it is **singular** in number. When a word refers to more than one person or thing, it is **plural** in number.

SINGULAR:	building	he	woman	knife	country
PLURAL:	buildings	them	women	knives	countries

A verb should always agree with its subject in number. Singular subjects take singular verbs.

The **dog barks** loudly.   Why **is he** laughing?

Plural subjects take plural verbs.

The **dogs bark** loudly.   Why **are they** laughing?

The number of the subject is not changed by a phrase following the subject.

The **packages** on the counter **are** hers.

Exercise A   Underline the verb in parentheses that agrees with the subject in each of the following sentences.

> EXAMPLE: [1] In Japan, noodle shops (resembles, <u>resemble</u>) our fast-food restaurants.

[1] These descriptions (tell, tells) how the noodles are prepared. [2] First, the noodle maker (roll, rolls) the dough out as thin as possible. [3] Then, the cook (slice, slices) the folded layers. [4] Next, each strand of noodles (is, are) separated and dusted with flour to prevent sticking. [5] After the noodles have dried a little, they (go, goes) into boiling water or broth to cook.

Exercise B   Underline the verb in parentheses that agrees with the subject in each of the following sentences.

> EXAMPLE: 1. The rules in this textbook (is, <u>are</u>) guidelines for using standard English.

1. Mastery of these rules (lead, leads) to improvement in speaking and writing.

2. The correct use of verbs (are, is) especially important.

3. Correct spelling, in addition to correct usage of verbs, (is, are) a useful writing skill.

4. People in the business world (look, looks) carefully at letters of application.

5. Letters with nonstandard English do not (makes, make) a good impression.

GRAMMAR/USAGE

Chapter 2: Agreement

Subject-Verb Agreement: Indefinite Pronouns

A pronoun that does not refer to a specific person, place, or thing is called an **indefinite pronoun**. The following indefinite pronouns are singular: *each, either, neither, one, everyone, everybody, everything, no one, nobody, nothing, anyone, anybody, anything, someone, somebody,* and *something*. When a singular indefinite pronoun is the subject of a sentence, it takes a singular verb.

> **Neither** of the contestants **knows** the answer.

The following indefinite pronouns are plural: *both, few, many,* and *several.*

> **Many** of the winners **are** in ninth grade.

The indefinite pronouns *all, any, most, none* and *some* may be either singular or plural. These pronouns are singular when they refer to singular words and plural when they refer to plural words.

> SINGULAR: **Most** of our vacation **is** over. [*Most* refers to the singular noun *vacation.*]
>
> PLURAL: **Most** of the days **have** passed. [*Most* refers to the plural noun *days.*]

Exercise A   Underline the subject of each verb in parentheses. Then underline the form of the verb that agrees with that subject.

> EXAMPLE: 1. <u>Several</u> of the kittens (has, <u>have</u>) been adopted.

1. All of the comedians (tries, try) to outdo each other.

2. Somebody on the bus (was, were) whistling.

3. (Is, Are) all of the apples spoiled?

4. Neither of these books (has, have) an index.

5. (Do, Does) everybody in the class have a pencil?

Exercise B   On each line, add a verb that agrees in number with each of the subjects below. Add any other words needed to create a clear sentence.

1. Most of the people _____

2. Some of the television program _____

3. Neither of the team captains _____

4. Both of the writers _____

Name _____ Date _____ Class _____

Subject-Verb Agreement: Compound Subjects

A **compound subject** consists of two or more nouns or pronouns that have the same verb. Two or more subjects joined by *and* usually take a plural verb.

> **Jovita** and **Jaime are** going to the dance.

A compound subject that names only one person or thing takes a singular verb.

> My best **friend** and my **hero is** my aunt. [One person is both my friend and my hero.]

Two or more singular subjects joined by *or* or *nor* take a singular verb.

> At bedtime, either **Mom** or **Dad reads** to my little sister. [One of them reads to her.]

When a singular subject and a plural subject are joined by *or* or *nor*, the verb agrees with the subject nearer the verb.

> Neither my **brothers** nor my **sister likes** swimming as much as I do.
>
> Neither my **sister** nor my **brothers like** swimming as much as I do.

Exercise A   Underline the correct form of the verb in parentheses in each of the following sentences.

> EXAMPLE: 1. (<u>Do</u>, Does) Josh and Brian enjoy football as much as Rachel does?

1. Tina and Betty (is, are) first cousins once removed.

2. Playing games or listening to old records (is, are) an enjoyable way to spend a rainy Saturday.

3. Either an apple or some grapes (are, is) my favorite snack.

4. Neither Eileen nor Greg (enjoy, enjoys) listening to music.

5. Both Mr. and Mrs. Chen (agree, agrees) to be chaperons for the dance.

Exercise B   In each blank below, write the correct form of the verb preceding the sentence.

> EXAMPLE: 1. *have*   Mr. Richards and Mrs. Urquides
> _*have*_ called a meeting.

1. *have*   _____ Yoko and Juan already seen that movie?

2. *raise*   My grandmother, my mother, and my aunts _____ tropical fish to earn extra money.

3. *have*   Neither the librarian nor the aides _____ found the missing book.

4. *make*   Black beans and rice _____ an inexpensive meal.

5. *be*   My aunt and uncle _____ planning a trip to Nairobi National Park in Kenya.

GRAMMAR/USAGE

Name _____ Date _____ Class _____

WORKSHEET 4

Other Problems in Agreement A

Two words combined into one, with one or more letters omitted is called a **contraction**. *Don't* is the contraction for *do not*. *Doesn't* is the contraction for *does not*. Contractions must always agree with their subjects.

With the subjects *I* and *you* and with plural subjects, use *don't (do not)*.

I **don't** speak Spanish well.   They **don't** listen carefully.

Mice **don't** like cats.   You **don't** want that book.

With other subjects, use the singular *doesn't (does not)*.

It **doesn't** matter.   She **doesn't** give up easily.

He **doesn't** eat meat.   One **doesn't** show up late there.

Collective nouns such as *chorus, crowd, faculty, family, group, public,* and *team* are singular in form, but they each name a group of persons or things. Collective nouns may be either singular or plural. Use a plural verb with a collective noun to indicate that the individual parts or members of the group are acting separately. Use a singular verb to indicate that the group is acting as a unit.

The committee **are** doing individual projects to raise funds.

The committee **is** planning a fund-raising project.

Exercise A   Write the correct form (*doesn't* or *don't*) for each of the following sentences.

EXAMPLE: 1. *Doesn't* that bouquet of roses look great?

1. This apple _____ taste sweet.

2. _____ he want to see the game?

3. These _____ impress me.

4. One of the players _____ plan to go.

5. _____ Jason and Tanya like the new band uniforms?

Exercise B   Select two of the following collective nouns. On the lines below, write a pair of sentences using each one. Use the noun with a singular verb in one sentence and with a plural verb in the other sentence.

　　band　　　class　　　crowd　　　family　　　jury　　　public　　　team

EXAMPLE: 1. *The jury is ready.*

The jury are still arguing among themselves.

1. _____

_____

2. _____

_____

Name _____ Date _____ Class _____

Other Problems in Agreement B

A verb agrees with its subject, not with its predicate nominative.

    S   PN
    Trees **are** a valuable addition to any property.

              S   PN
    A valuable addition to any property **is** trees.

When the subject follows the verb, as in sentences beginning with *here* and *there* and in questions, make sure the verb agrees with the subject.

    Here **is** the **book** to read.

    There **are** the **books** you wanted to read.

    Where **is** the **saw**?

    Where **are** the **tools**?

Words stating an amount are usually singular because a weight, measurement, or amount of money is usually thought of as a unit.

    Fifty dollars is required for a deposit.

However, sometimes an amount is thought of as individual pieces or parts and takes a plural verb.

    Four wonderful **days await** us in Hawaii.

Use a singular verb when the phrase *the number* comes before a prepositional phrase. Use a plural verb when the phrase *a number* comes before a prepositional phrase.

    The number of semesters before graduation **is** five.

    A number of classes **are** already full.

Exercise In the following sentences, underline the correct verb in parentheses.

             EXAMPLE: 1. Where (is, <u>are</u>) the tickets to the concert?

1. First prize (was, were) two tickets to Hawaii.

2. A number of doors (was, were) open in the hall.

3. My favorite exhibit at the museum (is, are) the dinosaurs.

4. Three quarters of the movie (was, were) over when we arrived.

5. Here (are, is) my contribution to the flowers.

6. Five of the missing books (was, were) returned.

7. Where (is, are) the paragraphs you wrote?

8. Four dollars (is, are) not enough to pay for the ticket.

9. There (isn't, aren't) enough money for the supplies.

10. The number of absentees (have, has) increased.

GRAMMAR/USAGE

Chapter 2: Agreement

Other Problems in Agreement C

Even if it is plural in form, the title of a creative work (such as a book, song, film, or painting) takes a singular verb. The name of an organization, a country, a city, or other geographical location also takes a singular verb.

> **"The Three Bears" is** her favorite children's story.
>
> **The United Nations has** a beautiful building in New York City.
>
> **New Orleans** is home to the Mardi Gras.

Every or *many a* before a subject calls for a singular verb.

> **Every** adult and teen **has** responsibility for the earth.
>
> **Many a** fire fighter **is** also an athlete.

A few nouns, although plural in form, take singular verbs.

> **Politics is** an interesting career choice.
>
> **Measles was** more prevalent before a vaccine was developed.

Exercise A   In the following sentences, underline the correct verb in parentheses.

> EXAMPLE: 1. *War and Peace* (<u>is</u>, are) a world-famous novel.

1. Mathematics (is, are) an important part of many activities.

2. Many a writer (have, has) puzzled over that problem.

3. *Romeo and Juliet* (has, have) been made into at least two movies.

4. Every student (need, needs) to be at the meeting.

5. Mumps (is, are) contagious.

Exercise B   Terence and Janeese are at the video store deciding what movies they will rent for the weekend. In the following sentences, wherever blanks appear, supply the name of a movie of your choice. Then underline the correct form of the verb in parentheses to complete each sentence.

> EXAMPLE: 1. Look, Terence. <u>*Horse Feathers*</u> (<u>is</u>, are) supposed to be
> very funny.

1. Terence: According to LaShonda, _____ (is, are) very exciting.

2. Janeese: Well, _____ (sounds, sound) more interesting to me.

3. Terence: Both _____ and _____ (are, is) good, but I've seen each of them twice.

4. Janeese: (Isn't, Aren't) _____ any good? I'm surprised.

5. Terence: All right, here's my vote. _____ (is, are) tonight's

   movie, and either _____ or_____ (is, are) the movie for Saturday night's party.

Name _____ Date _____ Class _____

Agreement of Pronoun and Antecedent

Usually, a pronoun refers to a noun or another pronoun used earlier. The word that a pronoun refers to is called its **antecedent**. In the previous sentence, for example, *its* is a pronoun that refers to the antecedent *pronoun*.

A pronoun should agree with its antecedent in number and gender. A few singular personal pronouns have forms that indicate the gender of the antecedent. Masculine pronouns *(he, him, his, himself)* refer to males; feminine pronouns *(she, her, hers, herself)* refer to females. Neuter pronouns *(it, its, itself)* refer to things and, often, to animals.

> Marcia played **her** guitar for us.

> The kitten enjoys **its** noisy toys.

Use a singular pronoun to refer to *each, either, neither, one, every, everyone, everybody, everything, no one, nobody, nothing, anyone, anybody, anything, someone, somebody,* or *something.* Use a singular pronoun to refer to two or more singular antecedents joined by *or* or *nor.*

> **Each** of the dogs has **its** own bowl.

> Neither **Wyatt** nor **Clinton** drove **his** own car.

When the antecedent of a personal pronoun is an indefinite pronoun, use both the masculine and feminine personal pronouns connected by *or.*

> Someone left **his** or **her** basketball at the courts.

Use a plural pronoun to refer to two or more antecedents joined by *and.*

> **Diane** and **Sheila** turned in **their** papers.

Exercise: Proofreading The following sentences contain errors in agreement between pronouns and their antecedents. Draw a line through the error, and write the correct pronoun above the error. If a sentence is correct, write C following the sentence.

> EXAMPLE: 1. All of us need to choose topics for ~~his or her~~ reports. *(our)*

1. Several of the people in our class have already submitted his or her topics.

2. Jerome and Ken are both going to write their papers on dinosaurs.

3. Either Jerome or Ken went to a dinosaur exhibit, and they can't stop talking about it.

4. Ms. Ruiz and Mr. O'Malley are letting his students write about movies.

5. Both of them are big movie fans themselves.

6. Neither Marisa nor Elena chose their own topic.

7. Each of this moviemaker's films has left their mark on the entertainment world.

8. Ginger and George have both chosen Walt Disney as the subject of his or her reports.

9. Does either George or Dominic know that they must use facts, not opinions?

10. Neither of them is used to holding back their opinion.

GRAMMAR/USAGE

Chapter 2: Agreement

WORKSHEET 8 *Review*

Exercise A Underline the correct form of the verb in parentheses in each of the following sentences.

        EXAMPLE: 1. Neither of the swans (are, <u>is</u>) on the pond.

1. Physics (is, are) one of Tracey's favorite subjects.

2. The question of taxes (is, are) always a main issue during an election year.

3. Not one of the ushers (knows, know) where the lounge is.

4. The team (is, are) on a winning streak.

5. Carol, as well as Ines, (writes, write) a column for the *East High Record*.

6. "Beauty and the Beast" (is, are) a folk tale that exists in many different cultures.

7. Ten pounds (is, are) far too much weight for a young child to carry in a backpack.

8. It is difficult to concentrate when there (is, are) radios and stereos blasting away.

9. (Has, Have) either of you read *To Kill a Mockingbird*?

10. In most situation comedies, there (is, are) a very wise character, a very foolish character, and a very lovable character.

Exercise B: Revising On the lines provided, rewrite the following sentences according to the directions given in parentheses. If necessary, change the forms of verbs, pronouns, or other words in the sentences.

        EXAMPLE: 1. Of all the students in my class, perhaps one or two enjoy being in the class play. (Change *perhaps one or two* to *only one*.)

                Of all the students in my class, only one enjoys being in the
                class play.

1. Most of the acting talent in our school is in the other classes. (Change *acting talent* to *talented actors*.) _____

    _____

2. Very few of my classmates think highly of their own acting ability. (Change *Very few* to *Not one*.) _____

    _____

3. Most of the students in the class have to be in the play, however. (Change *Most of the students* to *Almost every student*.) _____

    _____

Chapter 2, Worksheet 8, continued

4. There is at least one major speaking role in this year's play. (Change *at least one major speaking role* to *several major speaking roles*.) _____

_____

5. The hero and the heroine, naturally, have more lines than the supporting members of the cast. (Change *The hero and the heroine* to *The hero or the heroine*.) _____

_____

6. Therefore, both of the main roles are considered undesirable. (Change *both* to *either*.) _____

_____

7. A reluctant boy trying out for a main role usually takes care to do his worst. (Change *A reluctant boy* to *Reluctant boys*.) _____

_____

8. Two of my friends were late to the tryouts, so they were assigned to the stage crew. (Change *Two* to *One*.) _____

_____

9. In our town, rain and snow don't stop a school play. (Change *rain and snow* to *rain or snow*.)

_____

10. At the first performance of our play, two of my three lines were furnished to me by the prompter. (Change *two* to *one*.) _____

_____

Exercise C   Each numbered item below lists four expressions. Underline the one expression that is incorrect.

EXAMPLE: 1. there are a few, <u>nobody have</u>, she and I do, my team is

1. not many was, the soloists are, everybody is, they don't

2. anybody has, he and she is, it was they, what's this

3. here's my book, both was new, most of these are, they seem

4. both of them is, some of the men are, he or she goes, you or they have

5. roads that lead, if the class does its best, that's ours, here is several of them

Chapter 2, Worksheet 8, continued

Exercise D: Proofreading In most of the following sentences, a verb does not agree with its subject, or a pronoun does not agree with its antecedent. Underline each wrong verb or pronoun. Then write the correct form on the line provided. If the sentence is correct, write C on the line.

EXAMPLE: _*have*_ 1. Nancy and her sister <u>has</u> tickets to the play.

_____ 1. My aunt and I like to play tennis, although neither of us are really very good at it.

_____ 2. Everybody on the team would like to spend their free time at football practice.

_____ 3. Neither the teacher nor the students think that these problems are difficult.

_____ 4. Some of the prize-winning costumes was very original.

_____ 5. Mathematics are an easy subject for some students, but to most students either history or English seems easier.

Name _____ Date _____ Class _____

Principal Parts of Regular Verbs

The four **principal parts** of a verb are the **base form,** the **present participle,** the **past,** and the **past participle**. The present participle and the past participle require helping verbs (forms of *be* and *have*).

A **regular verb** forms its past and past participle by adding *–d* or *–ed* to the base form. Most regular verbs ending in *e* drop the *e* before adding *–ing* for the present participle.

Base Form	**Present Participle**	**Past**	**Past Participle**
hope	(is) hoping	hoped	(has) hoped

Exercise In the space provided, write the base form, past, past participle, or present participle of the verb shown to complete the sentence correctly. On the line before each sentence, identify the principal part of the verb you used. Write *B* for base form, *Pres P* for present participle, *P* for past, or *Past P* for past participle.

EXAMPLE: <u>Past P</u> 1. Many visitors to the National Museum of American History in Washington, D.C., have <u>seen</u> an exhibit called "American Encounters." (*see*)

_____ 1. The museum has _____ the exhibit to mark the five-hundredth anniversary of Columbus's arrival in America. (*create*)

_____ 2. The exhibit focuses on the influence that European cultures and the native civilizations of New Mexico _____ on each other. (*exert*)

_____ 3. Only half a century after Columbus came to America, the Zuni Indians were _____ Spaniards on their land. (*encounter*)

_____ 4. These first encounters marked the beginning of the Native Americans' ongoing struggle to _____ their identities. (*preserve*)

_____ 5. The exhibit features the culture of the *Kha p'on,* a people who have been _____ along the upper Rio Grande since 1350. (*live*)

_____ 6. The creators of the exhibit have _____ video recordings. (*include*)

_____ 7. I _____ learning about the Chimayó community. (*enjoy*)

_____ 8. This community has _____ from the Hispanic people of New Mexico. (*descend*)

_____ 9. The Hispanics in Chimayó have _____ to the modern world, yet still maintain a traditional village organization. (*adapt*)

_____10. Parts of the Chimayó village today look very much as they _____ a century ago. (*look*)

GRAMMAR/USAGE

Chapter 3: Using Verbs Correctly

Principal Parts
of Irregular Verbs

An **irregular verb** forms its past and past participle in some other way than by adding *-d* or *-ed*. Irregular verbs form their past and past participle in one of the following ways:

	Base Form	Past	Past Participle
vowel change	swim	swam	(has) swum
consonant change	send	sent	(have) sent
vowel and consonant change	think	thought	(have) thought
no change	burst	burst	(have) burst

Exercise A   On the lines provided, change each of the following verb forms to the form indicated in parentheses. Use *have* before the past participle form.

EXAMPLES: 1. eat (past)   *ate*

2. take (past participle) *have taken*

1. do (past)   _____

2. begin (past participle)   _____

3. see (past)   _____

4. ride (past participle)   _____

5. go (past participle)   _____

6. know (past)   _____

7. speak (past participle) _____

8. steal (past participle)   _____

9. bring (past)   _____

10. choose (past)   _____

Exercise B   Underline the correct form of each verb in parentheses.

EXAMPLE: I just [1] (<u>wrote</u>, written) a letter to my Russian pen pal!

Joining the Russian-American pen-pal club *Druzhba* is one of the most important things I have ever [1] (did, done). The founder of the club [2] (chose, chosen) the name *Druzhba* because it means friendship in Russian. This club has [3] (given, gave) American and Russian teenagers the chance to become friends. I [4] (began, begun) to write to my pen pal Vanya in April. It [5] (took, taken) six weeks to get his reply. I should have [6] (knew, known) that mail service to and from Russia might be slow. In his letters, Vanya has [7] (written, wrote) about his daily life, his family, and his thoughts. We have [8] (become, became) good friends, even though we have never [9] (spoke, spoken) to each other. I like to think that my correspondence with Vanya has [10] (brung, brought) our two nations closer together.

Chapter 3: Using Verbs Correctly

WORKSHEET 3 — *Tense*

The **tense** of a verb indicates the time of the action or state of being expressed by the verb. Every English verb has six tenses.

PRESENT TENSE: I ride, he rides

PAST TENSE: I rode, he rode

FUTURE TENSE: I will (shall) ride, he will ride

PRESENT PERFECT TENSE: I have ridden, he has ridden

PAST PERFECT TENSE: I had ridden, he had ridden

FUTURE PERFECT TENSE: I will (shall) have ridden, he will have ridden

Each of the six tenses has an additional form called the **progressive form,** which expresses continuing action. It consists of a form of the verb *be* plus the present participle of a verb.

PRESENT PROGRESSIVE: am, are, is riding

PAST PROGRESSIVE: was, were riding

FUTURE PROGRESSIVE: will (shall) be riding

PRESENT PERFECT PROGRESSIVE: has, have been riding

PAST PERFECT PROGRESSIVE: had been riding

FUTURE PERFECT PROGRESSIVE: will (shall) have been riding

Exercise   Fill in the blank in each of the following sentences with the correct form of the verb indicated to the left. Use the verb tense indicated in parentheses.

EXAMPLE: 1. *hide* The mouse ___*hid*___ under the stove. (*past*)

1. *play*   Mr. Jacobi _____ golf every Sunday. (*present*)

2. *organize*   I _____ a committee to reelect Alice Newman.
                 (*present perfect progressive*)

3. *take*   They _____ possession of their home by Friday.
                 (*future perfect*)

4. *jump*   Elizabeth _____ at the chance. (*past*)

5. *request*   Bob _____ a salary increase. (*present perfect*)

6. *invite*   I _____ Steve and Monica, but they were unable to
                 attend. (*past perfect*)

7. *rain*   It _____ by early evening. (*future progressive*)

8. *sponsor*   Mr. Newcomb _____ the annual bicycling
                 convention next spring. (*future*)

9. *cheer*   They _____ continuously for their team and had
                 lost their voices as a result. (*past perfect progressive*)

10. *study*   Shawn worked days and _____ at night. (*past*)

GRAMMAR/USAGE

Chapter 3: Using Verbs Correctly

Uses and Consistency of Tenses

Each of the six tenses has its own special uses:
- The **present tense** is used mainly to express an action or a state of being that is occurring now.
  She **attends** medical school.
- The **past tense** is used to express an action or a state of being that occurred in the past but that is not occurring now.
  We **stopped** at the mall.
- The **future tense** is used to express an action or a state of being that will occur.
  The choir **will sing** tomorrow.
- The **present perfect tense** is used to express an action or a state of being that occurred at some indefinite time in the past.
  She **has played** all the roles in that play.
- The **past perfect tense** is used to express an action or a state of being that was completed in the past before some other past action or event.
  Once the bell **had rung,** the teacher handed out the tests.
- The **future perfect tense** is used to express an action or a state of being that will be completed in the future before some other future occurrence.
  By the time you arrive, I **will have finished** my homework.

Changing verb tenses is sometimes necessary to show the order of events that occur at different times. However, do not change needlessly from one tense to another.

> NONSTANDARD: I open the door and walked outside.

> STANDARD: I **open** the door and **walk** outside.

Exercise   On the line provided, rewrite the italicized verb or verb phrase in the appropriate tense.

> EXAMPLE: 1. I *finished* the quilt by the time winter arrives.
> _will have finished_

1. When my little brother cried, he *wins* the argument.   _____

2. Jake *crosses* the finish line before his competitors reached the last hurdle.   _____

3. Sherry glanced at the test and *hands* it to the teacher.   _____

4. The parachuter secures his harness and *had prepared* to jump.   _____

5. We *reached* our destination, and now we are going to set up camp.   _____

Name _____ Date _____ Class _____

Active and Passive Voice

A verb in the **active voice** expresses an action done *by* its subject. A verb in the **passive voice** expresses an action done *to* its subject.

ACTIVE VOICE: Nat King Cole **sang** many beautiful songs.

PASSIVE VOICE: Many beautiful songs **were sung** by Nat King Cole.

The object of the active sentence [*songs*] becomes the subject of the passive sentence. The subject of the active sentence [*Nat King Cole*] becomes the object of a preposition. The verb in a passive sentence is always a verb phrase made up of a form of the verb *be* and the main verb's past participle.

Use the passive voice sparingly because it generally makes your writing sound weak and awkward. However, the passive voice is useful when you do not know or do not want to reveal the performer of the action or when you want to emphasize the receiver of the action.

Exercise A On the line provided, identify each of the following sentences as *active* or *passive*.

EXAMPLE: 1. In the morning, I am awakened by the alarm clock.
passive

1. The student body elects the council president. _____

2. Brian has been appointed captain of the team. _____

3. Angelo's courageous act prevented a tragedy. _____

4. W. C. Handy composed the famous jazz song "St. Louis Blues." _____

5. The half-time show was performed by the band. _____

6. The new bill was presented to Congress by Senator Thompson. _____

7. The Pittsburgh Pirates defeated Montreal, 8 to 2. _____

8. The delicate glass was dropped carelessly by Maria. _____

9. Enough weight was finally gained by the wrestler. _____

10. Excessive heat ruined the crops last summer. _____

Exercise B Five of the sentences in Exercise A contain verbs in the passive voice. On the lines below, rewrite each of the five sentences so that the verb is in the active voice.

1. _____ .

2. _____ .

3. _____ .

4. _____ .

5. _____ .

Chapter 3: Using Verbs Correctly

 **WORKSHEET 6** *Six Troublesome Verbs*

The verb *lie* means "to rest," "to stay,"or "to recline." *Lie* never takes an object. The verb *lay* means "to put (something) in a place." *Lay* usually takes an object.

   I will **lie** down for a nap.   Please **lay** my keys on the table.

The verb *sit* means "to rest in an upright, seated position." *Sit* rarely takes an object. The verb *set* means "to put (something) in a place." *Set* always takes an object.

   Please **sit** in that chair.   He will **set** your boots in the hall.

The verb *rise* means "to go up" or "to get up." *Rise* never takes an object. The verb *raise* means "to cause (something) to rise" or "to lift up." *Raise* usually takes an object.

   The sun **rises** around six o'clock.   **Raise** your hand to cast your vote.

Here are the principal parts of these verbs:

Infinitive	Present Participle	Past	Past Participle
lie (to rest)	lying	lay	(have) lain
lay (to put)	laying	laid	(have) laid
sit (to rest)	sitting	sat	(have) sat
set (to put)	setting	set	(have) set
rise (to go up)	rising	rose	(have) risen
raise (to move something up)	raising	raised	(have) raised

Exercise   Underline the correct form of the verb in parentheses in each of the following sentences.

   EXAMPLE: 1. Will you (sit, set) with me, Josh?

1. Please (rise, raise) and face the audience.

2. Our dog (sits, sets) in the sun whenever it can.

3. She has (lain, laid) on the couch all morning.

4. The moon (rose, raised) and slipped behind a cloud.

5. The price of fuel has (risen, raised) steadily.

6. We had (sat, set) still for almost an hour.

7. Mrs. Levine (sat, set) the menorah on the mantle.

8. (Lie, Lay) down and rest a while.

9. The stagehands (rose, raised) the curtain for each act.

10. Jennifer (lay, laid) the flowers on the table and looked for a vase.

Chapter 3: Using Verbs Correctly

WORKSHEET 7   *Review*

Exercise A   On the line provided, write the correct past or past participle form of the verb given for each sentence.

EXAMPLE: 1. *run*   Yesterday we ___*ran*___ around the track three times.

1. *sing*   Luther Vandross _____ last night.

2. *burst*   The car suddenly _____ into flames.

3. *drink*   Yesterday they _____ juice with their sandwiches.

4. *do*   They _____ their best to repair the damage.

5. *loan*   Grandma has _____ us some old photos.

6. *ring*   My alarm _____ at six o'clock.

7. *speak*   Toni has not _____ to me since our argument.

8. *fall*   A tree has _____ across the highway.

9. *throw*   Kerry should have _____ the ball to Lee.

10. *freeze*   Has the water _____ yet?

Exercise B   On the line provided, write the correct past or past participle form of each verb in parentheses in the following paragraph.

EXAMPLE: All my life I have [1] *(know)* _*known*_ that I must make my own choices.

I have never [1] *(choose)* _____ to be on a sports team because I am

not a very athletic person. On the other hand, my brother and sister have [2] *(drive)*

_____ themselves very hard and have [3] *(become)*

_____ excellent athletes. For example, my brother, Emilio,

[4] *(break)* _____ three swimming records this year alone. He has

[5] *(swim)* _____ better than anyone else in our school. He also [6] *(go)*

_____ out for tennis and track this year. My sister, Elena, is only a junior,

but she has already [7] *(run)* _____ the 100-yard dash faster than any

senior girl. I [8] *(use)* _____ to think I wanted to follow in my brother's

and sister's footsteps, but now I have [9] *(take)* _____ a different path in

life. My English teacher just [10] *(give)* _____ me a chance to lead the

debating team, and I am going to grab it!

GRAMMAR/USAGE

Chapter 3, Worksheet 7, continued

Exercise C On the line provided, identify the tense of each italicized verb in the following sentences. Use the identifications *Present, Past, Future,* and *Pres P, Past P,* and *Future P* for the three perfect tenses. Add *PF* if a tense is also in the progressive form.

EXAMPLE: 1. Marian Anderson *sang* her way out of poverty. __Past__

1. She *went* on to earn worldwide fame and the Presidential Medal of Freedom. _____

2. You *will find* her life very interesting. _____

3. I *have learned* that in 1955 Marian Anderson became the first African American singer to perform with the Metropolitan Opera in New York City. _____

4. She *began* her career as a child, singing hymns in church. _____

5. She *had studied* music in Europe before becoming an international star. _____

6. Many people *have been remembering* Anderson's career since her death in 1993. _____

7. Civil rights leaders *have noted* Anderson's achievements in overcoming racial barriers. _____

8. I *want* to listen to all of Anderson's recordings. _____

9. By the end of the year, I *will have heard* all of them. _____

10. I also *am reading* Anderson's autobiography, *My Lord, What a Morning.* _____

Exercise D: Proofreading On the line provided, rewrite each sentence to correct any errors in verb tense. In each sentence, make both verbs agree in tense.

EXAMPLE: 1. We waited for three hours and then leave the lake.
We waited for three hours and then left the lake.

1. I sing my song first and then you danced.

_____

2. Martha had been listening while he talks.

_____

3. I have finished before you got here.

_____

4. I never ridden a horse before you had taken me to the stables.

_____

5. Chris grabbed her coat and rushes out of the apartment.

_____

Exercise E   On the line provided, identify each of the following sentences as *active* or *passive*.

> EXAMPLE: 1. The horse is chasing the steer. *active*

1. Rodeo horses are specially trained for this work. _____

2. The mountains were covered by freshly fallen snow. _____

3. A sand crab lived in the seashell. _____

4. Tonight's movie premiere will be followed by a presentation by
    the director. _____

5. Hannah was surprised by a sudden rock slide. _____

6. The tennis match was delayed by heavy rains. _____

7. Edith Wharton wrote *Ethan Frome*. _____

8. Jeffrey had been elected honor-code counselor by the student body. _____

9. Lightning struck the boat. _____

10. Alex rode his bicycle everywhere. _____

Exercise F: Revising   Each of the following sentences contains a verb in the passive
voice. On the line provided, rewrite each sentence so that the verb is in the active voice.

> EXAMPLE: 1. The garden was overrun by weeds.
>
> *Weeds overran the garden.*

1. The bell was rung by Ramash.

   _____

2. The milk was poured by Clarence.

   _____

3. The mail was brought by our new carrier.

   _____

4. The curtains were ironed by Darob.

   _____

5. The cat was chased by the puppy.

   _____

GRAMMAR/USAGE

Chapter 3, Worksheet 7, continued

Exercise G   For each of the following sentences, underline the correct verb in parentheses.

EXAMPLE: 1. The number of European immigrants coming to the United States (<u>rose</u>, raised) steadily during the late 1800s.

1. I saw a photograph of a Hungarian mother (sitting, setting) with her children around 1910.

2. They were among thousands of immigrant families who (sat, set) their baggage on American soil for the first time at the immigration station on Ellis Island in New York Harbor.

3. (Lying, Laying) down was often impossible on the crowded ships that brought these immigrants to the United States.

4. Most immigrants were thankful to be able to (lie, lay) their few belongings on the deck and think of the future.

5. Their hopes must have (risen, raised) as they drew closer to the United States.

6. The history book (lying, laying) on the desk states that eleven million immigrants came to the United States between 1870 and 1899.

7. (Sit, Set) down and read more about the immigrants who came from Germany, Ireland, Great Britain, Scandinavia, and the Netherlands in the early 1800s.

8. After 1890, the number of immigrants from Austria-Hungary, Italy, Russia, Poland, and Greece (rose, raised).

9. Many United States citizens were (rising, raising) concerns that there would not be enough jobs for everyone in the country.

10. But we know now that immigrant workers helped the country to (rise, raise) to new industrial heights.

Name _____ Date _____ Class _____

 **WORKSHEET 1** *Pronoun Case*

Case is the form of a noun or a pronoun that shows how it is used. In English, there are three cases: **nominative**, **objective**, and **possessive**. Most personal pronouns have a different form for each case, as this chart indicates.

		Nominative	Objective	Possessive
SINGULAR	FIRST PERSON:	I	me	my, mine
	SECOND PERSON:	you	you	your, yours
	THIRD PERSON:	he, she, it	him, her, it	his, her, hers, its
PLURAL	FIRST PERSON:	we	us	our, ours
	SECOND PERSON:	you	you	your, yours
	THIRD PERSON:	they	them	their, theirs

Exercise A   Each of the following sentences contains a pronoun in italics. Identify the case form of the pronoun. On the line provided, write *NOM* for nominative case, *OBJ* for objective case, or *POS* for possessive case.

EXAMPLE: _NOM_ 1. Last weekend *we* went to a Chinese restaurant for a delicious meal called dim sum.

_____ 1. The waiter brought *us* a cart that had many bowls.

_____ 2. *I* lifted the lid off one bowl.

_____ 3. The cart had so many of *them*.

_____ 4. After the meal, *our* table contained many empty bowls.

_____ 5. After the waiter counted them, *we* paid the bill.

Exercise B   Each of the following sentences includes a description of a pronoun. On the line after each sentence, write the pronoun that completes the sentence correctly.

EXAMPLE: 1. Outdoor activities interest everyone in (first person plural, possessive) family. _our_

1. *(First person singular, possessive)* sister and I went hiking in the desert in Arizona. _____

2. Relatives who live there gave us good advice when *(third person plural, nominative)* said to carry plenty of water. _____

3. It surprised *(first person plural, objective)* that there were so many beautiful and interesting plants and animals. _____

4. Lizards of all sizes and colors scurried away if we approached *(third person plural, objective)*. _____

5. If *(second person singular, possessive)* family goes to the desert, take time to do some hiking. _____

GRAMMAR/USAGE

Name _____ Date _____ Class _____

The Nominative Case

Pronouns used as subjects are in the **nominative case**.

SUBJECT: **They** left after lunch.

COMPOUND SUBJECT: Diego and **I** played chess.

Pronouns used as *predicate nominatives* are also in the nominative case. A **predicate nominative** is a noun or a pronoun that follows a linking verb and that explains or identifies the subject of the verb. A pronoun that is used as a predicate nominative always follows a form of the verb *be: am, is, are, was, were, be,* or *been.*

PREDICATE NOMINATIVE: Once again the winner was **he**.

Exercise A For each sentence in the following paragraph, underline the correct form of the pronoun in parentheses.

EXAMPLE: [1] (They, Them) may be the most famous husband-and-wife team of scientists who ever lived.

Although Marie and Pierre Curie were both brilliant physicists, [1] (she, her) is better known than her husband is today. In fact, [2] (I, me) was surprised to learn that [3] (them, they) both received the Nobel Prize for physics in 1903. [4] (We, Us) tend to remember only Marie because [5] (her, she) was the first woman to win a Nobel Prize. In 1911, [6] (she, her) was again honored by the Nobel Committee when [7] (she, her) was awarded the prize for chemistry. Despite her individual honors, Marie Curie always felt that [8] (her, she) and her husband were a team. Working in a small laboratory in Paris, [9] (they, them) didn't have room for independent research. As a result, [10] (them, they) collaborated on almost every project.

Exercise B Complete the following sentences by adding pronouns used as predicate nominatives. Use a different pronoun in each sentence. Do not use *you* or *it*.

EXAMPLE: 1. It is __*she*__ who is most likely to be chosen.

1. Do you know if it was _____ ?

2. I thought it would be _____ .

3. The winner of the marathon will likely be _____ .

4. That is not _____ .

5. Can the valedictorian be _____ ?

Name _____ Date _____ Class _____

The Objective Case

Pronouns used as direct objects, indirect objects, and objects of prepositions are in the **objective case**. A **direct object** is a noun or a pronoun that follows an action verb. It tells *who* or *what* receives the action of the verb. A direct object may be compound.

> DIRECT OBJECTS: Luigi visited **us** in November.
>
> Pam met **her** and **me** at the bus stop.

An **indirect object** is a noun or a pronoun that tells *to whom, to what, for whom,* or *for what* something is done. An indirect object may be compound.

> INDIRECT OBJECTS: The guide gave **us** a tour.
>
> The guide gave **them** and **us** a tour.

A prepositional phrase begins with a preposition and ends with a noun or a pronoun called the **object of the preposition**. An object of a preposition may be compound.

> OBJECTS OF PREPOSITIONS: Beth trimmed the hedge for **them**.
>
> She lent the saw to **him** and **me**.

Exercise A   For each of the following sentences, underline the correct form of the pronoun in parentheses.

> EXAMPLE: 1. Give (<u>him</u>, he) and (I, <u>me</u>) a chance to solve the problem.

1. Hassan asked (she, her) the most difficult question.

2. Mrs. Yee handed the homework assignments to (they, them) and (me, I).

3. Please give (her, she) last week's assignment.

4. Writing letters to (he, him) gives (us, we) great pleasure.

5. Just between you and (I, me), this assignment is too difficult.

Exercise B   On the line provided before each of the following sentences, identify the pronoun. Write *DO* for direct object, *IO* for indirect object, or *OP* for object of a preposition.

> EXAMPLE: _OP_   1. Friends often lend books to *me*.

_____ 1. People gave *him* the nickname Prez.

_____ 2. I saw Charles and *him* at the meeting.

_____ 3. A messenger in a blue uniform handed a sealed package to *her*.

_____ 4. Most of *us* liked the new biology book.

_____ 5. Aunt Flo sent Howard and *me* a magazine subscription.

GRAMMAR/USAGE

Name _____ Date _____ Class _____

Special Pronoun Problems: Who and Whom

WORKSHEET 4

Who is used as a subject of a verb and as a predicate nominative. *Whom* is used as an object of a verb and as an object of a preposition. The pronouns *who* and *whoever* are in the nominative case; *whom* and *whomever* are in the objective case. The use of *who* or *whom* in a subordinate clause depends on how the pronoun functions in the clause. In the following example, notice how four simple steps reveal which pronoun to use in the sentence *Do you know (who, whom) is absent?* These steps can help you determine how the pronoun functions in a subordinate clause:

QUESTION: What is the subordinate clause in the sentence?

ANSWER: The subordinate clause is *(who, whom) is absent*.

QUESTION: How is the pronoun used in the clause—as subject, predicate nominative, object of the verb, or object of a preposition?

ANSWER: The pronoun is the subject of the verb *is*.

QUESTION: What is the correct case for this use of the pronoun?

ANSWER: A pronoun used as a subject is in the nominative case.

QUESTION: What is the correct form of the pronoun?

ANSWER: *Do you know* who *is absent?*

Exercise   For each of the following sentences, underline the correct form of the pronoun in parentheses.

EXAMPLE: 1. The friends (who, <u>whom</u>) I like best are the ones with goals.

1. Carol wondered (who, whom) she should ask for directions.

2. The artist (who, whom) painted that mural was Diego Rivera.

3. Is that the singer (who, whom) plays the guitar so well?

4. Lily couldn't figure out (who, whom) sent her the surprise package.

5. Jesse didn't know (who, whom) we were talking about.

6. You may invite (whoever, whomever) you wish.

7. Mr. Chow, (who, whom) is a real-estate broker, won the award.

8. (Whoever, Whomever) solves the mystery gets a free copy of the book.

9. Do you know (who, whom) your new neighbors are?

10. Sessue Hayakawa is the actor (who, whom) played that role.

Name _____ Date _____ Class _____

WORKSHEET 5

Pronouns Used as Appositives

An **appositive** is a noun or a pronoun placed next to another noun or pronoun to identify or explain it. Pronouns used as appositives are in the same case as the words to which they refer.

> The group leaders, Paula and **I,** set the practice times. [The pronoun is in the nominative case because it is used as an appositive of the subject, *leaders*.]

> The spelling champs are the youngest spellers, **he** and **she**. [The pronouns are in the nominative case because they are used as appositives of the predicate nominative, *spellers*.]

> The celebration is for the top competitors, Lin and **me**. [The pronoun is in the objective case because it is used as an appositive of *competitors*, the object of the preposition.]

> The principal praised the most-improved writers, Fran and **her**. [The pronoun is in the objective case because it is used as an appositive of the direct object, *writers*.]

Sometimes the pronouns *we* and *us* are followed by noun appositives.

> **We** students want to start an orienteering club.

> The lifeguard gave advice to **us** swimmers.

Exercise A   For each of the following sentences, underline the correct form of the pronoun in parentheses.

> EXAMPLE: 1. The principal named the winners, Julia and (I, <u>me</u>).

1. Kiole listed her favorite actors, Emilio Estevez, Tom Cruise, and (he, him).

2. Come to the game with (we, us) girls.

3. I want to go to the concert with two friends, Iola and (he, him).

4. The librarian gave the best readers, Craig and (I, me), two books.

5. The two forwards, Scarlett and (she, her), work well together on the basketball court.

Exercise B: Proofreading   Each of the following sentences contains an error in pronoun form. Revise each sentence to correct the error.

> EXAMPLE: 1. The band's rhythm section, Tito and ~~me,~~ *I* will practice at my house tonight.

1. Us waiters pool our tips with the cooks, Sharon and her.

2. The fastest runners, she and him, will run last in their relay teams.

3. Those two, he and she, have been looking enviously at we swimmers all afternoon.

4. She awarded the debate champions, Geraldine and he, their own trophies.

5. The two finalists in the street-basketball tournament are the Praying Mantises, Roberto and I, and the Wings, Eddie and him.

GRAMMAR/USAGE

Chapter 4: Using Pronouns

WORKSHEET 6

Pronouns in Incomplete Constructions

In a sentence with an **incomplete construction,** the case of the pronoun depends on how the omitted part of the sentence would be completed. After *than* and *as* introducing an incomplete construction, use the pronoun form that would be correct if the construction were completed. Notice in the following examples how changing the pronoun changes the meaning of the sentence.

> I called you earlier than **he** [called you].
>
> I called you earlier than [I called] **him.**

Exercise A   For each of the following sentences, underline the correct form of the pronoun in parentheses. If a sentence may be completed in two different ways, underline both alternatives.

> EXAMPLE: 1. That skater is more daring than (<u>she</u>, her).

1. Justin wants to go hiking more often than (I, me).

2. Did the puzzle confuse you as much as (we, us)?

3. My brother is taller than (he, him).

4. Have they studied as long as (we, us)?

5. We liked the older actress better than (she, her).

Exercise B   In each of the following sentences, complete the incomplete construction, beginning with *than* or *as,* by using the correct form of the pronoun. Then, tell whether the pronoun in the completed clause is a *subject* or an *object.* If a sentence may be completed in two different ways, provide both alternatives.

> EXAMPLE: 1. Marty was happier than (I, me).
>
> *than I was—subject*

1. Are you more creative than (he, him)?

   _____

2. Do they swim as fast as (I, me)?

   _____

3. I like Rene better than (they, them).

   _____

4. Many people are less fortunate than (we, us).

   _____

5. Are you as optimistic as (she, her)?

   _____

Chapter 4: Using Pronouns

WORKSHEET 7

Inexact Pronoun Reference: Ambiguous and General Reference

A pronoun should always refer clearly to its antecedent. Using a pronoun in such a way that it can refer to either of two antecedents produces an **ambiguous reference**.

> AMBIGUOUS: George missed his father while he was in California.
> [Who was in California?]
>
> CLEAR: While George's father was in California, George missed him.

Include a specific antecedent for each pronoun you use. Using a pronoun that refers to a general idea rather than to a specific noun produces a **general reference**. The pronouns commonly used in making general-reference errors are *it, that, this, such,* and *which.*

> GENERAL: Zeke swerved his bike, which caused an accident.
> [What caused the accident?]
>
> CLEAR: Zeke caused an accident when he swerved his bike.

Exercise A   On the blank provided, tell whether the inexact pronoun reference is an ambiguous-reference *(AMB)* or general-reference error *(GEN)*.

> EXAMPLE: _GEN_   1. This is difficult because I like both books.

_____ 1. Marian called Ruth when she was in Oregon.

_____ 2. Fu-Yen has mastered English in a year, which is impressive.

_____ 3. The rain clouds were dark. That made the search difficult.

_____ 4. My father told my brother he was going camping.

_____ 5. Helene lost the key to the house, which is a problem.

Exercise B: Revising   On the lines provided, rewrite the following sentences to eliminate inexact pronoun references.

> EXAMPLE: 1. After viewing Beth's ceramics and Anne's sculptures, the judges gave the award to her.
>
> *The judges awarded Beth the blue ribbon after viewing her ceramics and Anne's sculptures.*

1. The science club changed the day of the meeting to discuss the field trip. This will take place on Tuesday.

_____

2. When the boomerang hit the fence, it splintered into pieces.

_____

3. Ginny and Ms. Campos decided she would pay the car insurance.

_____

4. Ione went to see Katie on her birthday.

_____

GRAMMAR/USAGE

Chapter 4: Using Pronouns

Inexact Pronoun Reference: Weak Reference and Indefinite Reference

Using a pronoun to refer to a word or idea that is not specifically stated results in a **weak reference**.

WEAK: Mai has artistic talent, and she wants to make it her career. [*It* probably refers to drawing, painting, or some other form of art, but the writer has not given a specific antecedent for *it*.]

CLEAR: Mai is a talented artist, and she hopes to make painting her career.

Using the pronouns *it, they,* and *you* unnecessarily is common in informal conversation. Avoid using such **indefinite references** in more formal situations and in writing.

INDEFINITE: In the French Club's bylaws, it explains that a meeting is required every week. [The pronoun *it* is not necessary to the meaning of the sentence.]

CLEAR: The French Club's bylaws require a meeting every week.

Exercise: Revising   The following sentences contain weak or indefinite references. On the line provided, rewrite each sentence, correcting the inexact reference. Although these sentences can be corrected in more than one way, you need only give one revision.

EXAMPLE: 1. I'm not that good at softball, but I enjoy socializing with them.

I'm not that good at softball, but I enjoy socializing with the team.

1. In this book I am reading, it has a complicated plot.

_____

2. Carmen likes studying astronomy, although she has never seen one through a telescope.

_____

3. In the newspaper, it reported that the concert was sold out.

_____

4. Even though they don't always come out right, I enjoy cooking.

_____

5. In exchange for horseback-riding lessons, Lucy grooms them and cleans out their stables.

_____

Name _____ Date _____ Class _____

 **WORKSHEET 9** | *Review*

Exercise A   For each of the following sentences, underline the correct form of the pronoun in parentheses. On the line provided, give the pronoun's use in the sentence by writing *S* for subject, *PN* for predicate nominative, *OV* for object of the verb, or *OP* for object of the preposition.

EXAMPLE: _OP_ 1. He always hit the ball when it was pitched to (he, <u>him</u>).

_____ 1. My sister and (me, I) like to play chess.

_____ 2. Both of (we, us) play it rather well.

_____ 3. (We, Us) both played in local tournaments this year.

_____ 4. Compared with my parents, we can play much better than (they, them) can.

_____ 5. "This is a good game for (they, them)," my father said, "since they have plenty of time."

_____ 6. To (we, us) he appears indifferent toward the game.

_____ 7. It is (he, him) and Ahulani who most dislike losing.

_____ 8. "Play again," my mother says when (he, him) is beaten.

_____ 9. The most difficult player to beat is (she, her) because her game is always carefully played out.

_____10. My father doesn't challenge Ahulani or (I, me) very often.

Exercise B   On the line provided, write *who, whoever, whom,* or *whomever* to complete each of the following sentences correctly.

EXAMPLE: 1. *Whoever* wins this game will go to the tournament.

1. _____ was the first American grandmaster of chess?

2. To _____ would you go to learn this fact?

3. Our school librarian, _____ knows where to look, told us.

4. I wish I could defeat _____ I play.

5. _____ challenges me, however, gets a friendly welcome and a serious game.

Exercise C: Proofreading   Some of the following sentences contain errors in pronoun usage. Underline each pronoun error and write the correct pronoun on the line provided. If a sentence is correct, write *C* on the line provided.

EXAMPLE: 1. Was it my sister or <u>me</u> who first played chess well? ___*I*___

1. My father and us two beginners soon were playing to win. _____

2. It was he who first realized how complex a game it is. _____

GRAMMAR/USAGE

3. A bitter rivalry arose between my sister and me.   _____

4. Before long, my father and her were also rivals.   _____

5. The person whom enjoyed the rivalry least was Mother.   _____

Exercise D   Underline the correct pronoun in each sentence.

EXAMPLE: 1. Not many people take more risks than (he, him).

1. He competes more strenuously than (they, them).

2. His sister is even better at sports than (him, he).

3. Are you as strong as (he, him)?

4. No one here is quicker than (she, her).

5. Many people are less dedicated than (us, we).

6. Both of us, Sandy and (I, me), want to be writers.

7. Writers of great determination, (we, us) plan to become rich and famous.

8. We will give autographs to (they, them), our adoring fans.

9. But (we, us) best-selling authors will be humble.

10. As a high school student for now, however, (me, I) had better do my assignment.

Exercise E: Revising   Revise each of the following sentences by correcting the inexact pronoun reference. [Note: Although these sentences can be corrected in more than one way, you need to give only one revision.]

EXAMPLE: 1. She spent an hour at the hat store but didn't buy it.

She spent an hour at the hat store but didn't buy a hat.

1. In Arkansas they have the only diamond mine in the United States.

_____

2. When the car hit the tree, it was damaged.

_____

3. In the mid-eighteen-hundreds, you have the American Civil War.

_____

4. I ran and hiked and swam last weekend, and it made me feel better.

_____

5. I heard from my friend about a trip he took, which was a surprise.

_____

Name _____ Date _____ Class _____

 # Adjectives and Adverbs

A **modifier** is a word or group of words that makes the meaning of another word more definite. Two kinds of single-word modifiers are *adjectives* and *adverbs*.

Use an **adjective** to limit the meaning of a noun or a pronoun.

> Hubble sang a **cheerful** song. [The adjective *cheerful* limits the meaning of the noun *song*.]

Use an **adverb** to limit the meaning of a verb, an adjective, or another adverb.

> Hubble sang **cheerfully**. [The adverb *cheerfully* limits the meaning of the verb *sang*.]

A **linking verb,** such as *be, become, look, seem,* or *taste,* is often followed by a *predicate adjective*. A **predicate adjective** is a word that modifies the subject. Most linking verbs can also be used as action verbs. Whether to use an adjective or an adverb in a sentence depends on whether the verb is a linking verb or an action verb.

> That clock **appears slow**. [*Appears* is a linking verb. The predicate adjective *slow* modifies the subject *clock*.]

> The sun **appeared slowly** from behind the clouds. [*Appeared* is an action verb modified by the adverb *slowly*.]

If a word in the predicate modifies the subject, use the adjective form. If it modifies the verb, use the adverb form.

Exercise For each of the following sentences, underline the correct modifier in parentheses. Then underline the word it modifies.

> EXAMPLE: 1. Elvira <u>smiled</u> (happy, <u>happily</u>) as she opened the door.

1. The quiz bowl team's chances look (excellent, excellently) this year.

2. Last year they did (poor, poorly).

3. That greyhound is (fastly, fast)!

4. If we run (quick, quickly), we can catch this roller-coaster ride.

5. The celery soup is (absolute, absolutely) delicious.

GRAMMAR/USAGE

Chapter 5: Using Modifiers

WORKSHEET 2   *Comparison*

The forms of modifiers change to show comparison. Adjectives change form to compare one noun or pronoun with another noun or pronoun that has the same quality. Adverbs are used to make comparisons between verbs.

ADJECTIVE: Mount McKinley is **higher** than Mount Ranier.

ADVERB: Aaron ate **slowly**, but Alicia ate even **more slowly**.

There are three degrees of comparison: *positive, comparative,* and *superlative.* A one-syllable modifier regularly forms its comparative and superlative degrees by adding *–er* and *–est.* Some two-syllable modifiers form their comparative and superlative degrees by adding *–er* and *–est.* Other two-syllable modifiers form their comparative and superlative degrees with *more* and *most.* Modifiers that have more than two syllables form their comparative and superlative degrees with *more* and *most.*

	One-syllable Modifier	Two-syllable Modifier	Three-syllable Modifier
Positive	fast	hungry, cheerful	comfortable
Comparative	faster	hungrier, more cheerful	more comfortable
Superlative	fastest	hungriest, most cheerful	most comfortable

To indicate a decrease in a quality or degree, modifiers use the word *less* or *least.*

interesting   less interesting   least interesting

Exercise   On the lines provided, give the forms for the comparative and superlative degrees of the following words.

EXAMPLES: 1. bright *brighter, brightest*
2. quickly *more quickly, most quickly*

1. fast   _____

2. soon   _____

3. happy   _____

4. careful   _____

5. simple   _____

6. fabulous   _____

7. powerful   _____

8. wisely   _____

9. anxious   _____

10. pretty   _____

Chapter 5: Using Modifiers

WORKSHEET 3 | *Irregular Comparison*

Some modifiers do not follow the regular methods of forming their comparative and superlative degrees.

POSITIVE	COMPARATIVE	SUPERLATIVE
bad	worse	worst
good/well	better	best
little	less/littler	least/littlest
many/much	more	most

Do not add *–er* or *–est* to irregular comparative and superlative forms. For example, use *worse*, not *worser;* use *best*, not *bestest.*

Exercise   For the blank in each of the following sentences, write the correct form of the word in italics before that sentence.

EXAMPLE: 1. *bad* My notebook looks <u>worse</u> than Joshua's.

1. *well*   I can skate _____ now than I could last year.

2. *many*   She caught the _____ fish of anyone in our group.

3. *bad*   That is the _____ movie I have ever seen.

4. *much*   We have _____ homework than we had last week.

5. *good*   Felicia has the _____ attendance record in the class.

6. *many*   Justin's tree has the _____ peaches.

7. *bad*   The test results were _____ than we had expected.

8. *many*   You bought _____ clothes today than I've bought all year!

9. *good*   I have seen _____ illustrations in other books.

10. *little*   We raised far _____ money this year than last.

Chapter 5: Using Modifiers

Use of Comparative and Superlative Forms

Use the **comparative** degree when comparing two things. Use the **superlative** degree when comparing more than two.

COMPARING TWO: Artist Henry Ossawa Tanner is **more famous** now than he was a decade ago.

COMPARING MORE THAN TWO: One of Tanner's **most famous** works shows an old man giving a young boy a banjo lesson.

Exercise: Proofreading   Each of the following sentences contains a comparative or superlative modifier. If the form is correct for the number of items compared, write C on the line provided. If the wrong form is used, write the correct form.

EXAMPLE: 1. Nina's report on Native Americans' star legends was the more interesting report in the class. _most interesting_

1. Although Nina and I both researched our reports carefully, her report was the most thorough one. _____

2. The Native Americans' stories about the stars and the sky are even better than the Greek myths, in my opinion. _____

3. Nina told a dozen stories, but the six myths she told about the cluster of stars known as the Pleiades are the more fascinating. _____

4. The stranger tale, which is from the Monache Indians of central California, relates how a little girl and six women who wouldn't give up eating onions became the Pleiades. _____

5. The scariest of the tales is the Skidi Pawnee myth about six brothers and an adopted sister who fight the Rolling Skull. _____

6. That story was not only the most interesting but also the longer legend that Nina told. _____

7. Of all the earthly creatures in the stories Nina told, Coyote is perhaps the more important. _____

8. In fact, people often play a least important role than Coyote plays in some stories. _____

9. After class, I told Nina that compared with my report, hers was the best. _____

10. She said that telling the stories was easier than finding them. _____

Name _____ Date _____ Class _____

WORKSHEET 5

Other, Else/Double Comparisons/ Unclear Comparisons

Include the word *other* or *else* when comparing one thing with others in the same group.

NONSTANDARD: My brother Jack is taller than anyone in the family. [He can't be taller than himself.]

STANDARD: My brother Jack is taller than anyone **else** in the family.

A double comparison contains both *–er* and *more* (or *less*) or both *–est* and *most* (or *least*).

NONSTANDARD: That is the most silliest clown I've ever seen.

STANDARD: That is the **silliest** clown I've ever seen.

You can often make a comparison clearer by adding a word or phrase.

UNCLEAR: I wrote to him more than Yuri.

CLEAR: I wrote to him more than **I wrote** to Yuri.

CLEAR: I wrote to him more than Yuri **wrote to him**.

Exercise A: Proofreading   Correct each of the following sentences by inserting a caret (^) with either *other* or *else* above it at the appropriate point.

EXAMPLE: 1. Rodney spells better than anyone ^*else* in his class.

1. My grandmother is wiser than anyone I know.

2. Kumiko eats more slowly than anybody I've seen.

3. Flying is faster than any type of travel.

4. My sunflowers grew taller than any flowers I planted this year.

Exercise B: Revising   Rewrite each sentence on the line provided, correcting double comparisons and changing unclear comparisons into clear comparisons.

EXAMPLE: 1. Today is more colder than yesterday.
Today is colder than yesterday.

1. That is the most softest sweater that I have ever had.

_____

2. The part of the mushroom you see is much smaller than underground.

_____

3. She is the most fastest runner on the team.

_____

4. Milo writes me more frequently than Jake.

_____

5. Is Georgia more larger in area than any other state east of the Mississippi?

_____

GRAMMAR/USAGE

Chapter 5: Using Modifiers

 **WORKSHEET 6** *Dangling Modifiers*

A modifying phrase or clause that does not clearly and sensibly modify a word or a group of words in the same sentence is a **dangling modifier**. When a participial phrase comes at the beginning of a sentence, the phrase is followed by a comma. The word that the phrase modifies should come as closely as possible after the comma.

Reading Pearl Buck's *The Good Earth,* I became interested in Chinese history.

To correct a dangling modifier, rearrange the words in the sentence and add or change words to make the meaning logical and clear.

DANGLING: Looking out the window, a robin was singing.

CLEAR: Looking out the window, **I** saw a robin singing.

Exercise A   Write complete sentences, using the following list of introductory modifiers.

EXAMPLE: 1. Having solved one problem, *Seema found that another awaited her.*

1. Leaping from branch to branch, _____

2. Soaked by rain, _____

3. While eating our lunch, _____

4. Surrounded by the cheering crowd, _____

5. Worried that he would be late, _____

Exercise B: Revising   Each of the following sentences contains a dangling modifier. Revise each sentence to eliminate the dangling modifier.

1. Walking through the main gate, the swimming pool lies to your right.

   _____

2. Lost in the jungle for three weeks, the small village was a more than welcome sight.

   _____

3. To earn spending money, my neighbor gave me a job addressing envelopes.

   _____

4. Trying to study, my cat's howling annoyed me.

   _____

5. Walking in the woods, the sound of singing birds is an enjoyable experience.

   _____

Name _____ Date _____ Class _____

 **WORKSHEET 7** *Misplaced Modifiers*

A **misplaced modifier** is a phrase or clause that makes a sentence awkward or unclear because it modifies the wrong word or group of words. Modifying phrases and clauses should be placed as near as possible to the words they modify.

MISPLACED: The report is lying on my kitchen table that was due today.

CORRECTED: The report that was due today is lying on my kitchen table.

Exercise: Revising On the lines provided, revise the following sentences so that they make sense. Be sure that you do not misplace another modifier in revising a sentence.

EXAMPLE: 1. There was a bird in the tree that had a strange looking beak.

There was a bird with a strange looking beak in the tree.

1. I could see the scouts marching over the hill with my binoculars.

   _____

2. We gave the boxes of cereal to the children with prizes inside.

   _____

3. As a child, my grandmother taught me how to weave baskets.

   _____

4. One advertiser handed out roses to customers with dollar bills pinned to them.

   _____

5. I borrowed a radio from my sister with a weather band.

   _____

6. Did you look for a collection of hats worn by your grandmother in the attic?

   _____

7. Our cat was waiting patiently for us to come home on the front porch.

   _____

8. She ate two peaches and a plate of strawberries watching TV.

   _____

9. In a tank at the aquarium, we watched the seals playing.

   _____

10. There is a flower garden behind the shed that is planted with prize-winning dahlias.

   _____

GRAMMAR/USAGE

Chapter 5: Using Modifiers

 **WORKSHEET 8** *Review*

Exercise A On the line provided, write the comparative and superlative forms of each of the following modifiers.

	Positive	Comparative	Superlative
EXAMPLE: 1.	*bad*	*worse*	*worst*
1.	*good*		
2.	*closely*		
3.	*rich*		
4.	*useful*		
5.	*many*		

Exercise B: Proofreading Some of the sentences below contain errors in the use of modifiers. If the sentence is correct, write *C* on the line provided. If the sentence is incorrect, underline the incorrect modifier. Then write the correct modifier on the line provided. If a word is missing, draw a caret (^) where the word belongs. Then write the missing word on the line provided.

> EXAMPLES: 1. That is the <u>most brightest</u> light of all. *brightest*
>
> 2. Janeel is better at math than anybody in her class. *else*

1. My hometown is prettier than any town of its size in the state. _____

2. Her suggestion is a good one, but Paquito's is much better. _____

3. Who is tallest, you or Arlon? _____

4. I was relieved to find that some of the best students in the class did worser on the test than I did. _____

5. Our city park is much more cleaner than most of the parks in neighboring towns. _____

6. Which of the two high schools in your town is the largest? _____

7. My sister Marita is taller than anybody in my family. _____

8. Our new mayor works more hard than our last mayor did. _____

9. Both of the speeches were good, but I thought that Rajiv's was the better of the two. _____

10. The first half of the test was more easier than the second half. _____

Chapter 5, Worksheet 8, *continued*

Exercise C: Revising The sentences below contain dangling or misplaced modifiers. On the lines provided, rewrite the sentences with the modifier correctly placed.

EXAMPLE: 1. Lying in the middle of the road, I saw a large snake.

I saw a large snake lying in the middle of the road.

1. Looking up, the rain forest canopy blocked the sun.

_____

2. An elm fell across the house that had been uprooted in the storm.

_____

3. I bought a book from that store that describes the history of the Alamo.

_____

4. We looked for a map irritated by the delay.

_____

5. We saw the Taj Mahal looking down from an airplane.

_____

6. Coming home from the movies, the raccoon ran in front of us.

_____

7. The azalea belongs to my neighbor, which blooms early in the spring.

_____

8. Cawing and chirping, we heard the birds making their nests.

_____

9. My aunt served fish to Melvin and me broiled over hot coals.

_____

10. Barking at passing cars, I raced after my dog.

_____

Exercise D Each of the following sentences contains a misplaced modifier. Circle the misplaced modifier and then draw an arrow to show where it should go in the sentence.

EXAMPLE: 1. (At the age of six,) my father decided that I was ready for my first camping trip.

1. The campers watched the sunrise peacefully eating their breakfast.

2. We were nearly blinded as we came out of the tunnel by the sunlight.

3. A gift basket was carried into the living room which was filled to the top with fancy cheeses and crackers.

4. A huge plane roared over our house with its wheels down.

5. Circling the field, the women in the control tower watched the plane.

GRAMMAR/USAGE

Exercise E   You are writing a science fiction story. To help get started, jot down the following list of phrases and clauses:

roaring and breathing fire as it approached

that had a head on each finger

whether they had come in peace

to communicate with the aliens

which seemed to be everywhere

Now you can use these ideas to start the story. On the lines provided, use each of the phrases and clauses correctly as modifiers. Make sure that you don't have any dangling or misplaced modifiers.

EXAMPLE: to communicate with the aliens

To communicate with the aliens, Martin tried playing samba music at half-speed.

_____

_____

_____

_____

_____

Chapter 6: Phrases

Prepositional Phrases

A **phrase** is a group of related words that is used as a single part of speech and does not contain both a verb and its subject.

> have been riding [verb phrase; no subject]

> for you and me [prepositional phrase; no subject or verb]

A **prepositional phrase** is a group of words consisting of a preposition, a noun or a pronoun called the **object of the preposition**, and any modifiers of that object.

> at the post office   to school   from them   next to me

The object of a preposition may be compound.

> She looked **at the stamp and postmark**. [Both *stamp* and *postmark* are objects of the preposition *at*.]

Exercise A On the line provided, identify each of the following groups of words as *phrase* or *not a phrase*.

> EXAMPLES: 1. with a hammer *phrase*
> 2. because we agree *not a phrase*

1. was hoping   _____

2. if she really knows   _____

3. with Abdul and me   _____

4. will be writing   _____

5. since Donna wrote   _____

Exercise B In each sentence of the following paragraph, underline each preposition once and its object twice.

> EXAMPLE: [1] I've been studying Spanish <u>in</u> <u>school</u> <u>for</u> three <u>years</u>.

[1] Last Tuesday, my Spanish class went on a field trip to Juarez, Mexico, across the Río Grande from El Paso, Texas, where we live. [2] Señora Ayala, our teacher, wanted us to practice speaking and reading Spanish outside the classroom. [3] Everyone was supposed to speak only Spanish during the trip. [4] We first went to the *Muséo de Arte e Historia* and saw colorful displays of art and crafts as well as many archaeological exhibits. [5] Besides the museum, we visited the Pueblito Mexicano, a beautiful shopping area owned by the Mexican government.

SENTENCES

Chapter 6: Phrases

The Adjective Phrase

A prepositional phrase used as an adjective is called an **adjective phrase**. An adjective phrase always follows the noun or pronoun it modifies.

> The life cycle **of the piranha** is interesting. [The phrase *of the piranha* is used as an adjective that modifies *life cycle*.]

More than one adjective phrase may modify the same noun or pronoun. An adjective phrase may also modify the object of another prepositional phrase.

> Exhibits **of dangerous fish at the zoo** are fascinating. [The phrases *of dangerous fish* and *at the zoo* modify *Exhibits*.]

> Some frogs produce a poison **from glands in their skin**. [The phrase *from glands in their skin* modifies the noun *poison*. The phrase *in their skin* modifies *glands*, the object of the preposition *from*.]

Exercise A Underline each adjective phrase in the following sentences. Then draw an arrow from each adjective phrase to the word it modifies.

> EXAMPLE: 1. The mysteries of the world beneath the ocean interest us.

1. My visit to the aquarium was fascinating.

2. There you can find information about fish in the world's oceans.

3. The shark is not the only fish with a bad reputation.

4. For example, barracuda in South America's coastal waters can be dangerous.

5. You should also be careful ordering barracuda from a restaurant's menu.

Exercise B Underline the ten adjective phrases in the following paragraph. Then circle the word that each phrase modifies. [Note: Some sentences contain more than one phrase. Identify each phrase separately.]

> EXAMPLE: [1] You probably have seen(photographs)of Mount Rushmore National Monument.

[1] A few years ago our family visited South Dakota and saw a famous monument to great American leaders. [2] Our guide, Black Elk, took pictures of my brother and of me under the monument. [3] The images of George Washington, Thomas Jefferson, Theodore Roosevelt, and Abraham Lincoln are carved into the mountainside. [4] Nearly all visitors are impressed by the massive, noble faces of the four American presidents. [5] Tourists on the viewing terraces must gaze up nearly five hundred feet to see these works of art, which are approximately sixty feet tall. [6] Why did sculptor Gutzon Borglum create this gigantic memorial in granite? [7] He wanted to pay a lasting tribute to four great Americans who made giant contributions to our country's history.

WORKSHEET 3 *The Adverb Phrase*

A prepositional phrase used as an adverb is called an **adverb phrase**. Adverb phrases tell *when*, *where*, *how*, *why*, or *to what extent*. An adverb phrase modifies a verb, an adjective, or an adverb.

MODIFYING A VERB: The book was written **in the 1800s**. [The phrase modifies *was written*.]

MODIFYING AN ADJECTIVE: The writer is good **at description**. [The phrase modifies *good*.]

MODIFYING AN ADVERB: Mark Twain became popular early **in his career**. [The phrase modifies *early*.]

An adverb phrase may appear at various places in a sentence. More than one adverb phrase may modify the same word.

During his youth, Twain worked **as a newspaper writer**. [The adverb phrases *During his youth* and *as a newspaper writer* modify the verb *worked*.]

Exercise A   Underline the adverb phrase or phrases in each of the following sentences. Then underline twice the word or words each phrase modifies.

EXAMPLE: 1. Do you read poetry for relaxation?

1. In my literature class, we studied the Harlem Renaissance for two weeks.

2. I could read Langston Hughes's poetry for hours.

3. In this collection, you can find "A Dream Deferred."

4. Through his poetry, Hughes helped express the African American experience.

5. Although it ended around 1930, writers everywhere were influenced by the Harlem Renaissance.

Exercise B   Underline the ten adverb phrases in the following sentences. Underline twice the word or words each phrase modifies. Then draw an arrow from the adverb phrase to the word or words it modifies. [Note: Some sentences contain more than one phrase.]

EXAMPLE: [1] Time has inspired many artists over the years.

[1] In Chicago's Washington Park stands a weathered sculpture, *Fountain of Time*.

[2] The work shows humanity as it struggles through time. [3] Father Time appears as a mysterious outsider. [4] He stands apart from the other figures and gazes at their effort.

[5] Another artist's concept of time is displayed in New York City's Rockefeller Center.

[6] Three figures representing Past, Present, and Future are painted on the ceiling.

[7] Wherever you stand in the room, Past's eyes are turned away from you, while Future's eyes look upward. [8] The eyes of Present, however, always look straight at you.

SENTENCES

Chapter 6: Phrases

Participles and Participial Phrases

A **participle** is a verb form that can be used as an adjective. There are two kinds of participles. **Present participles** end in *–ing,* and **past participles** regularly end in *–d* or *–ed.* Some past participles are irregularly formed.

> The **pacing** lion made me nervous. [Present participle modifies *lion.*]
>
> The **hunted** animal camouflaged itself. [Past participle modifies *animal.*]
>
> The **broken** fence allowed it to escape. [Past participle modifies *fence.*]

A **participial phrase** is a phrase containing a participle and any complements or modifiers it may have. The entire participial phrase acts as an adjective.

> **Searching for food,** the dog roamed the neighborhood. [participle with adverb phrase *for food*]
>
> The dog, **walking slowly,** approached our house. [participle with adverb *slowly*]
>
> **Sniffing our clothing,** the dog seemed to trust us. [participle with direct object *clothing* and possessive pronoun *our*]

Exercise A   Underline the participles used as adjectives in each of the following sentences.

> EXAMPLE: 1. We searched the island for <u>buried</u> treasure.

1. The prancing horses were loudly applauded by the delighted audience.

2. The colorful flags, waving in the breeze, brightened the gloomy day.

3. Swaggering and boasting, he made us extremely angry.

4. The game scheduled for tonight has been postponed because of rain.

5. Branches tapping on the roof made an eerie sound.

Exercise B   For each blank in the following sentences, choose a participle that completes the meaning of the sentence.

> EXAMPLE: 1. The _rising_ tide washed over the beach.

1. Jan Evers, _____ in a recent magazine, describes the destruction of the rain forest.

2. The tiger, _____ by the hunters, swam across the river to safety.

3. _____ at the traffic light, the driver put on his sunglasses.

4. The poem describes a spider _____ on a thread.

5. We stumbled off the race course, _____ .

Chapter 6: Phrases

Gerunds and Gerund Phrases

A **gerund** is a verb form ending in *–ing* that is used as a noun. Like nouns, gerunds are used as subjects, predicate nominatives, direct objects, or objects of prepositions.

SUBJECT: Walking is good exercise.
PREDICATE NOMINATIVE: My favorite exercise is walking.
OBJECT OF PREPOSITION: I feel good after walking.
DIRECT OBJECT: Pablo loves walking.

A **gerund phrase** contains a gerund and any modifiers or complements it may have. The entire gerund phrase acts as a noun.

> **Finding a good place for a walk** is simple. [The gerund phrase is the subject of the verb *is*. The noun *place* is the direct object of the gerund *finding*. The adjective *good* and the adjective phrase *for a walk* modify the noun *place*.]

Exercise A   Underline each gerund in the following sentences. Then, above each underlined item, identify the gerund as *S* (subject), *PN* (predicate nominative), *DO* (direct object), or *OP* (object of a preposition).

OP
EXAMPLE: 1. Instead of <u>driving</u>, let's walk.

1. Her laughing attracted my attention.

2. By studying, you can improve your grades.

3. Why did the birds stop chirping?

4. Frowning, Dad said that we had to finish our work before we could begin skating.

5. Yvette's favorite exercise is hiking.

Exercise B   Underline the gerund phrases in the following sentences. Then, above each underlined item, identify the gerund phrase as *S* (subject), *PN* (predicate nominative), *DO* (direct object), or *OP* (object of a preposition).

DO
EXAMPLE: 1. I enjoyed <u>reading about Jane Addams</u>.

1. Founding Hull House in Chicago in 1889 was one of Addams's greatest achievements.

2. She began her work by obtaining a large building to house the community center.

3. Her work was encouraging young men and women in immigrant neighborhoods.

4. They enriched their lives by going to the community center.

5. Discovering help and empathy gave many poor immigrants courage.

SENTENCES

Infinitives and Infinitive Phrases

An **infinitive** is a verb form, usually preceded by *to*, that can be used as a noun, an adjective, or an adverb.

NOUN: **To sew** requires skill. [*To sew* is the subject of the verb *requires*.]

ADJECTIVE: The easiest thing **to sew** is a skirt. [*To sew* modifies the noun *thing*.]

ADVERB: The children were happy **to sew**. [*To sew* modifies the adjective *happy*.]

An **infinitive phrase** consists of an infinitive together with its modifiers and complements. The entire infinitive phrase can be used as a noun, an adjective, or an adverb.

Mario wants **to visit Spain again**. [The infinitive phrase is used as the direct object of the verb *wants*. The noun *Spain* is the direct object of *to visit*. The adverb *again* modifies *to visit*.]

Exercise A   Underline the infinitives and infinitive phrases in the following sentences. Then, above each underlined item, identify the infinitive as *N* (noun), *ADJ* (adjective), or *ADV* (adverb). A sentence may contain more than one infinitive or infinitive phrase.

ADJ
EXAMPLE: 1. Scott is the person <u>to elect</u>.

1. She wanted to join the chorus.

2. A good way to lose weight is to eat moderately.

3. After our long vacation, we needed to get back in training.

4. Juanita and Matt shopped to find the perfect gift.

5. He lives to swim and to water-ski.

Exercise B   Underline the infinitive phrases in the following sentences. Then, above each underlined item, identify the infinitive phrase as *N* (noun), *ADJ* (adjective), or *ADV* (adverb).

N
EXAMPLE: [1] <u>To create a miracle fabric</u> was chemist Joe Shivers's aim.

[1] He succeeded with spandex, and athletes of all shapes and sizes have learned to appreciate the qualities of his "power cloth." [2] This strong material has a fantastic ability to stretch and to snap back into shape. [3] Its sleek fit lessens friction to give the wearer faster movement through air or water. [4] Its slick surface makes an athlete such as a wrestler hard to hold on to. [5] To say that spandex has athletes covered is not stretching the truth.

Chapter 6: Phrases

Appositives and Appositive Phrases

An **appositive** is a noun or a pronoun placed beside another noun or pronoun to identify or explain it. An **appositive phrase** is made up of an appositive and its modifiers. Appositives and appositive phrases are usually set off by commas; however, an appositive that is essential to the meaning of the sentence is not set off by commas.

> The modern artist **Kandinsky** inspired many painters. [The appositive *Kandinsky* is essential to the sentence's meaning.]
>
> My art teacher, **Ms. Ortega,** showed us slides of Kandinsky's work. [The appositive *Ms. Ortega* is not essential to the meaning of the sentence.]
>
> Yuan Zuo, **a Chinese painter,** was influenced by Kandinsky. [appositive phrase]

An appositive or appositive phrase usually follows the noun or pronoun it refers to. Sometimes, however, an appositive phrase is placed in front of the word it refers to.

> **A tireless worker,** Joaquín studied every evening.

Exercise A Underline the appositive or appositive phrase in each of the following sentences. Then underline twice the word that each appositive identifies or explains.

> EXAMPLE: 1. My <u>uncle</u>, <u>a classics scholar</u>, studies Greek myths.

1. Agamemnon, a Greek leader, led his warriors to Troy to recapture Helen.

2. Menelaus' wife, Helen, had disappeared.

3. Paris, the king's son, had kidnapped Helen.

4. The god Zeus tried to remain impartial.

5. A brave Greek warrior, Achilles was eventually killed by a poisoned arrow.

Exercise B: Revising Using your imagination, create an appositive or an appositive phrase to explain or identify at least one of the nouns or pronouns in each of the following sentences.

> EXAMPLE: 1. Marquita Wiley has started a writers' club.
>
> <u>Marquita Wiley, a world-famous author, has started a</u>
> <u>writers' club.</u>

1. Ms. Wiley conducts the meetings as workshops.

_____

2. J. D. Ellis writes funny poems about bird-watching.

_____

3. Next week, we'll meet at our regular time.

_____

4. Our guest speaker will be Wanda Frazier.

_____

SENTENCES

Chapter 6: Phrases

WORKSHEET 8   *Review*

Exercise A   There are ten prepositional phrases in the following paragraph. Underline each prepositional phrase and then circle the object of the prepositional phrase. [Note: Some sentences do not contain any prepositional phrases, and others contain more than one. Even if one prepositional phrase contains another, identify each phrase separately. Do not identify a prepositional phrase that is part of a compound noun.]

EXAMPLE: [1] I especially like postage stamps featuring paintings <u>of famous (people.)</u>

[1] What is the story behind a United States commemorative stamp? [2] First, the idea for a new stamp comes from an interested citizen. [3] Then, the Postmaster General of the United States relays that idea to the Citizens' Stamp Committee. [4] The Citizens' Stamp Committee, a group of artists, stamp collectors, and businesspeople, considers the idea for the stamp. [5] The stamp is then approved by the Postmaster General. [6] Next, the Committee selects the stamp's artist. [7] This artist gives his or her artwork to an artist from the U.S. Bureau of Printing and Engraving. [8] This second artist creates the actual stamp design. [9] The new stamp will include the letters *USA*, the stamp's price, and a title that tells about the stamp.

Exercise B   There are ten prepositional phrases in the following paragraph. First, underline each prepositional phrase. Then, above each underlined item, identify the phrase as *ADJ* (adjective) or *ADV* (adverb).

ADV

EXAMPLE: [1] Each day I take time to write <u>in my journal</u>.

[1] For the past year I have been keeping a journal of my thoughts and ideas. [2] I generally write entries before bedtime. [3] Last week I wrote a story about an imaginary journey. [4] I described a fantastic train ride across the country. [5] In yesterday's entry I merely described an uneventful day. [6] My finest entry of fiction is an account of a young astronaut's moonwalk. [7] Someday I might send a copy to a magazine. [8] For now, I am my only reader.

Exercise C   Underline the participles and participial phrases in the following paragraph. Then, underline twice the words that the participles modify.

EXAMPLE: [1] <u>Cats</u>, <u>known for their pride and independence</u>, are not as hard to train as many people think.

[1] One day I was giving Chops, my very spoiled cat, treats. [2] Standing on her hind legs, she reached up with her paw. [3] Grabbing for my fingers, Chops tried to bring the tasty morsel closer. [4] I pulled my hand back a little and tugged gently on her curved paw, which made her step forward. [5] Praising my clever cat, I immediately gave her two more

treats. [6] The next time I held a treat up high, Chops, puzzled but eager, repeated the grab-and-step movement. [7] Soon Chops was taking steps toward treats held out of her reach. [8] I now have an educated cat who can walk on two legs. [9] Grabbing the treats, she has learned that certain moves always get her a snack. [10] Sometimes after Chops has had her treat, she just sits and looks at me, no doubt thinking that humans are truly a strange bunch!

Exercise D   For each of the following sentences, underline each verbal or verbal phrase. On the line provided, identify each verbal or verbal phrase as a *gerund*, a *gerund phrase*, an *infinitive*, an *infinitive phrase*, a *participle*, or a *participial phrase*.

> EXAMPLE: 1. Building the railroad across the United States in the
> late 1800s required thousands of workers. *gerund phrase*

1. The government commissioned two companies to build railway tracks between Omaha, Nebraska, and Sacramento, California.   _____

2. Building eastward from Sacramento, the Central Pacific Railroad relied on Chinese workers.   _____

3. One fourth of the Chinese immigrants in the United States in 1868 helped with laying the track.   _____

4. The terrain was difficult to cover, but the laborers rose to the challenge.   _____

5. Known for their dependability and endurance, the Chinese were strong workers who learned quickly.   _____

6. Complaining was a problem with some workers, but seldom with Chinese laborers.   _____

7. It was often necessary to blow up parts of mountains, and the Chinese workers became experts at this task.   _____

8. Chinese and Irish workers set a record on April 28, 1869, by spiking ten miles and fifty-six feet of track in twelve hours.   _____

9. The railroad company divided the Chinese immigrants into working groups, or gangs, each with twelve to twenty men.   _____

10. The Chinese workers had food shipped to them from San Francisco's Chinatown.   _____

Exercise E   Underline the infinitives and infinitive phrases in the following paragraph. Then, above each underlined item, identify the infinitive as a *noun*, an *adjective*, or an *adverb*. Use the abbreviations *N, ADJ*, and *ADV*.

>   ADJ
> EXAMPLE: [1] Laurel and Hardy were a comic team to remember.

[1] Slender Stan Laurel and roly-poly Oliver Hardy worked together to entertain us. [2] In their day, to be funny in the movies meant using body language. [3] To keep audiences laughing, they developed mannerisms that were unmistakably their own. [4] For his

SENTENCES

famous head scratch, Stan grew his hair long so that he could scratch and pull it to make a

comic mess. [5] Stan also developed a hilarious cry to show his character's childish nature.

[6] He would shut his eyes tightly, pinch up his face, and begin to wail. [7] Ollie used

different mannerisms to create his character. [8] For example, he put on a long-suffering

look to express frustration. [9] He would also wiggle his tie at a person he and Stan had

offended and then begin to titter. [10] Ollie's effort to make the person less angry only made

the situation worse.

Exercise F   Underline the ten verbal phrases and appositive phrases in the following
paragraph. Then, in the space above each line, identify the phrase as *participial, gerund,*
infinitive, or *appositive.*

> EXAMPLE: [1] At the 1988 Olympic Games, Florence Griffith Joyner and
> *appositive*
> Jackie Joyner-Kersee, two superstars of track, showed the
> *infinitive*
> world how to win big.

[1] Florence, called Flo-Jo by her fans, smashed the women's records in the 100-meter and the

200-meter dash at the games in Seoul, Korea. [2] Realizing that she was winning the 100-meter

race, Flo-Jo raised her arms in triumph. [3] This gesture and her brilliant smile, admired by

thousands of spectators, seem to illustrate perfectly her supreme confidence and talent. [4] Jackie

Joyner-Kersee, Flo-Jo's sister-in-law, gained fame by winning gold medals in the women's long

jump and heptathlon. [5] The heptathlon, combining seven different track and field events, is a

tough two-day competition in which athletes earn points for each event. [6] Earning a total of

7,291 points, Jackie broke the old world record. [7] Setting a furious pace in the 100-meter

hurdles, she showed the superb concentration, strength, and form that helped to win her the

medal for this exhausting event.

Chapter 7: Clauses

Kinds of Clauses

A **clause** is a group of words that contains a verb and its subject and is used as part of a sentence.

An **independent** (or **main**) **clause** expresses a complete thought and can stand by itself as a sentence.

> The king announced a feast. [The independent clause is used as a sentence.]

Independent clauses can be joined to *subordinate clauses* or to other independent clauses.

> After the feast was announced, preparations began. [one independent clause and one subordinate clause]

> The king announced a feast, **and** preparations began. [two independent clauses]

A **subordinate** (or **dependent**) **clause** does not express a complete thought and cannot stand alone. To make a complete sentence, a subordinate clause must be joined to an independent clause.

> The king made the plans **after he had talked to his court**. [The subordinate clause *after he had talked to his court* is linked to an independent clause.]

Exercise A   On the line provided in each sentence of the following paragraph, identify the clause in italics as *IND* for independent or *SUB* for subordinate.

> EXAMPLE: [1] *Whenever I read Gary Soto's poems*   _SUB_ , I am impressed by their quiet power.

[1] Gary Soto, *who was born in Fresno, California* _____ , describes his experiences as a

farm laborer and factory worker in his book of poems The Elements of San Joaquin.

[2] Soto's use of imagery is skillful; *his language is precise and vivid* _____ . [3] One poem *that*

reminds me of the desert _____ is "Wind." [4] *What happens to the land when the wind blows*

_____ is the subject of the poem. [5] *I also enjoy his poems "Stars" and "Sun"* _____ , which

describe other elements of the natural world.

Exercise B   On the line provided, attach each of the following subordinate clauses to an independent clause to create a sentence.

> EXAMPLE: 1. what the Queen ordered
>
> *I do not know what the Queen ordered.*

1. when spring is here

_____

2. that the price is too high

_____

SENTENCES

Chapter 7: Clauses

The Adjective Clause

An **adjective clause** is a subordinate clause used as an adjective to modify a noun or a pronoun. An adjective clause follows the word it modifies. An adjective clause is not set off by commas if it is necessary, or *essential*, to the meaning of a sentence. If a clause only gives additional information and is *nonessential* to the meaning of a sentence, it is set off by commas.

> Water **that has a strong current** is sometimes called white water. [The adjective clause *that has a strong current* modifies *water*. The clause is necessary to tell what kind of water is being referred to. Therefore, the clause is not set off by commas.]

> The water, **which was calm yesterday,** is rough today. [The clause *which was calm yesterday* modifies the noun *water*. The clause gives nonessential information and is therefore set off by commas.]

Adjective clauses are often introduced by **relative pronouns**: *who, whom, whose, which,* and *that.* (Occasionally, the relative adverb *where* or *when* may introduce an adjective clause.) A relative pronoun has its own function in the clause.

> Do you remember the ship **on which we sailed**? [The relative pronoun *which* relates the adjective clause to *ship. Which* also serves as the object of the preposition *on.*]

In many cases, the relative pronoun in the clause may be omitted. The pronoun is understood and still has a function in the clause.

> This is the model boat **[that] I bought**. [The relative pronoun *that* is understood; it serves as the direct object of the verb *bought* in the clause.]

Exercise Each sentence in the following paragraph contains an adjective clause. Underline the adjective clause once. Then underline twice the relative pronoun or relative adverb that introduces it.

> EXAMPLE: [1] Do you know anyone <u>who is familiar with *briffits,*</u>
> <u>*swalloops,* and *waftaroms*</u>?

[1] Cartoonists use a variety of unusual names for the symbols that commonly appear in funnies. [2] For example, a *briffit* is the little puff of dust hanging in the spot where a swiftly departing character once stood. [3] For times when cartoonists want to make something appear hot or smelly, they use wavy, rising lines called *waftaroms.* [4] *Agitrons* are the wiggly lines around an object that is supposed to be shaking. [5] The arm of a character who is taking a swing at something may be trailed by a set of curved lines called a *swalloop.* [6] *Plewds,* which look like flying droplets of sweat, are drawn around a worried character's head. [7] Just about everyone who likes to doodle and draw has probably used some of these symbols. [8] Professional cartoonists, however, have symbols to suggest almost all motions and emotions that can be found in cartoons. [9] Look at your favorite comic strip to find places where the cartoonist has used *briffits, plewds,* or other symbols. [10] Congratulations! Now you know a "language" that almost nobody outside the cartooning profession knows!

Chapter 7: Clauses

WORKSHEET 3 *The Adverb Clause*

An **adverb clause** is a subordinate clause that modifies a verb, an adjective, or an adverb. An adverb clause tells *how, when, where, why, to what extent (how much),* or *under what condition.* An adverb clause may be located anywhere in a sentence.

MODIFYING A VERB: **When people enter a museum,** they sometimes don't know where to go first. [The clause tells *when* people don't know where to go.]

MODIFYING AN ADJECTIVE: The renovated museum is much larger **than it used to be**. [The clause modifies the adjective *larger,* telling *to what extent* the museum is larger.]

MODIFYING AN ADVERB: You know the artists better **than I do**. [The clause modifies the adverb *better,* telling *how much* better you know the artists.]

Adverb clauses are introduced by **subordinating conjunctions**. Some common subordinating conjunctions are *after, although, as, as if, as long as, as soon as, because, before, even though, if, in order that, once, since, so that, than, though, unless, until, when, where, whether,* and *while.*

Exercise Each sentence in the following paragraph contains an adverb clause. Underline the adverb clause once. Then circle the subordinating conjunction that introduces it.

EXAMPLE: [1] (Even though) he was world famous, Mohandas K. Gandhi was a simple man.

[1] If you look through newspapers from the first half of this century, you will see many pictures of Mohandas K. Gandhi. [2] This man led India to independence from Britain, and he took his spinning wheel wherever he went. [3] He did so because he viewed spinning as a symbol of the peaceful, native Indian lifestyle. [4] He also hoped to encourage the Indian people to make their own clothes so that they would not have to depend on British industry. [5] Gandhi persisted in using such nonviolent actions against the British until India gained its independence in 1947.

SENTENCES

Name _____ Date _____ Class _____

WORKSHEET 4 — *The Noun Clause*

A **noun clause** is a subordinate clause used as a noun. A noun clause may be used as a subject, a complement (predicate nominative, direct object, or indirect object), or an object of a preposition.

SUBJECT: **That you tried your best** is what matters.

PREDICATE NOMINATIVE: The winner is **whoever has the fastest time.**

DIRECT OBJECT: I don't know **when the awards ceremony is.**

INDIRECT OBJECT: The organization gives **whoever needs help the most** a helping hand.

OBJECT OF PREPOSITION: Ted and I volunteered to help with **whatever needs doing.**

Noun clauses are usually introduced by *that, what, whatever, when, where, whether, who, whoever, whom, whose,* or *why.* A noun clause sometimes has an understood introductory word rather than a stated one.

The word that introduces a noun clause may or may not have a function in the noun clause.

She knows **who won the race.** [*Who* is the subject of the noun clause.]

I hoped **that you would win.** [*That* has no function in the noun clause and may be omitted: *I hoped you would win.*]

Exercise   Underline each noun clause in the following paragraph. Some sentences do not contain noun clauses. Above each clause, write how the clause is used: *S* for subject, *PN* for predicate nominative, *DO* for direct object, *IO* for indirect object, or *OP* for the object of a preposition.

EXAMPLE: [1] We moved to Massachusetts and did not know <u>what we would find there.</u>   *DO*

[1] What surprised me first were the yellowish-green fire engines. [2] I had thought that fire engines were always red. [3] Our neighbors explained that the odd color kept the fire engines from being confused with other large red trucks. [4] My sister Michelle got a surprise at the bowling alley. [5] The small grapefruit-sized bowling balls with no holes were not what she was used to! [6] Whoever can knock down the pins with one of those bowling balls must be an expert. [7] We learned that this sport is called candlepin bowling. [8] Later on, I was pleasantly surprised by the delicious baked beans. [9] They should give whoever invented Boston baked beans an award. [10] Now, after we have lived in New England for a year, both Michelle and I are happy in our new home.

Chapter 7: Clauses

 **WORKSHEET 5**   *Review*

Exercise A   On the lines provided, write *I* for each of the following clauses that is independent and *S* for each clause that is subordinate.

EXAMPLE: ___*S*___ 1. when the peoples were united by the Islamic religion

_____ 1. the term *Arab* applies to Arabic-speaking peoples

_____ 2. even though it was not used until the seventh century

_____ 3. who live on the Arabian Peninsula

_____ 4. most of the world's Arabs live in the Middle East and North Africa

_____ 5. because the Arabian Peninsula is their ancestral home

_____ 6. the Arabic language originated there

_____ 7. wherever Arabs settled

_____ 8. Mecca is a holy city on the Arabian Peninsula

_____ 9. what the Arabs want

_____ 10. that occur in the United Arab Emirates

Exercise B   Underline the subordinate clauses in the following paragraph. Above each clause, identify the clause as an adjective *(ADJ)*, adverb *(ADV)*, or noun clause *(N)*.

EXAMPLE: [1] In paintings created before 1880, horses are usually shown
                                               ADJ
            in poses <u>that now look quaint and unnatural.</u>

[1] If you stop to think about it, you can see why painters had a problem. [2] Stop-action photography had not yet been invented, and when painters looked at rapidly moving horses, they could not see where the legs and hooves were at any one instant. [3] Whenever painters wanted to portray a galloping horse, they made up a position that they thought suggested speed. [4] The horse in one painting that I have seen has both front legs extended far to the front and both hind legs stretched far out behind. [5] Today, we know instantly that this is an impossible position for a horse. [6] Stop-action photography was first used in the 1870s by a Californian named Eadweard Muybridge, who took a famous series of photographs of a galloping horse. [7] Along a racetrack, he set up many cameras whose shutters were controlled by threads stretched across the track. [8] As the horse ran by, it broke the threads and tripped the cameras' shutters one after the other. [9] Painters of the time thought this new technology was truly amazing! [10] They were the first artists in history to know what a horse really looked like at each point in its stride.

Exercise C   On the line provided, identify the subordinate clause or clauses in each of the following sentences. Tell whether each clause is used as an *adjective,* an *adverb,* or a *noun.* If a clause is used as an adjective or an adverb, write the word(s) the clause modifies. If a clause is used as a noun, write *SUB* for subject, *DO* for direct object, *IO* for indirect object, *PN* for predicate nominative, or *OP* for object of a preposition.

EXAMPLE: 1. When our science teacher described insect-eating plants, we listened with amazement.

When our science teacher described insect-eating plants—
adverb—listened

1. Plants that eat insects usually live in swampy areas.

   _____

2. Because the soil in these regions lacks nutrients, these plants do not get enough nitrogen through their roots.

   _____

3. The nitrogen that these plants need comes from the protein in insects.

   _____

4. How these plants catch their food is interesting.

   _____

5. A pitcher plant's sweet scent attracts whatever insect is nearby.

   _____

6. The insect thinks that it will find food inside the plant.

   _____

7. What happens instead is that the insect drowns in the plant's digestive juices.

   _____

8. The Venus' flytrap has what look like small bear traps at the ends of its stalks.

   _____

9. When a trap is open, an insect can wander in and trigger the trap to shut.

   _____

10. The insect is then digested by the plant in a process that takes several days.

   _____

Name _____ Date _____ Class _____

 **Sentences and Fragments**

A **sentence** is a group of words that contains a subject and a verb and expresses a complete thought. A sentence always begins with a capital letter and ends with a period, a question mark, or an exclamation point. If a group of words does not express a complete thought, it is a **fragment,** or a piece of a sentence.

> FRAGMENT: the entire issue of the magazine
>
> SENTENCE: The entire issue of the magazine was devoted to Mexico.

Exercise A   Identify each of the following groups of words as a sentence or a fragment. On the line, write *S* for sentence or *F* for fragment.

> EXAMPLE: ___F___ 1. About the country of Mexico.

_____ 1. Cuernavaca, a city in Mexico

_____ 2. The Spaniards founded it in 1521.

_____ 3. From the writer's room at the Las Mañanitas.

_____ 4. With its tropical climate and hot springs, the resort.

_____ 5. The Palace of Cortes is probably named for the famous soldier.

Exercise B   Decide whether each of the following groups of words is a sentence or a fragment. If the word group is a sentence, correct its capitalization and punctuation on the lines provided. If the word group is a fragment, revise it to make a complete sentence. Be sure to add correct capitalization and punctuation.

> EXAMPLES: 1. here are your glasses
>
>   *Here are your glasses.*
>
>   2. before going out
>
>   *Before going out, I always turn off the lights.*

1. on Monday or later this week

_____

2. patiently waiting for the mail carrier

_____

3. just yesterday I discovered

_____

4. two strikes and no one on base

_____

5. give me a hand

_____

SENTENCES

Chapter 8: Sentence Structure

WORKSHEET 2 — *Subject and Predicate*

A sentence consists of two parts: the subject and the predicate. The **subject** is the part that names the person or thing spoken about in the rest of the sentence. The subject may come at the beginning, in the middle, or at the end of the sentence. The **predicate** is the part that says something about the subject. A subject and a predicate may each be more than one word.

SUBJECT: **A leaf of gold** is less than one millimeter thick.

PREDICATE: It **is thinner than a sheet of paper.**

Exercise A   Decide whether the italicized group of words in each of the following sentences is the subject or the predicate. On the line, write *S* for subject or *P* for predicate.

EXAMPLE: _____P_____ 1. Gold *melts at 1064.43 degrees Celsius.*

_____ 1. *Ancient Egyptians* crafted jewelry from gold earlier than 3500 B.C.

_____ 2. Gold items over 5,000 years old *have been found in Iraq.*

_____ 3. During the Middle Ages, *alchemists* tried to manufacture gold.

_____ 4. *Copper and silver* may be combined with gold to make jewelry.

_____ 5. *Was* El Dorado, the legendary city of gold, *ever discovered?*

_____ 6. *The first gold rush in America* was in Georgia in 1828.

_____ 7. *In 1849 came* the famous California gold rush.

_____ 8. In the 1960s, *the largest discovery of gold in this century* was made in Nevada.

_____ 9. *Since 1937,* most of the gold in America *has been kept underground at Fort Knox.*

_____10. When did *the United States* stop minting gold coins?

Exercise B: Revising   On the lines provided, make each of the following fragments a complete sentence by adding a subject or a predicate. Proofread for correct capitalization and punctuation.

EXAMPLE: 1. Mr. Leopold and his son Frank

Mr. Leopold and his son Frank lived in Africa for two years.

1. the trouble with my class schedule

_____

2. the legs of the table

_____

3. appeared deserted

_____

4. thousands of screaming fans

_____

Chapter 8: Sentence Structure

WORSHEET 3

Complete Subjects and Simple Subjects

The **simple subject** is the main word or group of words in the complete subject. The **complete subject** consists of the simple subject and any words, phrases, or clauses that modify the simple subject.

SENTENCE: World-class bicycle racing requires skill and stamina.

COMPLETE SUBJECT: World-class bicycle racing

SIMPLE SUBJECT: bicycle racing

Exercise A   Underline the complete subject of each sentence in the following paragraph.

EXAMPLE: [1] <u>The art of quilting</u> has been popular in America for many years.

[1] Ever since colonial times, Americans have made quilts. [2] Traditional designs, with names like Honeycomb, Tumbling Blocks, and Trip Around the World, have been handed down from generation to generation. [3] Many modern quilters, however, make their own designs. [4] Quilting techniques have stayed basically the same for well over a hundred years. [5] Small scraps of bright cloth are still painstakingly stitched together to create each block.

Exercise B   Make each of the following fragments a sentence by adding a complete subject. Underline each simple subject.

EXAMPLE: 1. Did <u>*your little brother*</u> watch the Super Bowl?

1. _____ was baying at the moon.

2. _____ can make the pizza.

3. _____ is needed for this recipe.

4. Was _____ the person who won the match?

5. _____ rose and soared out over the sea.

6. _____ stood on the stage singing.

7. _____ were late for their classes.

8. Over in the next town is _____ .

9. Buzzing around the room was _____ .

10. In the middle of the yard grew _____ .

SENTENCES

Chapter 8: Sentence Structure

Complete Predicates and Simple Predicates

The **simple predicate,** or **verb,** is the main word or group of words in the complete predicate. The simple predicate may be a single verb or a **verb phrase** (a verb with one or more helping verbs). The **complete predicate** consists of the verb and any words, phrases, or clauses that modify the verb or complete the meaning of the verb.

SENTENCE: I have been reading a collection of short stories.

COMPLETE PREDICATE: have been reading a collection of short stories

SIMPLE PREDICATE: have been reading

Exercise A   For each sentence in the following paragraph, underline the complete predicate once and the verb or verb phrase in each complete predicate twice.

EXAMPLE: [1] Surfing and snow skiing <u>are different in many ways</u>.

[1] The warm-weather sport of surfing is powered by the force of incoming waves. [2] The wintertime activity of snow skiing relies instead on gravity. [3] Surfers can pursue their sport with only a surfboard, a flotation vest, a swimsuit, and a safety line. [4] A skier's equipment includes ski boots, skis with bindings, safety cables, ski poles, warm clothing, and perhaps goggles. [5] Surfers paddle out to their starting place under their own power. [6] Skiers must usually buy tickets for a ski-lift ride to the top of the mountain. [7] Oddly enough, some important similarities exist between surfing and skiing. [8] Both depend on the cooperation of nature for pleasant weather and good waves or good snow. [9] Both sports require coordination and balance more than strength. [10] In fact, each of these sports would probably make an excellent cross-training activity during the other's off-season.

Exercise B   On the lines provided, write complete sentences by supplying complete predicates for the following subjects. Be sure to use correct capitalization and punctuation.

EXAMPLE: 1. that famous painting

That famous painting sold for three million dollars.

1. justice

_____

2. some commercials

_____

3. the store on the corner

_____

4. the woman next door

_____

5. one way to study

_____

Name _____ Date _____ Class _____

 **WORKSHEET 5** *Finding the Subject*

The best way to find the subject of a sentence is to find the verb first. Then ask "Who?" or "What?" in front of the verb. The following sentence structures can make it difficult to locate the subject:

(1) sentences that begin with prepositional phrases

On Tuesday of next week is the test. [What is? The *test* is. Note: The subject of a verb is never in a prepositional phrase.]

(2) sentences that ask questions

Are these paintings very old? [What are? The *paintings* are.]

(3) sentences beginning with *there* or *here*

There goes our bus. [What goes? *Bus* goes.]

(4) sentences, such as requests or commands, in which *you* is the understood subject

Please get in line. [Who gets in line? *You* get in line.]

Exercise   On the lines provided, identify the subjects and the verbs in the following sentences. Show an understood subject in parentheses.

EXAMPLE: 1. Please help me study for my history test.

(you)—subject; help—verb

1. There are many questions on American history in my book.

_____

2. In the book, too, are many answers. _____

3. Under whose flag did Columbus sail? _____

4. Where is Plymouth Rock? _____

5. Tell me about the Lost Colony. _____

6. What does *squatter's rights* mean? _____

7. In what area did most of the early Dutch colonists settle?

_____

8. Was there disagreement among settlers in Massachusetts?

_____

9. Remember the facts about colonial schools. _____

10. Here is a book about travel in colonial America. _____

SENTENCES

Chapter 8: Sentence Structure

WORKSHEET 6

Compound Subjects and Verbs

A **compound subject** consists of two or more subjects that are joined by a conjunction and have the same verb. A **compound verb** consists of two or more verbs that are joined by a conjunction and have the same subject. Both the subject and the verb may be compound.

COMPOUND SUBJECT: Neither **Josie** nor **Beth** had read the book.

COMPOUND VERB: Hank **has read** the book and **written** his report.

COMPOUND SUBJECT: **Tao, Rudy,** or **Seth** will present the next report.

COMPOUND VERB: Paul **stood** up, **walked** to the podium, and **began** his speech.

COMPOUND SUBJECT AND VERB: The **students** and the **teacher like** Paul's report and **are saying** so.

Exercise   On the lines provided, identify the subjects and verbs in the following sentences.

EXAMPLE: 1. Should I buy this pair of jeans now or wait for a sale?
I—subject; Should buy, wait—verbs

1. Toshiro sings, acts, and dances in the show.

_____

2. At the fair, Dan and Frank ran faster than the other boys and tied for first prize.

_____

3. Moles and bats supposedly have very poor eyesight.

_____

4. April, May, and June are the best months for studying wildflowers in Texas.

_____

5. Kettles of soup and trays of sandwiches were prepared and delivered.

_____

6. Both you and I should go downtown.

_____

7. Geraldo rewound the cassette and then pressed the playback button.

_____

8. The newborn calf rose unsteadily to its feet and stood for the first time.

_____

9. Will you and Jan walk home or wait for the four o'clock bus?

_____

10. This kitchen appliance will slice, dice, or chop.

_____

Name _____ Date _____ Class _____

 **Subject Complements**

A **subject complement** is a noun, a pronoun, or an adjective that follows a linking verb and describes or identifies the subject. A **predicate nominative** is a noun or pronoun in the predicate that renames or identifies the subject of a sentence or a clause. A **predicate adjective** is an adjective in the predicate that modifies the subject of a sentence or a clause. Subject complements may be compound.

> PREDICATE NOMINATIVE: Lasagna is my favorite **food**. [noun]
>
> PREDICATE NOMINATIVE: The best Italian cooks are **they**. [pronoun]
>
> PREDICATE ADJECTIVE: The kitchen smells **wonderful**.
>
> COMPOUND PREDICATE
> ADJECTIVE: Her marinara sauce tastes **rich** and **tangy**.

To find the subject complement in an interrogative sentence, rearrange the sentence to make a statement.

> Was Jane the first speaker? [Jane was the first *speaker*.]

To find the subject complement in an imperative sentence, insert the understood subject *you*.

> Be energetic! [(You) be *energetic*!]

The subject complement may precede the subject of a sentence or a clause.

> I saw what a good runner you are. [*Runner* is a predicate nominative identifying *you*.]

Exercise   Each of the following sentences has at least one subject complement. On the lines provided, give the complement or complements for each sentence. Then tell whether each is a *predicate nominative* or a *predicate adjective*.

> EXAMPLE: 1. Gloria is my favorite character on the show.
>
> *character—predicate nominative*

1. Does the lemonade taste too sour?

   _____

2. Our candidate for the city council was the winner in the primaries.

   _____

3. Will the club president be Pablo or Tammy?

   _____

4. Soft and cool was the grass under the catalpa tree.

   _____

5. Be a friend to animals.

   _____

SENTENCES

Chapter 8: Sentence Structure

WORKSHEET 8 — *Objects*

Objects complete the meaning of transitive action verbs, not linking verbs.

A **direct object** is a noun or pronoun that receives the action of the verb or shows the results of the action. It answers the question "Whom?" or "What?" after a transitive action verb.

> Gayle visited her **grandparents** in Florida. [The direct object *grandparents* receives the action of the verb *visited* and tells *whom* Gayle visited.]

An **indirect object** is a noun or pronoun that precedes the direct object and usually tells *to whom* or *for whom* (or *to what* or *for what*) the action of the verb is done.

> Give **me** your ticket. [The indirect object *me* tells *to whom* you should give your ticket.]

Both direct and indirect objects may be compound.

> DIRECT OBJECTS: Michael built the **table** and **chairs**.

> INDIRECT OBJECTS: He sold **Jessica** and **me** the furniture.

Exercise   In the following sentences, underline the direct objects once and the indirect objects twice. You will not find an indirect object in every sentence. Make sure that you give all words in compound direct and indirect objects.

> EXAMPLE: 1. Sometimes I read my little <u>brother</u> <u>stories</u> from Greek mythology.

1. In one myth, a famous artist and inventor named Daedalus built the king of Crete a mysterious building known as the Labyrinth.

2. The complicated passageways of this building give us the word *labyrinth*, meaning "a confusing maze of possibilities."

3. After the completion of the Labyrinth, the king imprisoned Daedalus and his son, whose name was Icarus.

4. To escape, Daedalus made Icarus and himself wings out of feathers and beeswax.

5. He gave Icarus careful instructions not to fly too near the sun.

6. But Icarus soon forgot his father's advice.

7. He flew too high, and when the sun melted the wax in the wings, he plunged to his death in the ocean.

8. Though heartbroken by the death of his son, Daedalus flew on and reached Sicily safely.

9. Mythology tells us many other stories of Daedalus's fabulous inventions.

10. Even today, the name Daedalus suggests genius and inventiveness.

Chapter 8: Sentence Structure

Classifying Sentences by Purpose

Sentences may be classified as *declarative, imperative, interrogative,* or *exclamatory.*

(1) A **declarative** sentence makes a statement. It is followed by a period.

I'm looking for a summer job.

(2) An **imperative** sentence gives a command or makes a request. It is usually followed by a period. A strong command may be followed by an exclamation point.

Read the classified section of the paper.

Don't throw that paper away**!**

(3) An **interrogative** sentence asks a question. It is followed by a question mark.

Where will you work this summer**?**

(4) An **exclamatory** sentence expresses strong feeling. It is followed by an exclamation point.

Oh, I can't believe that you found a job as a circus clown!

Exercise   Decide what kind of sentence each of the following sentences is. Then on the line provided, write *DEC* if the sentence is declarative, *IMP* if it is imperative, *INT* if it is interrogative, or *EX* if it is exclamatory. Then add the necessary punctuation.

EXAMPLE: _DEC_   1. There are many delicious foods from India.

_____ 1. Do you like spicy food

_____ 2. *Palek alu* is a spicy dish of potatoes

_____ 3. Watch out for the hot chilies

_____ 4. Be sure to add the curry and other spices to the onions

_____ 5. Wow, wait until you taste this rice-and-banana pudding

_____ 6. Have you ever been to an Indian restaurant

_____ 7. How I wish there were one in my town

_____ 8. Some people don't like trying different ethnic foods

_____ 9. Billy Ray, please sample some Indian appetizers

_____10. What is the name of your delicious drink

SENTENCES

Chapter 8: Sentence Structure

Classifying Sentences by Structure

WORKSHEET 10

Sentences are classified as *simple, compound, complex,* or *compound-complex.*

(1) A **simple sentence** has one independent clause and no subordinate clauses. It may have a compound subject, a compound verb, and any number of phrases.

The Philippines was under American control from 1898 to 1946.

(2) A **compound sentence** has two or more independent clauses but no subordinate clauses. The independent clauses may be joined by a comma and a coordinating conjunction, by a semicolon, or by a semicolon and a conjunctive adverb, such as *however* or *therefore.*

Education for Filipinos had previously been restricted under Spanish rule, but the restrictions were abolished by the United States.

(3) A **complex sentence** has one independent clause and at least one subordinate clause.

When Admiral Dewey sailed into Manila Bay, Filipinos welcomed the Americans.

(4) A **compound-complex sentence** contains two or more independent clauses and at least one subordinate clause.

Most Philippine immigrants to the United States speak English very well; however, in their homes they regularly use their homeland's other official language, which is Tagalog.

Exercise   On the lines provided, classify the following sentences as *S* for simple, *CD* for compound, *CX* for complex, or *CD-CX* for compound-complex.

EXAMPLE: __CD__   1. In all the world, there is only one art museum for children's art, and it is located in Norway.

_____ 1. The International Museum of Children's Art is in Oslo.

_____ 2. The museum features artworks by young artists up to age seventeen.

_____ 3. Many of the 100,000 works, which come from 150 countries, deal with objects from nature, but a few focus on manufactured objects.

_____ 4. Of course, a few of the paintings depict troubles or problems, but most of the works express happiness and energy.

_____ 5. The museum's director says a child's first meeting with art is very important.

_____ 6. Children who visit the museum see that a museum can be cheerful.

_____ 7. The museum certainly is not dusty, and it isn't boring, either.

_____ 8. It is nice that some paintings are hung at toddler's eye level.

_____ 9. Young visitors are excited when they learn the artwork was created by children, and they are often inspired to start painting.

_____10. I wish there were a museum like this one in the United States.

Chapter 8: Sentence Structure

 **WORKSHEET 11** *Review*

Exercise A   On the line provided, identify each of the following word groups as either a sentence *(S)* or a fragment *(F)*.

> EXAMPLE: __*S*__ 1. The talented musicians played well together.

_____ 1. Jazz music filled the room.

_____ 2. Supporting the other instruments, the piano carried the melody.

_____ 3. The saxophonist, with lazy, lingering notes.

_____ 4. Beside him, the bass player added depth to the band.

_____ 5. The young woman who played the trumpet.

Exercise B   Each of the following sentences is a familiar saying. For each sentence, draw a line between the complete subject and the complete predicate. Watch for compound subjects and compound predicates.

> EXAMPLE: 1. Haste|makes waste.

1. A bird in the hand is worth two in the bush.

2. All work and no play makes Jack a dull boy.

3. Too many cooks spoil the broth.

4. You can't make a silk purse out of a sow's ear.

5. A rolling stone gathers no moss.

Exercise C   For each sentence in the following paragraph, underline the simple subject once and the verb twice, including all helping verbs and all parts of a compound verb. Write in an understood subject and underline it once.

> EXAMPLE: [1] Quicksand can be dangerous to a hiker.

[1] In quicksand, you need to remain calm. [2] Violent movement, such as kicking your legs, will only worsen the situation. [3] There are several steps to follow to escape from quicksand. [4] First, discard your backpack or any other burden. [5] Next, gently fall onto your back and spread your arms. [6] In this position, you will be able to float. [7] Only then should you slowly bring your feet to the surface. [8] Perhaps a companion or someone else nearby can reach you with a pole or a rope. [9] Are you alone? [10] Then you should look for the shortest distance to solid ground and paddle slowly toward it.

SENTENCES

Chapter 8, Worksheet 11, continued

Exercise D   On the lines provided, identify the subject complements and the objects in the following sentences. Identify each as PN *(predicate nominative)*, PA *(predicate adjective)*, DO *(direct object)*, or IO *(indirect object)*. Some sentences may have no subject complements or objects; others may have more than one.

> EXAMPLE: [1] My brother Bill gave Mom a birthday surprise.
>
> 1. *Mom—indirect object; surprise—direct object*

[1] My brother made Mom a birthday cake. [2] However, the project soon became a fiasco. [3] First, Bill cracked three eggs into a bowl. [4] But bits of the shells went in, too. [5] Then he added the flour and other dry ingredients. [6] The electric mixer whirled the batter right onto the ceiling. [7] The batter was so sticky that it stayed there and didn't fall off. [8] Bill didn't clean the ceiling, and the sticky substance hardened overnight. [9] Mom was not angry, but she did give Bill a suggestion for a gift. [10] "A clean kitchen would be a great present," she said.

1. _____   6. _____

2. _____   7. _____

3. _____   8. _____

4. _____   9. _____

5. _____   10. _____

Exercise E   On the lines provided, classify the following sentences according to purpose. Write INT *(interrogative)*, DEC *(declarative)*, EX *(exclamatory)*, or IMP *(imperative)*.

> EXAMPLE: _INT_ 1. Have you studied a foreign language?

_____ 1. Spanish is one of the Romance languages.

_____ 2. Did you know that French is a Romance language, too?

_____ 3. If you speak Spanish, you will find French easier to understand.

_____ 4. You could become a multilinguist in no time!

_____ 5. Please take a foreign language.

Exercise F   On the lines provided, classify the following sentences according to structure. Write *S* for simple, *CD* for compound, *CX* for complex, or *CD–CX* for compound-complex.

> EXAMPLE: _S_ 1. Barbara Sneyd lived more than one hundred years ago.

_____ 1. Her wealthy family lived in the English countryside, where they loved to ride.

_____ 2. Barbara had a governess, and although she kept Barbara very busy studying, Barbara did have time to pursue her greatest passion, which was riding.

_____ 3. Barbara's mother encouraged her to keep a diary about her life.

_____ 4. When Barbara was fourteen, she started her diary.

_____ 5. It took the form of a sketchbook, and in it she recorded her family's life.

Name _____ Date _____ Class _____

 **Sentence Fragments**

A **sentence** is a word group that has a subject and a verb and expresses a complete thought. If you punctuate a part of a sentence as if it were a complete sentence, you create a **sentence fragment**.

> FRAGMENT: Is an honor student. [*Who* is an honor student?]
>
> SENTENCE: Tanya is an honor student.

To find out whether a word group is a complete sentence or a sentence fragment, use this simple three-part test:

1. Does the group of words have a subject?
2. Does it have a verb?
3. Does it express a complete thought?

If you answer *no* to any of these questions, your word group is a fragment.

Exercise A   For each word group below that is a complete sentence, write *C*. If the word group is missing a subject, write *S*. If the word group is missing a verb, write *V*. If the word group is not a complete thought, write *I*.

> EXAMPLE: __*S*__   1. Is an important document.

_____ 1. A step toward democracy in England.

_____ 2. Later called the Magna Carta.

_____ 3. While King John put his seal on the document.

_____ 4. The first step in the fight of the English people for self-rule.

_____ 5. The Magna Carta signaled the beginning of democracy in England.

Exercise B: Revising   On the lines provided, rewrite each fragment as a complete sentence.

> EXAMPLE: 1. In studying United States history.
>
> *Do you have an interest in studying United States history?*

1. A deep faith in freedom and equality. _____

   _____

2. Fought and died for our great country and its freedoms. _____

   _____

3. Signed the Declaration of Independence. _____

   _____

4. Because rights must be protected. _____

   _____

5. The carefully worded phrases of the Constitution. _____

   _____

Chapter 9: Writing Complete Sentences

◆ **WORKSHEET 2** *Verbal Phrase Fragments*

A **phrase** is a group of words that does not have both a subject and a verb. One kind of phrase that is often mistaken for a complete sentence is a *verbal phrase*.

Verbals are forms of verbs that are used as other parts of speech. Some verbals typically end in *–ing*, *–d*, or *–ed* and don't have helping verbs (such as *is*, *were*, or *have*) in front of them. One type of verbal includes the word *to* with a form of the verb. A **verbal phrase** is a phrase that contains a verbal. By itself, a verbal phrase is a fragment because it doesn't express a complete thought.

FRAGMENT: Hearing the legend of Romulus and Remus.

SENTENCE: I enjoyed **hearing the legend of Romulus and Remus.**

FRAGMENT: Wrapped in silver paper.

SENTENCE: The presents **wrapped in silver paper** looked tempting.

FRAGMENT: To get tired.

SENTENCE: Mr. Botan started **to get tired.**

Exercise A   For each word group below that is a verbal phrase, write *VP*. If the word group is a complete sentence, write C.

EXAMPLE: ___VP___ 1. To study the poetry of Langston Hughes.

_____ 1. Reading Hughes's poem "A Dream Deferred."

_____ 2. Included in most poetry anthologies.

_____ 3. Hughes's work could be termed realistic.

_____ 4. Working on a steamer around Africa and Europe.

_____ 5. To use the speech of the black community.

Exercise B: Revising   On the lines provided, rewrite each verbal phrase as a complete sentence.

EXAMPLE: 1. Discussing "A Dream Deferred" in class.

I especially enjoyed discussing "A Dream Deferred" in class.

1. To appreciate Langston Hughes. _____

_____

2. Memorizing the poem. _____

_____

3. Talking about what does happen to a dream deferred. _____

_____

4. To read more of Hughes's poetry. _____

_____

Name _____ Date _____ Class _____

WORKSHEET 3

Appositive and Prepositional Phrase Fragments

An **appositive** is a noun or pronoun that identifies or explains another noun or pronoun in the same sentence. An **appositive phrase** is a phrase made up of an appositive and its modifiers. By itself, an appositive phrase is a fragment because it does not contain the basic parts of a sentence.

> FRAGMENT: The proud captain.
>
> SENTENCE: Jean, **the proud captain,** smiled at her teammates.

A **prepositional phrase** is a group of words that includes a preposition, a noun or pronoun called the object of the preposition, and any modifiers of that object. A prepositional phrase can't stand alone as a sentence because it doesn't express a complete thought.

> FRAGMENT: In the afternoon.
>
> SENTENCE: We made fajitas **in the afternoon.**

Exercise A   For each group of words below that may be used as an appositive phrase, write *AP*. For each prepositional phrase, write *PP*.

> EXAMPLE: ___AP___   1. a famous African leader

_____ 1. during the last game

_____ 2. the only pyramid that we visited

_____ 3. for the corn harvest

_____ 4. in the gumbo

_____ 5. the best hotel in town

Exercise B: Revising   On the lines provided, rewrite each appositive phrase or prepositional phrase fragment as a complete sentence.

> EXAMPLE: 1. A friend of my mother.
>
> *Debra, a friend of my mother, is visiting us.*

1. On a ranch in Argentina. _____

_____

2. A successful architect. _____

_____

3. A South American country. _____

_____

4. For each of us. _____

_____

SENTENCES

Chapter 9: Writing Complete Sentences

Subordinate Clauses and Series Fragments

A **clause** is a group of words that has a subject and a verb. An **independent clause** expresses a complete thought and can stand on its own as a sentence. A **subordinate clause** does not express a complete thought. It is a fragment and can't stand by itself as a sentence.

FRAGMENT: when Ashley returned from her trip

SENTENCE: **When Ashley returned from her trip,** she was tired.

A series of items, a **series fragment,** can easily be mistaken for a sentence.

FRAGMENT: Oil paints, brushes, canvases, and a dropcloth.

To correct a series fragment, you can (a) make it into a complete sentence or (b) link it to the previous sentence with a colon.

SENTENCE: For art class I bought **oil paints, brushes, canvases, and a dropcloth.**

or

I bought supplies for art class: **oil paints, brushes, canvases, and a dropcloth.**

Exercise   On the line provided after each word group in the following paragraph, identify the word group as a subordinate clause *(SC)*, a series fragment *(SF)*, or a complete sentence *(C)*.

EXAMPLE: [1] People have been using cosmetics for thousands of years.
_____C_____

[1] In Africa the ancient Egyptians used cosmetics. _____ [2] Perfumes, hair dyes, and makeup. _____ [3] That they made from plants and minerals. _____ [4] While they often used cosmetics to make themselves more attractive. _____ [5] They also used cosmetics to protect their skin from the hot sun. _____ [6] Today, cosmetics are made from over five thousand different ingredients. _____ [7] Waxes, oils, and dyes. _____ [8] The cosmetics business is a huge industry. _____ [9] Advertisers sell cosmetics. _____ [10] That appeal to our desire to be attractive. _____

Chapter 9: Writing Complete Sentences

 **WORKSHEET 5** *Run-on Sentences*

A **run-on sentence** is two or more complete sentences run together as one. There are two kinds of run-ons. In a **fused sentence** the sentences have no punctuation between them. In a **comma splice,** the other kind of run-on, only a comma separates the sentences from one another.

FUSED: I saw the movie with my friend I liked it but Rhonda didn't.

CORRECTED: I saw the movie with my friend. I liked it, but Rhonda didn't.

COMMA SPLICE: The tourist went to the mosque, he didn't take any photos.

CORRECTED: The tourist went to the mosque. He didn't take any photos.

Here are three ways to make a compound sentence out of a run-on:

(1) Use a comma and a coordinating conjunction—*and, but, for, nor, or, so,* or *yet.*

The tourist went to the mosque, **but** he didn't take any photos.

(2) Use a semicolon.

The tourist went to the mosque; he didn't take any photos.

(3) Use a semicolon and a conjunctive adverb—a word such as *therefore, instead, meanwhile, still, also, nevertheless,* or *however.* Follow a conjunctive adverb with a comma.

The tourist went to the mosque; however, he didn't take any photos.

Exercise: Revising   On the lines provided, revise the following run-on sentences. Use the method given in parentheses after each sentence.

EXAMPLE: 1. I like movies I see one a week. *(two sentences)*

I like movies. I see one a week.

1. Hollywood is still a center of American movie making fine films are made in other places, too. *(comma and coordinating conjunction)*

_____

2. Movies entertain millions of people they are popular the world over. *(two sentences)*

_____

3. Many films take years to make they require the skills of hundreds of workers. *(comma and coordinating conjunction)*

_____

4. The movie director is in charge the actors follow his or her instructions. *(semicolon)*

_____

5. The director makes many decisions, the producers usually take care of the business end of moviemaking. *(semicolon and conjunctive adverb)*

_____

SENTENCES

Chapter 9: Writing Complete Sentences

WORKSHEET 6 **Review**

Exercise A Some of the following word groups are complete sentences. Some are fragments. On the lines provided for each, write *S* for sentence or *F* for fragment.

_____ 1. Many people enjoy a variety of leisure activities.

_____ 2. Such as swimming, running, and tennis, as well as reading and cooking.

_____ 3. Other people, including my uncle Reynard, concentrate on one particular hobby.

_____ 4. Driving home from work, Reynard often speaks into a tape recorder.

_____ 5. On which he records ideas for songs he is writing.

_____ 6. Although not one of Reynard's many songs has been recorded by a major star.

_____ 7. Reynard still devotes most of his free time to songwriting and cutting demo tapes to send to recording companies.

_____ 8. Knowing how good many of the songs are.

_____ 9. The family often asks Reynard to play at family get-togethers.

_____ 10. Still haven't been returned by the record company executives who are considering whether or not to purchase them.

Exercise B: Revising Most of the following items contain sentence fragments. On the lines provided, revise each fragment and make it part of a complete sentence, adding commas where necessary. When you find a complete sentence that doesn't need revision, write *C*.

EXAMPLE: 1. Originally raised to hunt badgers. Dachshunds are now popular as pets.

Originally raised to hunt badgers, dachshunds are now popular as pets.

1. Humans have kept dogs as pets and helpers. For perhaps ten thousand years.

_____

_____

2. Herding sheep and cattle and guarding property. Many dogs more than earn their keep.

_____

_____

3. Descended from wolves. Some dogs are still somewhat wolflike.

_____

_____

4. There are over one hundred breeds of dogs now. The cocker spaniel, greyhound, Siberian husky, and collie.

_____

_____

5. The Saint Bernard is popular. One of the largest dogs.

_____

_____

6. Because Yorkshire terriers are very tiny. Many people keep them as pets.

_____

_____

7. Since they are all born blind and unable to take care of themselves. Puppies need their mothers.

_____

_____

8. Most dogs are fully grown by the time they are one year old.

_____

_____

9. Dogs live an average of twelve years. Although many live to be nearly twenty.

_____

_____

10. If you like dogs. Consider having one for a pet.

_____

_____

Exercise C: Revising   Identify each run-on sentence below as a fused sentence (*FS*) or a comma splice (*CS*). Then correct each run-on by creating a compound sentence in the space provided. Note: There is more than one correct way to revise each item. You need to give only one revision.

EXAMPLE: _FS_   1. Today we learned about the Ojibwa we were fascinated.

Today we learned about the Ojibwa, and we were fascinated.

_____ 1. The Ojibwa collected sap for syrup they also grew corn.

_____

_____ 2. They used birch bark for canoes, canoes were their transportation.

_____

SENTENCES

Chapter 9, Worksheet 6, continued

_____ 3. They used toboggans in the winter they also used snowshoes.

_____

_____ 4. Bearskins made good beds they hunted bear.

_____

_____ 5. They planted corn in the spring they collected wild rice in the fall.

_____

Chapter 10: Writing Effective Sentences

Sentence Combining A: Inserting Words

A long, unbroken series of short sentences can sound choppy. One method to combine short sentences is to insert a key word from one sentence into another. You usually need to cut some words in sentences that are combined. You may also need to change the form of the key word.

USING THE SAME FORM

ORIGINAL: Joan Baez is a talented folk singer. She is a Mexican American.

COMBINED: Joan Baez is a talented, Mexican American folk singer.

CHANGING THE FORM

ORIGINAL: I attended a Joan Baez concert. There was much excitement at the concert.

COMBINED: I attended an exciting Joan Baez concert.

Exercise: Revising   On the line provided, combine each of the following sets of sentences by inserting a word or words into the first sentence. There may be more than one way to combine each set; do what sounds best to you. Add commas and change the forms of words where necessary.

EXAMPLE: 1. Luis Valdez is a famous playwright. He is a Mexican American.

Luis Valdez is a famous Mexican American playwright.

1. Valdez was born in Delano. Delano is in California.

   _____

2. He grew up in a family of farm workers. They were migrant workers.

   _____

3. As a child, Valdez began to work in the fields. He was six years old.

   _____

4. He champions the cause of underpaid migrant farm workers. He also champions the cause of migrant farm workers who suffer from overwork. _____

   _____

5. He organized the Farm Workers' Theater, a troupe of actors and musicians. The troupe travels.

   _____

SENTENCES

Chapter 10: Writing Effective Sentences

Sentence Combining B: Inserting Phrases

You can combine closely related sentences by inserting prepositional phrases, participial phrases, or appositive phrases from one sentence into another. You usually need to eliminate some words in sentences that are combined.

ORIGINAL: You can hear African rhythms. The rhythms are in Carlos Santana's music.

COMBINED: You can hear African rhythms **in Carlos Santana's music.** [prepositional phrase modifying the verb phrase *can hear*]

ORIGINAL: Linda Ronstadt is a famous singer. She is known for a variety of styles.

COMBINED: Linda Ronstadt is a famous singer **known for a variety of styles.** [participial phrase modifying the noun *singer*]

ORIGINAL: Ron Howard is a former child actor. He directed the film *Parenthood*.

COMBINED: Ron Howard, **a former child actor,** directed the film *Parenthood*. [appositive phrase identifying the noun *Ron Howard*]

Exercise: Revising   Combine each of the following sets of sentences to create one sentence that includes the type of phrase in parentheses. Add commas as needed.

EXAMPLE: 1. I looked through a book of famous scientists. I learned about Auguste Piccard. *(participial phrase)*

Looking through a book of famous scientists, I learned about Auguste Piccard.

1. Auguste Piccard was a Swiss physicist who studied the upper atmosphere. He studied the atmosphere from balloons. *(prepositional phrase)*

_____

2. Auguste Piccard was born in Switzerland. He was an inventor, a scientist, and an explorer. *(appositive phrase)*

_____

3. Piccard once spent sixteen hours in a balloon. The balloon was floating across Germany and France. *(participial phrase)*

_____

4. Piccard attended a famous institute in Zurich, Switzerland. The institute was the Swiss Institute of Technology. *(appositive phrase)*

_____

5. Piccard was a young man when he became a professor. He became a professor at the Swiss Institute. *(prepositional phrase)*

_____

Name _____ Date _____ Class _____

Sentence Combining C: Using Compound Subjects and Verbs

You can combine sentences by using compound subjects and verbs. Just look for sentences that have the same subject or the same verb. Then make the subject, verb, or both compound by adding a coordinating conjunction such as *and, but, or, nor,* or *yet.*

ORIGINAL: Alexandra worked at the frozen yogurt shop. Anthony worked at the frozen yogurt shop.

COMBINED: **Alexandra and Anthony** worked at the frozen yogurt shop. [compound subject]

ORIGINAL: Alexandra cleaned the yogurt machine. She assembled the machine.

COMBINED: Alexandra **cleaned and assembled** the yogurt machine. [compound verb]

ORIGINAL: Alexandra tasted the new yogurt. Anthony tasted the new yogurt. They did not like it.

COMBINED: **Alexandra and Anthony tasted** the new yogurt but **did** not **like** it. [compound subject and compound verb]

Exercise: Revising On the line provided, combine each set of short sentences into one sentence that has a compound subject, a compound verb, or a compound subject and a compound verb.

EXAMPLE: 1. Konane's family grows bananas and coconuts. Suke's family also grows bananas and coconuts.

Konane's family and Suke's family grow bananas and coconuts.

1. Bananas are a tropical fruit. Coconuts are also a tropical fruit.

_____

2. Brazil produces bananas. India produces bananas. Both countries export bananas.

_____

3. Some bananas are cooked like vegetables. They are eaten like vegetables.

_____

4. By A.D. 600, the Egyptians were eating coconuts. Indians and Koreans were also eating coconuts.

_____

5. Coconuts are not a major crop in the United States. Bananas are not a major crop in the United States, either.

_____

SENTENCES

Chapter 10: Writing Effective Sentences

Sentence Combining D: Creating a Compound Sentence

You can combine two sentences by creating a **compound sentence**. A compound sentence is really two or more simple sentences linked by a comma and a coordinating conjunction, a semicolon, or a semicolon and a conjunctive adverb.

ORIGINAL: Frank read about Syria. Jorge read about Lebanon.

REVISED: Frank read about Syria, **but** Jorge read about Lebanon. [comma and coordinating conjunction]

Frank read about Syria; Jorge read about Lebanon. [semicolon]

Frank read about Syria; **however,** Jorge read about Lebanon. [semicolon and conjunctive adverb]

Exercise: Revising   On the line provided, combine each of the following pairs of sentences to create compound sentences.

EXAMPLE: 1. At first, Tom and Patwin wandered aimlessly through the exhibit of Mexican art. Then, a painting by Diego Rivera attracted their attention.

At first, Tom and Patwin wandered aimlessly through the exhibit of Mexican art; then, a painting by Diego Rivera attracted their attention.

1. Tom was familiar with Diego Rivera's work. Patwin was not familiar with the artist.

_____

2. Some of Rivera's paintings tell a story. The story is not always easy to understand.

_____

3. Rivera was influenced by painters from other countries. His themes are distinctly Mexican.

_____

4. Rivera liked Mexican folk painting. He used some of its themes in his works.

_____

5. Rivera is very well-known as a muralist. José Clemente Orozco is regarded by many as the greatest of the Mexican muralists.

_____

Name _____ Date _____ Class _____

WORKSHEET 5

Sentence Combining E: Creating a Complex Sentence

A **complex sentence** includes one independent clause and one or more subordinate clauses. An independent clause can stand alone as a sentence, but a subordinate clause cannot.

Make a sentence into an **adjective clause** by replacing the subject with *who*, *which*, or *that*. Then use the clause to modify a noun or pronoun in another sentence.

> ORIGINAL: Neil Armstrong took a giant step for humankind. Neil Armstrong was the first human to walk on the moon.

> REVISED: Neil Armstrong, **who was the first human to walk on the moon,** took a giant step for humankind.

Turn one sentence into an **adverb clause** by adding a subordinating conjunction (such as *after*, *although*, *because*, *if*, *when*, or *where*) at the beginning of the sentence. Then use the clause to modify a verb, an adjective, or an adverb in another sentence.

> ORIGINAL: We don't celebrate Leif Eriksson Day. Leif Eriksson probably sailed to America before Christopher Columbus.

> REVISED: We don't celebrate Leif Eriksson Day **although Leif Eriksson probably sailed to America before Christopher Columbus.**

Make a sentence into a **noun clause** and insert it into another sentence just like a noun. A noun clause begins with a word such as *that*, *which*, *how*, *what*, *whatever*, *who*, or *whoever*.

> ORIGINAL: Something puzzles me. I don't know how the lock broke.

> REVISED: **How the lock broke** puzzles me.

Exercise: Revising   On the line provided, combine each of the following pairs of sentences into a single complex sentence as directed in parentheses.

> EXAMPLE: 1. I enjoy singing. I studied the history of opera. *(adverb clause)*
> *Because I enjoy singing, I studied the history of opera.*

1. Lucrezia Bori was a well-known opera singer. Lucrezia Bori was born in 1888 in Valencia, Spain. *(adjective clause)* _____

_____

2. She first performed in the United States in 1912. Audiences cheered her. *(adverb clause)*

_____

3. Lucrezia Bori helped to save the Metropolitan Opera. The Metropolitan Opera faced economic problems during the Great Depression. *(adjective clause)* _____

_____

4. Bori was the first woman opera singer to be elected a member of the Board of Directors of the Metropolitan Opera. This event was historic. *(noun clause)* _____

_____

SENTENCES

Chapter 10: Writing Effective Sentences

Improving Sentence Style A: Using Parallel Structure

When you combine several related ideas in one sentence, it's important to make sure that your combinations are parallel. You create parallelism, or **parallel structure,** in a sentence by using the same form or part of speech to express each idea. For example, you balance a noun with a noun, a phrase with a phrase, and a clause with a clause.

> NOT PARALLEL: Learning to swim is easier in a pool than the ocean.
>
> PARALLEL: Learning to swim is easier in a pool than in the ocean. [two parallel phrases: *in the pool, in the ocean*]

Exercise: Revising   On the line provided, revise each of the following sentences by putting the ideas in parallel form.

> EXAMPLE: 1. Ann wanted to visit India, and returning to Indonesia was a dream, too.
>
> *Ann wanted to visit India and to return to Indonesia.*

1. Jesse Jackson answered the question slowly, carefully, and with thoroughness.

   _____

2. Naturally graceful and because she has confidence, Lani will be a good gymnast.

   _____

3. The teacher suggested holding a concert and that we make a music videotape.

   _____

4. Clive loves to sing, to dance, and playing music.

   _____

5. Losing the game was difficult for the players, but it also caused difficulty for the coach.

   _____

6. Governor Ann Richards spoke confidently and with logic to the Texas legislature.

   _____

7. He liked both eating in the cafeteria and to eat at home.

   _____

8. Convincing Mom to take me to the game is easy, but to convince Dad is difficult.

   _____

9. Chow took little time to do research; writing the report took a long time.

   _____

10. The collection in our public library is better than many college libraries.

   _____

Chapter 10: Writing Effective Sentences

Improving Sentence Style B: Revising Stringy and Wordy Sentences

A **stringy sentence** usually has too many independent clauses strung together with coordinating conjunctions like *and* or *but*. To fix a stringy sentence, you can break the sentence into two or more sentences, or turn some of the independent clauses into subordinate clauses or phrases.

STRINGY: I learned that some Vietnamese Americans save money, and they buy a boat, and they become shrimpers and live on the coast.

REVISED: I learned that some Vietnamese Americans save money to buy a boat. Then they become shrimpers on the coast.

Extra words and unnecessarily difficult words make your writing hard to follow. To make sentences less wordy, use as few words as possible; avoid fancy words where simple ones will do; and don't repeat yourself unless it's absolutely necessary.

WORDY: At this point in time the situation is improving quickly and rapidly.

REVISED: The situation is now improving rapidly.

Exercise: Revising On a separate sheet of paper, revise the writer's stringy or wordy sentences.

EXAMPLE: [1] I must let you know about and inform you of my decision.

1. *I must tell you my decision.*

Dear Mr. and Mrs. Wilson:

[1] At this point in time, it is my unhappy duty to inform you of a certain fact, and that fact is that I will no longer be available to baby-sit with Charles, and this is a decision that I will not change. [2] On the evening of July 13, I was hired by you to perform the duties of baby sitter for your three-year-old son, and these duties were performed by me to the best of my ability. [3] However, I do not feel that any baby sitter should be in a position of having to deal with the threat of harm to the baby sitter's person. [4] I feel that Charles's hurling of objects at my person and his action of locking me in the closet were possible threats to my safety. [5] The situation being what it is, I feel that I cannot safely perform my duties, and I will no longer place myself in danger by sitting with your son.

Sincerely,

Miguel Garza

Miguel Garza

SENTENCES

Name _____ Date _____ Class _____

Improving Sentence Style C: Varying Sentence Beginnings and Structures

Many sentences begin with a subject followed by a verb (for example, *Ann read the letter.*). You can use the following methods to vary this type of beginning.

SINGLE-WORD MODIFIER: **Happily,** Ann read the letter. [adverb]

PHRASE: **With reluctance,** Ann read the letter. [prepositional phrase]

SUBORDINATE CLAUSE: **Because she couldn't wait any longer,** Ann read the letter. [adverb clause]

Vary the structure of your sentences to make your writing livelier. Instead of using all simple sentences, you can use a mix of simple, compound, complex, and compound-complex sentences.

SIMPLE SENTENCES: The dog chased cars. The dog's owners kept it in the fenced yard. The dog was much safer there.

VARIED STRUCTURES: **Because it chased cars,** the dog's owners kept it in the fenced yard. The dog was much safer there. [one complex sentence, one simple sentence]

Exercise: Revising   On the lines provided, vary the beginnings or structures of the following sentences. The notes in parentheses tell you whether to start your revised sentence with a single-word modifier, a phrase, or a clause, or whether to create compound, complex, or compound-complex sentences.

EXAMPLE: 1. Animals are in danger of extinction in many different parts of the world. *(phrase)*

In many different parts of the world, animals are in danger of extinction.

1. The aye-aye is a small animal. It is related to the monkey. *(complex sentence)*

_____

2. The aye-aye is endangered because the rain forest on its home island is being destroyed. *(subordinate clause)*

_____

3. The desman is a water-dwelling mammal. You can find it in the Pyrenees, Portugal, and the former Soviet Union. *(compound sentence)*

_____

4. People are threatening the desmans' survival by damming mountain streams. *(phrase)*

_____

5. The giant otter is protected. It lives in South America. Poachers continue to threaten its survival. *(compound-complex sentence)*

_____

Chapter 10: Writing Effective Sentences

Review

Exercise A: Revising   In the following sets of sentences, some words have been italicized. On the line provided, combine each of the following sets of sentences by inserting the italicized word or words into the first sentence. Where necessary, directions in parentheses will tell you how to change word forms. Add commas where needed.

EXAMPLE: 1. Edgar Allan Poe was a writer who wrote stories and poems. Edgar Allan Poe was an *American* writer.

Edgar Allan Poe was an American writer who wrote stories and poems.

1. Poe's mother died three years after he was born. His mother was *an actress.*

_____

2. Poe was taken in by Mrs. John Allan and her husband. He was taken in *later.* Their taking him in was *fortunate.* (Add *–ly* to *fortunate.*)

_____

3. Poe created stories. He created *detective* stories.

_____

4. Poe inspired Sir Arthur Conan Doyle, the author. Doyle was the author *of the Sherlock Holmes stories.*

_____

5. Poe had original theories about the writing of fiction. Poe was *known for his creativity.*

_____

Exercise B: Revising   On the lines provided, combine the following sentences according to the directions given in parentheses.

EXAMPLE: 1. We strolled through the woods. We found several unusual ferns. *(compound verb)*

We strolled through the woods and found several unusual ferns.

1. My brother is always on the lookout for poison ivy. He is very allergic to it. *(Use who to create a complex sentence.)*

_____

2. He also worries about snakes. My sister worries about snakes, too. *(compound subject)*

_____

3. He has other fears, too. He is afraid of bees and spiders. *(Use for instance to create a compound sentence.)*

_____

SENTENCES

4. He worries so much about these things. He doesn't enjoy the woods nearly as much as I do. *(Use* since *to create a complex sentence.)*

_____

5. I especially enjoy the woods in the fall. Joanne likes the woods in the fall, too. We like to go hiking then. *(compound subject in the first part of a compound sentence joined by* and*)*

_____

Exercise C: Revising   On the line provided, expand each of the following sentences. Using your imagination, add the type of word or word group indicated in parentheses.

> EXAMPLE: 1. I still watch silent movies. *(subordinate clause)*
>
> *Whenever I get the chance, I still watch silent movies.*

1. He watched the silent movie. *(prepositional phrase)*

_____

2. The stars of these old films had to be very talented in their use of gestures. *(subordinate clause)*

_____

3. To supply sound, someone played a piano. *(prepositional phrase)*

_____

4. People thronged to the movie theaters every Saturday. *(single-word modifier)*

_____

5. They laughed, cried, and applauded just as audiences do today. *(participial phrase)*

_____

Exercise D: Revising   The sentences in the following passage are wordy and stringy. On the lines provided, rewrite the passage to eliminate this problem.

> EXAMPLE: [1] Camping experiences can be humorous and funny, and you probably know that.
>
> 1. *You probably know that camping experiences can be funny.*

[1] There were four rainy days all in a row, and we campers got tired of singing songs and singing more songs, and we also got tired of playing charades, and we announced that we wanted to do something different. [2] One of the counselors suggested a contest in which people eat pies, and naturally we accepted the idea enthusiastically. [3] I ate seven pieces of pie, and I got halfway through the eighth piece, but then I terminated the experience. [4] Rafael was the winner, but he was not at all thrilled when he saw his prize, and it was a big blueberry pie! [5] I can certainly tell you, and I will, that I am glad that I did not become the winner of that particular contest!

Name _____ Date _____ Class _____

1. _____

   _____

2. _____

   _____

3. _____

   _____

4. _____

   _____

5. _____

   _____

Exercise E: Revising   On the line provided, make each of the following sentences parallel.

EXAMPLE: 1. At the park, my little sister likes to feed the birds and riding on the swings.

At the park, my little sister likes to feed the birds and to ride on the swings.

1. Captain Picard commands his ship with intelligence and in a fair way.

   _____

2. William Shakespeare's sonnets are more famous than Ben Jonson.

   _____

3. In Florida you can go to Sea World, tour Everglades National Park, or shopping for exotic seashells.

   _____

4. I like working crossword puzzles more than to mow the lawn.

   _____

5. Some architects prefer designing homes to office buildings.

   _____

Exercise F: Revising   The sentences in the following passage are unnecessarily short, monotonous, or rambling. Combine ideas in the passage to create smooth sentences. Vary sentence beginnings and sentence structures. Write your improved version on the lines provided. You may supply a few words of your own if necessary.

The Siamese is a distinctive-looking cat. Most people recognize Siamese cats instantly. The Siamese is noted for its counterpoint coat. It is also noted for its deep-blue eyes. It is a medium-sized feline. The Siamese cat has a long body. It has a thin tail. It has a wedge-shaped head.

SENTENCES

Chapter 10, Worksheet 9, continued

It is highly intelligent. Its cries are loud and plaintive. It effectively communicates its needs to the person who owns it. In effect, it "owns" its owner.

_____

_____

_____

_____

_____

_____

_____

_____

_____

Name _____ Date _____ Class _____

First Words

Capitalize the first word in every sentence.

> **A** high school in Washington, D.C., is named after Paul Laurence Dunbar. **He** was a famous African American poet and novelist. **Many** of his poems reflect the experiences of rural life.

Capitalize the first word of a direct quotation.

> Twyla said, "**Please** look over these results."

Traditionally, the first word of a line of poetry is capitalized.

> **Hector,** the old gray cat,
> **Nobly** stared and sat.

Capitalize the first word both in the salutation and in the closing of a letter.

> **Dear** Cora,   **Sincerely,**

Exercise: Proofreading   Circle the twenty words that should be capitalized in the following letter.

> EXAMPLE: (please) call next weekend. (we) will be home.

dear Melanie,

   yesterday I read a newspaper article about a new kind of laser radar instrument that I thought would interest you. you recently said that lasers fascinate you. this instrument would be especially useful for people with visual impairments. how does the radar work? a laser device, which is small enough to fit onto an eyeglass frame, emits invisible infrared light beams. when the light strikes an object, the light bounces back to a receiver placed in the ear of the person with a visual impairment. the receiver, in turn, sounds a small tone. with this sort of device, the person with a visual impairment can "hear" any object nearby. the device is very promising. in fact, it may one day replace the cane or the guide dog as an aid for persons with visual impairments. there are few better examples of how beneficial laser research can be.

   my sister Sara asked me to send her poem to you. this is it:

   the bluebird reminded me of you
   because it sings and is happy, too.

   Beth sends her love. she also sends this message: "you must come for Thanksgiving this year. we missed you so much last year." I agree.

                         lovingly yours,

                         Clay

Chapter 11: Capitalization

I *and* O

The pronoun *I* is always capitalized.

Carmen said that **I** was an excellent public speaker.

The interjection *O*, usually used in invocations, is always capitalized. Generally, it is followed by the name of the person or thing being addressed.

Guide our ship toward shore, **O** great spirit of the sea.

The interjection *oh* requires a capital letter only at the beginning of a sentence.

Oh, I'm really thrilled to have won the contest.

The game is supposed to start, but **oh**, look at the rain coming down!

Exercise: Proofreading   In each of the following sentences, circle the letters that should be capitalized, and underline any letters that are capitalized but should not be.

EXAMPLES: 1. In "Jazz Fantasia," the speaker tells the musicians, "Go to it, ⓞjazzmen."
2. The quotation is short, but O̲h, does it inspire me!

1. Yesterday i learned two psalms that begin, "Bless the Lord, o my soul."

2. i haven't really decided about my future, but Oh, how i'd like to be an astronaut.

3. In the poem "The Fool's Prayer," the jester pleads, "o Lord, be merciful to me, a fool!"

4. The car had to stop suddenly, and Oh, was i glad my seat belt was fastened!

5. My favorite lines from *Romeo and Juliet* are
    "See how she leans her cheek upon her hand!
    o, that I were a glove upon that hand,
    That i might touch that cheek!"

Chapter 11: Capitalization

Common Nouns, Proper Nouns, and Proper Adjectives

A **common noun** is a general name for a person, a place, a thing, or an idea. A common noun is not capitalized unless it begins a sentence or a direct quotation or is part of a title. A **proper noun** names a particular person, place, thing, or idea and should always be capitalized. A **proper adjective** is formed from a proper noun and is always capitalized.

COMMON NOUN	PROPER NOUN	PROPER ADJECTIVE
continent	South America	a South American poet

All words in compound proper nouns and proper adjectives are capitalized except articles (*a, an, the*), prepositions of fewer than five letters (such as *of* and *with*), coordinating conjunctions (*and, but, for, nor, or, yet*), and the sign of the infinitive (*to*).

Exercise   In the following phrases underline each common noun once and each proper noun or adjective twice. Then, on the line provided, capitalize the proper nouns and adjectives.

EXAMPLE: 1. a city in north dakota *North Dakota*

1. a sandwich from main street cafe _____

2. an african nation _____

3. my team, the houston oilers _____

4. a south carolina city _____

5. a book titled *learning to swim* _____

6. a haitian restaurant _____

7. a vietnamese village _____

8. the mayflower hotel _____

9. 12 state street, ames, iowa _____

10. the first monday in may _____

11. a fourth of july parade _____

12. the institute for agriculture and trade policy _____

13. a book by langston hughes _____

14. the miami young republicans club _____

15. the hispanic artist _____

16. a hike up mount whitney _____

17. an inlet of the indian ocean _____

18. beaches on the gulf of mexico _____

19. a palestinian leader _____

20. of alexander the great _____

MECHANICS

Chapter 11: Capitalization

Proper Nouns and Proper Adjectives A

Proper nouns name a particular person, place, thing, or idea. **Proper adjectives** are formed from proper nouns. Names of persons and animals are proper nouns and are always capitalized.

Jean's brother is named Jacques.

Abbreviations such as *Ms., Mr., Dr.,* and *Gen.* should always be capitalized. Capitalize the abbreviations *Jr. (junior)* and *Sr. (senior)* after a name, and set them off with commas.

Dr. Bell said that he would see Samuel Portnoy, **Jr.,** in the morning.

Geographical names are **proper nouns** and are always capitalized. These include names of towns and cities; counties, townships, and parishes; states, countries, continents, islands, landforms, and features (such as **Carlsbad Caverns**); bodies of water, parks, and regions; roads, streets, and highways. Words such as *north, west,* and *southeast* are not capitalized when they indicate direction.

She lives **north** of **East St.** Louis, **Illinois,** on the **Mississippi River.**

Exercise: Proofreading Circle the letters that should be capitalized in each of the following sentences.

EXAMPLE: 1. The earliest Ⓐfrican Ⓐmerican folk tales have their roots in Ⓐfrica.

1. Our teacher, mr. elias samuels, jr., told us that the africans who were first brought to america enjoyed folk tales that blended their own african songs with stories they heard in america.

2. According to mr. samuels, african americans created new tales that reflected their experiences as slaves and their desire for freedom.

3. Many of these tales are about animals, especially the small but clever character named brer rabbit.

4. Zora neale hurston collected and published a number of these stories in *Mules and Men*.

5. Brer rabbit, who was especially popular in the south in the 1800s, constantly plays tricks on brer fox and brer wolf.

6. In some later tales, the main character isn't a rabbit but a slave, john, who outsmarts the slave owner.

7. Virginia hamilton tells other tales in *The People Could Fly: american Black Folktales*.

8. The title of ms. hamilton's book refers to another popular kind of folk tale that developed during the years of slavery.

9. In those tales, the people have magic powers and fly away from their troubles, mr. samuels said.

10. When I was growing up near the mississippi river in tennessee, I used to hear such folk tales.

Name _____ Date _____ Class _____

Proper Nouns and Proper Adjectives B

A **proper noun** names a particular person, place, thing, or idea. **Proper adjectives** are formed from proper nouns. Proper nouns include the names of organizations, teams, business firms, institutions, buildings and other structures, and government bodies; historical events and periods, holidays, special events, and other calendar items; nationalities, races, and peoples; brand names; ships, trains, aircraft, spacecraft, monuments, awards; and other particular places, things, or events.

the Boy Scouts of America	the Henley High School Senior Prom
the Chicago Bulls	Thanksgiving
Sears, Roebuck and Company	Mexican literature
the United States Senate	a Chrysler sedan
Texas Tech University	the Washington Monument
the Civil War	the Nobel Prize

The word *earth* is capitalized only when it is used with the names of other heavenly bodies.

How on **earth** did you get in!

The planet Venus is about the same size as Earth.

Do *not* capitalize the names of school subjects except for languages or course names followed by a number.

I am taking Spanish, Art 101, English, biology, and World History II.

Exercise: Proofreading   Circle the letters that should be capitalized in each of the following sentences.

EXAMPLE: 1. I wonder if people will ever walk on (m)ars.

1. On our trip during the memorial day weekend, we drove over the golden gate bridge.

2. My oldest brother, who is studying law at harvard university, dreams of serving on the supreme court.

3. Did you get tickets to see the dallas cowboys play on saturday?

4. Some wheaties cereal and a glass of orange juice are my usual breakfast.

5. What is the name of that musical about the french revolution?

6. Virginia Hamilton, an african american, has won the newbery medal and the national book award.

7. For my european history course, I read a book about the sinking of the *lusitania* off the coast of Ireland.

8. It's a beautiful, clear july night, and we should be able to see the big dipper.

9. We saw the space shuttle *discovery* being moved to its launch pad.

10. The teacher of our russian course spoke to the students in art history 104.

MECHANICS

Name _____ Date _____ Class _____

WORKSHEET 6 *Titles*

Capitalize the title of a person when it comes before the person's name. Do not capitalize a title that is used alone or following a person's name, especially if the title is preceded by *a* or *the*.

> Patricia Elliot, a **d**octor from Tennessee, appeared on a documentary about traditional remedies.
>
> The **s**enator from Maine met with **S**enator Burns.

When a title is used alone in direct address, it is usually capitalized.

> Thank you for meeting with me, **S**enator.

Capitalize words showing family relationship when used with a person's name but *not* when preceded by a possessive.

> My **u**ncle Bert is married to **A**unt Flora.

Capitalize the first and last words and all important words in titles of books, periodicals, poems, stories, essays, speeches, plays, historical documents, movies, radio and television programs, works of art, musical compositions, and cartoons.

> The song "**A Very Nice Prince**" is from the play *Into the Woods*.

Capitalize names of religions and their followers, holy days and celebrations, holy writings, and specific deities.

> One of the most sacred days for **C**hristians is **E**aster.

Exercise: Proofreading   Circle the letters that should be capitalized in each of the following sentences.

> EXAMPLE: 1. The citizens' group spoke with **g**overnor Richards.

1. One of the finest American novels is *the great gatsby* by F. Scott Fitzgerald.

2. With professor Chang's direction, Ruben studied the history of buddhism.

3. His aunt Carmelita works as an assistant to judge Rosetti.

4. Kiyo and Noburu submitted their report to the *Houston chronicle*.

5. Sheila asked, "Have you seen the play *the fantasticks*, uncle Marcus?"

6. The jewish members of the squadron met with rabbi Kolwitz.

7. Former Philadelphia district attorney Arlen Specter became a senator.

8. The movie *howard's end* was reviewed by *newsweek*.

9. Thank you, uncle, for the tape of Mozart's opera *the marriage of figaro*.

10. One of my favorite poems by Richard Wilbur is "first snow in alsace."

Name _____ Date _____ Class _____

Review

Exercise A   Circle the letter of the correctly capitalized sentence in each of the following pairs.

> EXAMPLE: 1. a. Drive Northeast until you get to new Haven.
> (b.) Drive northeast until you get to New Haven.

1. a. Anica and inés hiked through the grand Canyon.
    b. Anica and Inés hiked through the Grand Canyon.

2. a. Nectar-eating bats eat from hummingbird feeders in Arizona.
    b. Nectar-eating Bats eat from hummingbird feeders in arizona.

3. a. I like the following poem, from an old new England saying:
       Use it up, wear it out;
       make it do, or do without.
    b. I like the following poem, from an old New England saying:
       Use it up, wear it out;
       Make it do, or do without.

4. a. She spoke at the Women's Rights Convention in Akron, Ohio.
    b. She spoke at the women's rights convention in akron, Ohio.

5. a. Did ms. Jee say, "read *On Being a Writer*"?
    b. Did Ms. Jee say, "Read *On Being a Writer*"?

6. a. Letters to my favorite Uncle begin with "dear Unk" and end with "bye, now."
    b. Letters to my favorite uncle begin with "Dear Unk" and end with "Bye, now."

7. a. Atlanta is a fast-growing City in the Southern United States.
    b. Atlanta is a fast-growing city in the southern United States.

8. a. Pensacola is on the gulf of Mexico, i think.
    b. Pensacola is on the Gulf of Mexico, I think.

9. a. Write to the author at 95 coral street in Athens.
    b. Write to the author at 95 Coral Street in Athens.

10. a. Laredo is on the Mexican Border in Webb county.
    b. Laredo is on the Mexican border in Webb County.

Exercise B: Proofreading   Circle the letters that should be capitalized in the following sentences.

> EXAMPLE: 1. Most of the students in (m)iss Amundsen's (e)nglish class had
> already read "The (l)egend of Sleepy Hollow."

1. in tuesday's class, mrs. garcía explained that the diameter of earth is only 405 miles more than that of venus.

2. this year's juniors will be required to take more courses in english, science, and math than did prior juniors at briarwood county high school.

Chapter 11, Worksheet 7, continued

3. in chicago we visited wrigley field and the museum of science and industry, which are known all over the world.

4. Aboard the space shuttle *columbia* in january 1986, franklin Chang-Díaz became the first astronaut to send a message in spanish back to earth.

5. in kentucky, one of the border states between the north and the south, you can visit mammoth cave, churchill downs, and the abraham lincoln birthplace national historic site.

Exercise C   If the capitalization in a phrase below is correct, write C on the line provided. If the capitalization is incorrect, rewrite the phrase with correct capitals.

EXAMPLE: 1. dr. Huang *Dr. Huang*

1. hindu temple _____

2. "Home on The Range" _____

3. the *Texas Monthly* magazine _____

4. chosen president _____

5. chairperson Brown _____

6. knew the Greek Goddess athena _____

7. my sister and aunt Kaloma _____

8. his Grandfather's mother _____

9. the oscar won by Clint Eastwood _____

10. *the Diary of Anne Frank* _____

Exercise D   On the line provided, correctly use each of the following words in a sentence of your own.

EXAMPLES: 1. beach *The beach was deserted this morning.*
            2. Beach *Zuma Beach is beautiful this time of year.*

1. river _____

2. River _____

3. motel _____

4. Motel _____

5. street _____

6. Street _____

7. park _____

8. Park _____

9. west _____

10. West _____

Chapter 12: Punctuation

WORKSHEET 1   *End Marks*

End marks—*periods, question marks,* and *exclamation points*—indicate a sentence's purpose.

A **statement** (or **declarative sentence**) is followed by a period.

    Yo-Yo Ma is a renowned cello player**.**

A **question** (or **interrogative sentence**) is followed by a question mark.

    Can we get tickets for the Saturday concert**?**

An **exclamation** (or **exclamatory sentence**) is followed by an exclamation point.

    Wow**!** What a fine musician he is**!**

A **command** or **request** (or **imperative sentence**) is followed by either a period or an exclamation point.

    Please take your seats**.**   Stop making that noise**!**

An abbreviation is usually followed by a period.

    Dr. C. Linda Solomon   Rand Corp.   5 pts.   7:00 A.M.   400 B.C.

Exercise: Proofreading   Add appropriate end marks to the sentences below. On the lines provided, identify the kinds of sentences used.

          EXAMPLE: [1] Are you familiar with lacrosse, a field game**?**
                 1. *interrogative*

[1] Just listen to what I found out about lacrosse [2] My friend, J D Elliott, told me about lacrosse [3] What a rough sport lacrosse seems to be [4] Did you know that Native Americans developed this game [5] Before Columbus came to the Americas in AD 1492, the Iroquois were playing lacrosse in what is now upper New York State and Canada [6] Do you realize that lacrosse is the oldest organized sport in America [7] Lacrosse is played by two opposing teams [8] Players use sticks to catch, carry, and throw a ball, which is about 8 in around [9] The head of the stick looks like a bishop's cross, which is where the name of the game comes from (French, *la crosse*) [10] Lacrosse is especially popular in Canada, the British Isles, and Australia, and it is played in the US, too

1. _____   6. _____

2. _____   7. _____

3. _____   8. _____

4. _____   9. _____

5. _____   10. _____

Name _____ Date _____ Class _____

Commas with Items in a Series

A **comma** separates words or groups of words so that the meaning of a sentence is clear.

Use commas to separate items in a series. The items may be words, phrases, or clauses.

Items of folk art are often found in **closets, attics,** and **barns.** [words]

Old quilts, thick pottery, and **wooden ware** are good examples. [phrases]

Our exhibit has encouraged people **who tell stories, who sew quilts,** and **who carve toys** to share their talents. [clauses]

When the last two items in a series are joined by *and,* the comma before the *and* may be omitted if the comma is not necessary to make the meaning clear.

Items of folk art are often found in **closets, attics** and **barns.**

(1) If all items in a series are joined by *and* or *or,* do not use commas to separate them.

Diamonds or **flowers** or **stars** are good quilt block designs for a beginner.

(2) Short independent clauses may be separated by commas.

Plan your design, collect scraps, and **seek good advice.**

Use commas to separate two or more adjectives preceding a noun.

See the **loud, bright** colors in her design!

Exercise: Proofreading   Add commas where needed in the following sentences. Circle the number of any sentence that is correct.

EXAMPLE: 1. Rita plays soccer‚volleyball and softball.

or

1. Rita plays soccer‚volleyball‚and softball.

1. Dr. Charles Drew worked as a surgeon developed new ways of storing blood and was the first director of the Red Cross blood bank program.

2. I am going to take English science social studies algebra and Spanish.

3. The loud insistent smoke alarm woke us just before dawn this morning.

4. Please pass those delicious pancakes the margarine and the raspberries.

5. My twin sister can run faster jump higher and do more push-ups than I can.

6. Where is a store that sells newspapers magazines and paperbacks?

7. Horns tooted tires screeched a whistle blew and sirens wailed.

8. Steel is made from iron and other metals and small amounts of carbon.

9. The clown wore a long blue raincoat; big red gloves; and floppy yellow shoes.

10. Robert Browning says that youth is good that middle age is better and that old age is best.

Name _____ Date _____ Class _____

Commas with Independent Clauses

Use commas before *and, but, or, nor, for, so,* and *yet* when they join independent clauses.

Marina must pass the test**, or** she'll have to repeat the course.

NOTE: A comma may be omitted before *and, but, or,* or *nor* when the independent clauses are very short and when there is no possibility of misunderstanding.

Ms. Caruso offered her help **and** Marina accepted.

Exercise: Proofreading   Where a comma should be used in each of the following sentences, write the word preceding the comma, the comma, and the conjunction following it on the line provided. If a sentence is correct, write *C*.

EXAMPLE: 1. Accident-related injuries are common but many of these injuries could be prevented. *common, but*

1. I studied first aid and I enjoyed it.   _____

2. It is important to know first aid for an accident can happen at any time.   _____

3. More than eighty-five thousand people in the United States die in accidents each year and many millions are injured.   _____

4. Many household products can cause illness or even death yet these products are often stored where small children can reach them.   _____

5. Biking accidents are common wherever cars and bicycles use the same road so many communities provide bicycle lanes.   _____

6. Car accidents are the leading cause of childhood fatalities but seat belts have saved many lives.   _____

7. Everyone should know what to do in case of fire and different escape routes should be tested beforehand.   _____

8. To escape a fire, stay close to the floor, and be very cautious about opening doors.   _____

9. An injured person should not be allowed to get up nor should liquid be given to an unconscious victim.   _____

10. Always have someone with you when you swim or you may find yourself without help when you need it.   _____

MECHANICS

Chapter 12: Punctuation

WORKSHEET 4

Commas with Nonessential Elements

A **nonessential** (or **nonrestrictive**) clause or participial phrase adds information that is not needed to understand the main idea in the sentence. Use commas to set off nonessential clauses and nonessential participial phrases.

Dr. Laker, **who drives a yellow van,** is his advisor. [nonessential clause]

My brother, **hoping to get a job,** asked him for a reference. [nonessential phrase]

An **essential** (or **restrictive**) clause or phrase cannot be left out of a sentence without changing the main idea. Commas are *not* used.

The girl **who won third place** is my teammate. [essential clause]

The runner **wearing the red shirt** came in first. [essential phrase]

Exercise: Proofreading   Add commas where they are needed in the following sentences, and circle unnecessary commas. Circle the number of any sentence that is correct.

EXAMPLES: 1. My mother who is a Celtics fan has season tickets to the home games.

2. The girls in that picture are my sisters.

1. *Doonesbury* which is my favorite comic strip makes me think as well as laugh.

2. Elizabeth Blackwell completing her medical studies in 1849 became the first female doctor in the United States.

3. Our math teacher who also teaches gym will leave in January.

4. The amusement rides that are the most exciting may be the most dangerous.

5. Players breaking training will be dismissed from the team.

6. Students, planning to go on the field trip, should bring lunches.

7. Many of the first settlements in California were founded by Father Junípero Serra who liked to take long walks between them.

8. People who carry credit cards should keep records of their account numbers.

9. The movie's star who hates publicity appeared on three magazine covers this week.

10. People, visiting the reservation, will be barred from burial sites, which are considered holy by Native Americans.

Chapter 12: Punctuation

Commas After Introductory Elements

Use commas after certain introductory elements.

(1) Use commas after words such as *next, yes,* and *no* and after introductory interjections such as *why, well,* and *oops* when they express mild emotion.

No, I'm not busy tonight.

Well, let's ask Chun Ping to come along.

(2) Use a comma after an introductory participial phrase.

Jogging along her usual path, she came upon a furry creature.

(3) Use a comma after a series of introductory prepositional phrases.

At the side of the road, she came upon a furry creature.

(4) Use a comma after an introductory adverb clause.

Whenever I go to the bank, I stop at my aunt's office.

Exercise: Proofreading   Add commas where they are needed after introductory elements in the following sentences.

> EXAMPLE: 1. When Marco Polo visited China in the thirteenth century,
> he found an advanced civilization.

1. Although there was a great deal of poverty in China the ruling classes lived in splendor.

2. Valuing cleanliness Chinese rulers took baths every day.

3. Instead of using coins for currency the Chinese used paper money.

4. After marrying a Chinese woman lived in her mother-in-law's home.

5. Well I read that one Chinese emperor was buried with more than eight thousand statues of servants and horses.

6. Respected by all their descendants elderly people were highly honored.

7. Built around 200 B.C. the main part of the Great Wall is about four thousand miles long.

8. Until modern freeways were built the Great Wall was the world's longest construction.

9. In Chinese art from centuries ago people are very small and are usually shown in harmony with nature.

10. Yes Chinese landscapes look different from those done by Western artists.

Chapter 12: Punctuation

Commas with Interrupters

Use commas to set off elements that interrupt a sentence, such as appositives, nouns of direct address, and parenthetical expressions. Use two commas when the "interrupter" is in the middle. Use one comma when it comes at the beginning or the end.

(1) Appositives and appositive phrases are usually set off by commas.

My lab partner, **Richard Jackson,** did most of the experiment.

Dr. Okimo, **the new PTA president,** asked parents to become active.

NOTE: A **restrictive** appositive is so closely related to the word it identifies or explains that it is not set off by commas.

Mexican American performer **Dr. Loco** is also an anthropologist.

(2) Words used in direct address are set off by commas.

Please hang up your jacket, **Greta.**

(3) *Parenthetical expressions* are set off by commas. **Parenthetical expressions** are remarks that add minor information or that relate ideas to each other. Commonly used parenthetical expressions include *after all, however, I believe, in fact, nevertheless,* and *of course.*

Some of us, **I believe,** already recycle a large percentage of our trash.

Of course, not all trash can be recycled.

Exercise A: Proofreading   Correctly punctuate each appositive or appositive phrase below.

EXAMPLE: 1.   My cousin consulted Dr. Moniz, an allergy specialist, about the harmful effects of pollution.

1. *Ecology* a little-known word thirty years ago has become a popular term today.

2. The word's origin is *oikos* the Greek word meaning "house."

3. Ecology is the study of an enormous "house" the world of all living things.

4. Ecologists study the bond of a living organism to its environment the place in which it lives.

5. Our neighbor Dr. Alicia Montez is an ecologist.

Exercise B: Proofreading   Correctly punctuate the following sentences containing parenthetical expressions and words of direct address.

EXAMPLE: 1.   Gladys, have you read any stories by Toni Cade Bambara?

1. Toni Cade Bambara is I think a fine writer.

2. Perhaps Gladys you have read the story "My Delicate Heart Condition."

3. That story is by Bambara of course.

4. I know Ms. Reaves that you read Bambara's book *The Black Woman*.

5. In fact you said that you had read it three times.

Name _____ Date _____ Class _____

Commas in Conventional Uses and Unnecessary Commas

Use commas in certain conventional situations.

(1) Use a comma to separate items in dates and addresses.

Aunt Virginia was born on June 15, 1943, in Michigan.
She just moved to 125 Central St., Farmingdale, New York.

(2) Use a comma after the salutation of a friendly letter and after the closing of any letter.

Dear Aunt Virginia,   Sincerely yours,

(3) Use a comma after a name followed by an abbreviation such as *Jr., Sr.,* or *M.D.* Follow such an abbreviation with a comma unless it ends the sentence.

Alex M. Jorgensen, Jr., is my uncle.

Do not use unnecessary commas. Too much punctuation is just as confusing as not enough punctuation, especially in the case of commas.

CONFUSING: Your sister, Alice, lent me her skates, but now, I can't find them.

CLEAR: Your sister Alice lent me her skates, but now I can't find them.

Exercise A: Proofreading   Add commas where they are needed in the following sentences. Circle the number of any sentence that is punctuated correctly.

EXAMPLE: 1. On July 14, 1789, the French people destroyed the Bastille.

1. My friend Marybeth Correio lives at 1255 S.E. 56th Street Bellevue Washington.

2. On April 6 1909 Matthew Henson, assistant to Commander Robert E. Peary, reached the North Pole.

3. I glanced quickly at the end of the letter, which read, "Very sincerely yours Alice Ems Ph.D."

4. The Constitution of the United States was signed on September 17 1787 eleven years after the adoption of the Declaration of Independence on July 4 1776.

5. Did you go on a field trip to the desert in March or April of 1991?

Exercise B: Proofreading   Draw a line through any unnecessary commas in the following sentences.

EXAMPLE: 1. Please explain/why so many children enjoy using computers.

1. John Wayne, whose real name was Marion Morrison, won an Academy Award, for *True Grit*.

2. People who come to the game, early, will be allowed to take pictures.

3. In the story, "The Gift of the Magi," two characters who are deeply in love, make sacrifices in order to buy gifts, for each other.

4. Dad, why can't I go, to the movies, tonight?

Chapter 12: Punctuation

Semicolons A

Use a semicolon between independent clauses in a sentence if they are not joined by *and, but, or, nor, for, so,* or *yet.*

   Maria's latest tape is selling rapidly**;** she may become a major star.

Use a semicolon between independent clauses joined by a conjunctive adverb or a transitional expression. Conjunctive adverbs include *however, meanwhile, also, instead, otherwise,* and *nevertheless.* Common transitional expressions are *as a result, in fact, for example, in addition,* and *in other words.*

   I've called him repeatedly**; however,** I've not been able to reach him.

   Julio seems tired**; in fact,** he seems completely exhausted.

Exercise: Proofreading   Cross out incorrect punctuation, and add semicolons as needed to punctuate the following sentences correctly.

   EXAMPLE: 1. My mother and I usually go to Massachusetts in late

   summer**;**/however, last year we went in July.

 1. My grandparents live near Cape Cod, therefore, we visit there often.

 2. I miss my friends and sometimes find the yearly trip to Cape Cod boring, besides, my cousins in Massachusetts are all older than I am.

 3. To my great surprise, we had a good time last year, we even did some sightseeing in Boston and Plymouth.

 4. One hot day my grandparents and my mother and I went to the beach, my grandfather immediately went down to the water for a swim.

 5. My grandfather loves the water and is a strong swimmer, nevertheless, we worried when we saw that he was swimming out farther and farther in the choppy sea.

 6. Grandpa finally turned around and swam back to shore, he was astonished that we had been worried about him.

 7. While he was in the water, Mom had gathered driftwood and built a fire in a shallow pit in the sand, Grandma had put lobsters and potatoes on the coals.

 8. By the time we had finished eating, it was quite late, consequently, everyone else on the beach had gone home.

 9. We didn't leave for home right away, instead, we spent the evening watching the darkening ocean and listening to the whispering waves.

10. I enjoyed the outing, in fact, I look forward to going again soon.

Name _____ Date _____ Class _____

 **WORKSHEET 9**   *Semicolons B*

A semicolon (rather than a comma) may be needed to separate independent clauses joined by a coordinating conjunction when there are commas within the clauses.

> CONFUSING: Bert, Ray, and Jette joined us, and Pat and Bo arrived later.
>
> CLEAR: Bert, Ray, and Jette joined us; and Pat and Bo arrived later.

Use a semicolon between items in a series if the items contain commas.

> CONFUSING: The club officers are Kiyo Okaya, president, Lois Gould, secretary, and Maria Columbo, treasurer.
>
> CLEAR: The club officers are Kiyo Okaya, president; Lois Gould, secretary; and Maria Columbo, treasurer.

Exercise: Proofreading   Some of the following sentences are punctuated incorrectly. Cross out incorrect punctuation, and add semicolons as needed. Circle the number of any sentence that is punctuated correctly.

> EXAMPLE: 1. For the opinion survey, Billie will call the Grays, the
>
> Mitchells, and the Millers; and Jesse will call the Chuns,
>
> the Van Horns, and the Schmidts.

1. In the fifteenth century, the kings of France, England, and Spain grew stronger.

2. Gloria will go with Sal, and Bob, Fred, and Tyrone will come later.

3. Africa's once-powerful kingdoms included Mali, on the Niger River, Benin, in what is now Nigeria, and Karanga, in southern Africa.

4. The Incas in Peru planted crops, such as corn, domesticated animals, such as the llama, and developed crafts, such as weaving.

5. I've planted new parsley, chives, and dill, and basil is already in the garden.

6. The Mohawks, Senecas, Oneidas, Onondagas, and Cayugas banded together in the late 1500s to advance peace, civil authority, and righteousness.

7. Mrs. Gillis said that we could choose to write about Dekanawidah, the Huron founder of the Iroquois League, Mansa Musa, the Muslim emperor of Mali, Tamerlane, the Mongol conqueror of the Ottoman Turks, or Alexander the Great, the Macedonian conqueror of Greece and the Persian Empire.

8. Ahmad was surprised to see Juana, Michelle, and Carlos; but Erik, Faith, and I were not surprised at all.

9. In class today, we discussed the contributions of Gutenberg, the inventor of the printing press, Galileo, the inventor of the first complete astronomical telescope, and Newton, the discoverer of the laws of gravity.

10. At the concert I sat with Eli, Bill, and Earl, and May, Ruth, and Jo sat with Dad.

Chapter 12: Punctuation

Colons

Use a colon to mean "note what follows."

(1) In some cases a colon is used before a list of items, especially after the expressions *the following* and *as follows*.

> Please submit copies of the following documents: your driver's license, birth certificate, and Social Security card.

If a word is followed by a list of appositives, use a colon to make the sentence clear.

> I have the autographs of three stars: Danny Glover, Mel Gibson, and Cher.

Do not use a colon before a list that follows a verb or a preposition.

(2) Use a colon before a long, formal statement or a long quotation.

> The director made these remarks: "I am proud of the finished film and its message that people can overcome serious problems. We don't have to accept problems and their results; we can call upon our inner strengths, however dormant, to combat them and get us back on the right track."

Use a colon in certain conventional situations: between the hour and the minute, between chapter and verse in referring to passages from the Bible, and after the salutation of a business letter.

> At 10:30 the Reverend Dr. Torres will analyze Matthew 3:8.

> Dear Mr. Ames:

Exercise: Proofreading   The following excerpt from a business letter contains five errors in punctuation. To correct the letter, add five colons as needed. Insert the colons into the letter and circle them.

> EXAMPLE: A dinner for conference participants will begin at 7⊙30 P.M.

Dear Professor Liu

Thank you for accepting our invitation to discuss the biblical story of David and Goliath. I understand that the text of your discussion will be I Samuel 17 20–50. The session will be held on Monday, February 10, at 11 25 A.M. Other non-biblical stories that we will be discussing are the following *Sir Gawain and the Green Knight,* "Wanjiru," and "Cupid and Psyche." Dr. Frank Evans had this to say about our conference "It will be a scholarly meeting with much discussion about the literary, religious, and philosophical merits of the works and selections; but it also will be an informal gathering at which interested persons from all backgrounds can exchange knowledge and ideas."

Chapter 12: Punctuation

 **Review**

Exercise A: Proofreading Correct the following sentences by adding periods and other end marks as needed. Circle the periods that you add.

> EXAMPLE: 1. Chinese people have made important contributions to our society⊙

1. What a fine program Connie Chung presented

2. Maya Lin designed the Vietnam Veterans Memorial

3. Have you heard about the architecture of I M Pei

4. I like the East Building of the National Gallery of Art in Washington, DC

5. Go see the building tomorrow at 9 AM

Exercise B: Proofreading Insert commas where they belong in the following sentences.

> EXAMPLE: 1. Do you like to explore,to travel,and to discover new places?

1. Yes people still search for buried treasure in Florida for there is supposedly much pirate gold buried there.

2. Two years ago Tina Gregson my best friend asked me to go treasure hunting with her.

3. Agreeing to go I asked her what kind of equipment I would need.

4. She said that we didn't need any equipment except of course a shovel.

5. Because I'd lost things before my mother warned me to bring our shovel back.

6. We decided to dig on a flat empty beach that was a few blocks east of us.

7. Tina who is always optimistic carried a sack for the buried treasure.

8. In the hope of having more privacy and avoiding the heat of midday we set out early.

9. What a wonderful morning it was Sandra!

10. The sun sparkled on the sea and the sand and the air was so clear that we could see for miles.

11. Looking for signs of pirate activity we gazed intently at the long stretch of sand.

12. Since Miami's beaches seemed empty of such signs we chose a spot at random.

13. Soon we had a wide deep hole but we found no chest of pirate treasure.

14. We did find a number of rusty nails pieces of broken bottles and similar items.

15. I haven't bothered to hunt for treasure since then and Tina hasn't mentioned going treasure hunting again.

MECHANICS

16. Tina and I however still have adventures together and they are always fun.

17. Tina who lives near Los Angeles California invited me to go with her and her uncle Aaron Miller Jr. to a New Year's Day concert.

18. Before accepting her invitation I checked with my family.

19. My mother was glad I believe to learn that the concert was in the afternoon.

20. She smiled my father nodded and my brothers yelled.

Exercise C: Proofreading   Draw a line through any unnecessary commas in the following sentences.

> EXAMPLE: 1. Hanukkah, which is also called the Feast of Lights, is a major/Jewish celebration.

1. Hanukkah celebrates the rededication of the Temple of Jerusalem, in 165 B.C., and the word *Hanukkah*, in fact, means, "dedication."

2. This event followed the Jewish people's victory, over the Syrians, who were led by a pagan, king.

3. During the first Hanukkah, according to traditional lore, the Jews had a one-day supply of lamp oil, that lasted for eight days.

4. Modern Jews, celebrating the memory of this miraculous event, light one candle, on the menorah, each day, of the eight-day festival.

5. The menorah, which is an eight-branched candlestick, is a symbol, of the original festival.

Exercise D: Proofreading   Correct the following sentences by adding semicolons and colons where they are needed. Circle the colons or semicolons you add.

> EXAMPLE: 1. Mrs. Hughes named the three students who had completed extra project⊙Marshall, Helena, and Regina.

1. Because the club has run out of funds, the following supplies must be brought from home pencils, erasers, paper, and envelopes.

2. Sojourner Truth, a former slave, could neither read nor write however, this accomplished woman spoke eloquently against slavery and for women's rights.

3. A rabbi, a minister, and a priest discussed their interpretations of Isaiah 2 2 and 5 26.

4. In his speech Dr. Fujikawa quoted from several poets Rudyard Kipling, David McCord, and Nikki Giovanni.

5. From 1853 to 1865, the United States had three presidents Franklin Pierce, a Democrat from New Hampshire James Buchanan, a Democrat from Pennsylvania and Abraham Lincoln, a Republican from Illinois.

Chapter 13: Punctuation

Underlining (Italics)

Use underlining (italics) for titles of books, plays, long poems, films, periodicals, works of art, recordings, long musical works, television series, trains, ships, aircraft, and spacecraft.

BOOKS AND PLAYS:	*The Pearl*	*Romeo and Juliet*
LONG POEMS:	*Hiawatha*	*The Divine Comedy*
FILMS:	*Fantasia*	*Star Trek—The Motion Picture*
PERIODICALS:	*Newsweek*	*Los Angeles Times*
WORKS OF ART:	*American Gothic*	*The Thinker*
RECORDINGS, LONG MUSICAL WORKS:	*The Last Spring*	*Messiah*
TELEVISION PROGRAMS:	*Nova*	*Northern Exposure*
TRAINS, SHIPS:	*Texas Eagle*	*Santa Maria*
AIRCRAFT, SPACECRAFT:	*Memphis Belle*	*Discovery*

Use underlining (italics) for words, letters, and figures referred to as such and for foreign words not yet a part of English vocabulary.

When Myra's *t*'s aren't crossed, they look like *l*'s.

Merci means "thank you" in French.

Exercise: Proofreading Underline all the words and word groups that should be italicized in the following sentences.

> EXAMPLE: 1. We gave Mom a subscription to <u>Working Woman</u> magazine.

1. Shari asked if she could borrow my copy of Sports Illustrated.

2. Mrs. Hopkins said that if she had to describe me in one word, the word would be loquacious.

3. I've always wanted to read Tennyson's epic Idylls of the King.

4. My favorite painting is Georgia O'Keeffe's Black Iris; my favorite sculpture is Constantin Brancusi's Bird in Space.

5. We sang songs from Miss Saigon, a Broadway musical.

6. When voting, be sure your X's fill the entire box.

7. The Sea Witch was one of the fastest clipper ships.

8. Much Ado About Nothing is a fine film based on a Shakespeare play.

9. In Search of Dracula is a book about the famous Count Dracula.

10. Do you know what the French word maison means?

Chapter 13: Punctuation

Direct and Indirect Quotations

Use **quotation marks** to enclose a **direct quotation**—a person's exact words. Do not use quotation marks for **indirect quotations,** which are not the speaker's exact words.

> DIRECT QUOTATION: "The meeting was a success," said Mr. Kulas.

> INDIRECT QUOTATION: Mr. Kulas said that the meeting was a success.

An interrupting expression is not part of a quotation; it should not be inside quotation marks.

> "The meeting," Mr. Kulas said, "was a success."

When two or more sentences by the same speaker are quoted together, use only one set of quotation marks.

> Mr. Kulas said, "The meeting was a success. We accomplished all our objectives."

Exercise: Revising In the exercise below, change direct quotations to indirect quotations, and change indirect quotations to direct quotations. Use the lines provided.

1. "I think we will all enjoy seeing the castles of England," Mom said.

   _____

2. Our tour book says that Colchester Castle, built in 1080, is a good place to start.

   _____

3. My little brother Jason asked whether the castles were haunted.

   _____

4. "No," said Mom, "but we'll stay together so that you won't be afraid."

   _____

5. In England, Jason told Mom that he wanted to swim in a moat.

   _____

6. "Warwick Castle," said our guide, "is one of England's most beautiful castles."

   _____

7. "One of the towers," he went on to say, "was built in 1066."

   _____

8. "Is it still the home of the Earls of Warwick?" I asked.

   _____

9. The guide said that the castle contains many beautiful works of art.

   _____

10. "I like the collection of suits of armor best," said Jason.

   _____

Chapter 13: Punctuation

Punctuating Quotations A

A direct quotation begins with a capital letter.

Veronica remarked, "These elevators are very slow."

When a quoted sentence is divided into two parts by an interrupting expression, the second part begins with a small letter.

"I reported it," said Chuck, "but nothing has been done."

If the second part of a quotation is a new sentence, a period (not a comma) follows the interrupting expression, and the second part begins with a capital letter.

"The building has a manager," said Luis. "Why don't we call her?"

A direct quotation is set off from the rest of the sentence by a comma, a question mark, or an exclamation point.

"That's a fine idea," Dora agreed.   "Let us out!" we yelled.

Exercise A: Proofreading   Correctly punctuate and capitalize the following sentences.

EXAMPLE: 1. Pam said, "my sister and I remember playing with Modeling clay."

1. As a child, did you play with modeling clay asked our teacher.

2. yes, I did, replied Sanjay I made funny animals.

3. I used it for play food said Josephine, When I fed my dolls.

4. Mother would say, don't put it in your mouth.

5. I put it in my mouth once said Sanjay, it tasted terrible.

Exercise B: Proofreading   Rewrite the following passage on the lines provided, adding correct punctuation and capitalization.

EXAMPLE: [1] Are you going to the fiesta" Diego asked.

"Are you going to the fiesta?" Diego asked.

[1] I hope said Diego that it doesn't rain during the fiesta. [2] He continued to talk. [3] "in fact he said if it rains, the fiesta may be canceled.
[4] I may not be able to attend the fiesta said Annette if I have to baby-sit.
[5] Well, Diego said we'll just have to see what happens.

_____

_____

_____

_____

_____

Chapter 13: Punctuation

 **WORKSHEET 4** *Punctuating Quotations B*

When used with quotation marks, other marks of punctuation are placed according to the following rules:

(1) Commas and periods are always placed inside closing quotation marks.

"By the way," I said to Marta, "I'm interested in your holidays." ·

(2) Semicolons and colons are always placed outside the closing quotation marks.

She told me, "Breaking a piñata at parties is a Mexican tradition"; then she told me how piñatas are filled.

(3) Question marks and exclamation points are placed inside the closing quotation marks if the quotation is a question or an exclamation; otherwise, they are placed outside.

"Would you like to come to our party?" Hector asked.

How happy I was when Hector said, "Here is an invitation to our party"!

Exercise: Proofreading   Insert necessary quotation marks in the following sentences.

EXAMPLE: 1. ˇ"Birthday parties are such fun! ˇexclaimed Olga.

1. Olga asked, What's usually inside a piñata?

2. In addition to candy, replied Nina, there are little toys.

3. Toys! Kyoko exclaimed. They are such fun.

4. In Japan, she said, the third, fifth, and seventh birthdays are the most important.

5. Was that third, fifth, and seventh? Nina asked.

6. Yes, Kyoko replied, the children wear their best kimonos on those birthdays.

7. What do Russian children do on birthdays? asked Phil.

8. After Natasha told us, Somebody bakes a birthday pie, I yelled, Great!

9. Should I tell you what Hindus do at Holi, their spring festival? asked Helga.

10. She said, They throw colored water at each other; we all thought that sounded like fun.

Name _____ Date _____ Class _____

Quotations with Dialogue and Quoted Passages

When you write dialogue (a conversation), begin a new paragraph every time the speaker changes.

"When you went to Niagara Falls last summer," Lynn asked, "did you view the falls from both the American and Canadian sides?"

"We went to both sides, but the view was much better on the Canadian side," Anthony said.

When a quoted passage consists of more than one paragraph, put quotation marks at the beginning of each paragraph and at the end of the entire passage. Do not put quotation marks after any paragraph but the last.

"Niagara Falls must be seen to be believed," read the brochure. "You simply cannot imagine the quantity and power of the falling water.

"People sometimes marvel at the falls for hours. Come marvel with them!"

Use single quotation marks to enclose a quotation within a quotation.

Art said, "Ellie wrote, 'Our door is always open to you.'"

Exercise   On the lines provided, use the following information to write a five-paragraph conversation between two people. Follow the rules for indenting paragraphs and using quotations in dialogue. Include at least one quoted passage of two paragraphs and at least one quotation within a quotation.

Bill Cosby is a humorist, actor, and author. He was born in Philadelphia on July 12, 1937. His books include *Fatherhood* (1986) and *Love and Marriage* (1989). Both were bestsellers. He is known as the star of the television series *The Cosby Show*. He also starred with Robert Culp in the television series *I Spy* in the 1960s. For that series, Cosby won three Emmy awards. His Saturday morning cartoon series, *Fat Albert and the Cosby Kids*, premiered in 1972. He began as a stand-up comic in the early 1960s.

EXAMPLE: *"Of course, you have seen Bill Cosby on television for years," Marcie said.*

"Yes, but I never knew he was also an author," William said.

_____

_____

_____

_____

_____

_____

_____

_____

_____

MECHANICS

Chapter 13: Punctuation

Other Uses of Quotation Marks

Use quotation marks to enclose titles of articles, short stories, essays, poems, songs, individual episodes of TV shows, chapter titles, and other parts of books and periodicals.

ARTICLE:	"How Wall Street Works"
SHORT STORY:	"The Seeing Stick"
ESSAY:	"On Honesty"
POEM:	"Opposites"
SONG:	"When You Were Sweet Sixteen"
TV EPISODE:	"A Trip on the Trans-Siberian Railroad"
CHAPTER:	"Learning About Compositions"

Use quotation marks to enclose slang words, technical terms, and other special uses of words.

When my dad likes something, he says it's "far out."

Exercise: Proofreading   Insert the necessary quotation marks in the following sentences.

EXAMPLE: 1. The article ⌣How to Win at Soccer⌣ was given to players on the team.

1. W. W. Jacobs' short story The Monkey's Paw is a terrifying tale.

2. Here Comes the Sun is a song recorded by the Beatles.

3. I just finished the chapter Improving Your Vocabulary.

4. Have you read Judith Viorst's poem If I Were in Charge of the World?

5. My brother always describes anything he likes as rad.

6. Next week's episode of the TV show *All Creatures Great and Small* is Food for Thought.

7. As we drove through the mountains, there was a lot of interference, or static, on the car radio.

8. Your assignment is to write an essay titled Why Voting Is Important.

9. Did you read the article How to Overcome Prejudice?

10. Please find a copy of Alice Walker's short story Everyday Use.

Chapter 13: Punctuation

 **WORKSHEET 7** *Review*

Exercise A: Proofreading   Add underlining (italics) and quotation marks where needed in the following sentences.

EXAMPLE: 1. Tyrel asked, "Didn't Shirley Temple star in <u>Heidi</u>, a movie based on the book?"

1. The Bay Area Youth Theater is presenting Lorraine Hansberry's A Raisin in the Sun, which I consider a totally gnarly play.

2. Tyrone announced that he is going to sing Some Enchanted Evening from the musical South Pacific.

3. Here are tickets to the opera Carmen, said Karen, and one is for you; I accepted immediately.

4. The Spanish word for goodbye is adiós; the Swahili word is kwa heri.

5. My favorite story by Sir Arthur Conan Doyle is The Adventure of the Dying Detective, which is included in the anthology The Complete Sherlock Holmes.

6. Ms. Loudon said, I like your report on Ernest Hemingway. Remember, however, that Ernest is spelled without an a.

7. In her review of The King and I, the drama critic for the Los Angeles Times commented, This production is an excellent revival of a play that never seems to wear thin.

8. In my paper, which I titled The Hispanic Soldier in Vietnam, I cited several passages from Luis Valdez's play The Buck Private.

9. Ms. Howard asked, In Julius Caesar, who said, This was the noblest Roman of them all? Which Roman was being described?

10. Have you read Hannah Armstrong, one of the poems in the Spoon River Anthology by Edgar Lee Masters?

Exercise B: Proofreading   The following dialogue contains errors in punctuation and capitalization. Insert the correct punctuation and capitalization where necessary.

EXAMPLE: [1] As she watched me pack, my mother noted, "It's getting late."

[1] did you take everything on the list Kim asked.

[2] Yes, I think so I said, looking at the list again. [3] It seems like an awful lot of stuff for a week's trip.

[4] That may be Kim agreed but you'll find that you need everything.

[5] especially the insect repellent Mom chimed in, the bugs can be fierce at night.

[6] I'm not sure I'm prepared for this I said doubtfully.

[7] A whole week in the woods Kim commented eating your own cooking and
sleeping in a tent. [8] I don't know if you'll make it.

[9] Nonsense Mom cried, handing me my knapsack. You'll have a great time.

[10] Just be sure Kim added To watch out for rattlesnakes.

Exercise C: Proofreading   On the lines provided, rewrite the following conversation.
Add punctuation, indentions, underlining (italics), and quotation marks where necessary.

EXAMPLE: [1] Are all of these books by or about Benjamin Franklin?
asked Bonnie Lou.

"Are all of these books by or about Benjamin Franklin?"
asked Bonnie Lou.

[1] Yes, Bonnie Lou, Mr. Reyes answered. [2] There's even one, Ben and Me by Robert
Lawson, that's a biography written from the point of view of Amos, Franklin's pet mouse.
[3] This one, The Many Lives of Benjamin Franklin by Mary Pope Osborne, sounds really
interesting, said Jasmine.
[4] It is, Mr. Reyes said. [5] And that's exactly what we're going to talk about today—the
many sides of this early American genius. [6] Who can tell me about one of them?
[7] He invented electricity, didn't he? asked Liang.
[8] Well, he didn't exactly invent electricity, corrected Mr. Reyes, but his experiment proved
that lightning is a form of electricity.
[9] Franklin also helped draft some of our important historical documents, and he was a
diplomat, a printer, and a publisher. [10] Franklin's writings, his Autobiography and Poor
Richard's Almanack, have given us many well-known sayings.

_____

_____

_____

_____

_____

_____

_____

_____

_____

_____

_____

_____

_____

_____

_____

Chapter 14: Punctuation

Apostrophes and the Possessive Case of Nouns

The **possessive case** of a noun or pronoun shows ownership or relationship.

Derek's backpack   **our** bicycles   **my** shirt   **her** pen

To form the possessive case of a singular noun, add an apostrophe and an *s*.

hiker's boots   **baby's** bottle   **student's** lunch   **dog's** toy

NOTE: For a proper name ending in *s*, add only an apostrophe if the name has two or more syllables or if the addition of *'s* would make the name awkward to pronounce. For a singular common noun ending in *s*, add both an apostrophe and an *s* if the added *s* is pronounced as a separate syllable.

Kansas' capital   **Nicholas'** helmet   the **boss's** orders

To form the possessive case of a plural noun ending in *s*, add only the apostrophe.

wheels' rims   two **raccoons'** tracks   **teachers'** union

Some plural nouns are irregular and do not end in *s*. To form the possessive of such nouns, add an apostrophe and –*s*.

the **geese's** pond   **women's** department   **moose's** habitat

Exercise A   On the lines provided, form the possessive case of each of the following words. After each possessive word, give an appropriate noun.

EXAMPLE: 1. Theresa *Theresa's pencil*

1. men _____
2. Mr. Chan _____
3. year _____
4. elves _____
5. class _____

6. Terry _____
7. princesses _____
8. cattle _____
9. uncle _____
10. Miss Williams _____

Exercise B   On the lines provided, revise the following phrases by using the possessive case.

EXAMPLE: 1. parties for seniors *the seniors' parties*

1. prizes for winners _____
2. manners for teenagers _____
3. yokes of oxen _____
4. duties of nurses _____
5. names of players _____

Name _____ Date _____ Class _____

Possessive Personal and Indefinite Pronouns

Possessive personal pronouns do not require an apostrophe.

Possessive Personal Pronouns

my, mine	our, ours
your, yours	their, theirs
his, her, hers, its	

The red van is **ours.**   Which bicycle is **yours**?   **Hers** is a mountain bike.

NOTE: The possessive form of *who* is *whose,* not *who's.* Similarly, do not write *it's* for *its,* or *they're* for *their.*

Whose footballs are these?   **Who's** [*Who is*] on your team this year?

Indefinite pronouns in the possessive case require an apostrophe and an *s.*

somebody's helmet   **another's** idea   **no one's** fault

Exercise A   In each of the following sentences, underline the correct form of the pronoun in parentheses.

EXAMPLE: 1. Ralph Ellison, (who's, <u>whose</u>) book *Invisible Man* won a National Book Award, studied music at Tuskegee Institute.

1. That copy of Ellison's book of essays *Shadow and Act* is (ours, ours').

2. Doesn't your copy of *Invisible Man* have a picture of Ellison on (it's, its) back cover?

3. Uncle Levy and Aunt Sasha showed me (their, they're) collection of books by famous African American authors such as Ellison.

4. (Hers, Hers') is the report about Richard Wright's influence on Ellison.

5. (Whose, Who's) picture of Ellison is this?

Exercise B: Proofreading   Most of the following sentences contain errors in the use of the possessive form. Circle the incorrect form, and write the correct form on the line provided. If a sentence is correct, write *C.*

EXAMPLE: 1. It wasn't (anyones') fault that we missed the bus yesterday. *anyone's*

1. The reward is your's.   _____

2. Someones' choir robe was left on the bus.   _____

3. The loss was nobody's fault.   _____

4. Their's is the best frozen yogurt in town.   _____

5. Everybodys' trees must be irrigated.   _____

Chapter 14: Punctuation

WORKSHEET 3   *Compounds*

MECHANICS

In compound words, names of organizations and businesses, and word groups showing joint possession, only the last word is possessive in form.

COMPOUND WORDS: ceiling **fan's** breeze   sister-in-**law's** job

ORGANIZATION: Diabetes **Association's** letter

BUSINESS: Sleepytime **Inn's** swimming pool

ACRONYM: **UNICEF's** headquarters

JOINT POSSESSION: Cindy and **Mark's** report

When one of two words showing joint possession is a pronoun, both words should be possessive in form.

Benjy's and **my** report [a report we shared]

To avoid awkward possessive forms, use a phrase beginning with *of* or *for*.

AWKWARD: the president of our club's parents

BETTER: the parents of the president of our club

When two or more persons possess something individually, each of their names is possessive in form.

Mr. Lee's and **Mr. Ray's** classes [the classes of two different people]

Exercise: Revising   On the lines provided, revise the following phrases by using the possessive case.

EXAMPLE: 1. the book owned by Natalie and Stan

Natalie and Stan's book

1. the ticket of Sylvia and the ticket of Eric _____

2. a report from the CIA _____

3. the duet of Gwen and Carl _____

4. a uniform belonging to the master sergeant _____

5. the history of the Grand Canyon _____

6. the job shared by Rachel and me _____

7. an agent for the Acme Life Insurance Company _____

8. one tractor belonging to my uncle and one to us _____

9. the award given by the sales department _____

10. the house of Dan's mother-in-law and the house of his cousin _____

Chapter 14: Punctuation

 **WORKSHEET 4** *Apostrophes in Contractions*

A **contraction** is a shortened form of a word, a figure, or a group of words.

Use an apostrophe to show where letters, words, or numerals have been omitted in a contraction.

> they are—**they're**   of the clock—**o'clock**
> are not—**aren't**   1994—**'94**

Ordinarily, the word *not* is shortened to *n't* and added to a verb without any change in the spelling of the verb. Exceptions: will not—*won't*; cannot—*can't*

Do not confuse contractions with the possessive pronouns *whose, its, your, theirs,* and *their.*

> **Who's** [*Who is*] at the door?   **Whose** dog is this?

Exercise A On the lines provided, identify the contractions in the following sentences, and add the apostrophes.

> EXAMPLE: 1. "The stores about to close," said the clerk. *store's*

1. She gets up at 6 oclock.   _____

2. Im very glad to meet you.   _____

3. Dont you play chess?   _____

4. Whos going to the store?   _____

5. Jesse was born in 78.   _____

Exercise B Underline the correct word in each set of parentheses in the following paragraph.

> EXAMPLE: [1] (Your, <u>You're</u>) likely to see fiestas in Mexican American
> communities across the United States on September 16.

[1] (It's, Its) a day of celebration that includes parades, speeches, music, and colorful folk dances. Of course, [2] (theirs, there's) plenty of food, including stacks of tortillas and bowls of beans and soup. [3] (Who's, Whose) to say how late the merrymaking will last on this holiday? [4] (It's, Its) a joyful day of fun, but everyone remembers [5] (it's, its) importance, too. Mexican Americans know that [6] (they're, their) celebrating the beginning of Mexico's rebellion to gain independence from Spain. On this date in 1810, Father Miguel Hidalgo y Costilla gathered his forces for the rebellion and uttered [7] (its, it's) first battle cry. Father Hidalgo, [8] (who's, whose) parish was in west central Mexico, led an army across the country. If [9] (your, you're) in Mexico City on the eve of September 16, you can hear the president of Mexico ring what is believed to be the bell that Hidalgo rang to summon his people for [10] (they're, their) historic march.

Chapter 14: Punctuation

 **WORSHEET 5** *Apostrophes in Plurals*

To prevent confusion, use an apostrophe and an *s* to form the plurals of all lowercase letters, some capital letters, and some words that are referred to as words.

I must remember to dot my *i*'**s** and *j*'**s**.

Add *and*'**s**, *but*'**s**, and *so*'**s** to the compound sentences.

NOTE: You may add only an *s* to form the plurals of such items (except lowercase letters) if the plural forms won't be misread.

How many **TVs** does your family have?

Exercise A   On the lines provided, write the plural forms of the underlined items.

EXAMPLE: *ABC's*   1. Has your little brother learned his <u>ABC</u>?

_____ 1. Your *q* look like *g*.

_____ 2. Why do you put <u>U</u> at the end?

_____ 3. She made all <u>A</u> and <u>B</u>.

_____ 4. The paper has unclear pronoun references for *his*.

_____ 5. You haven't dotted your *i*.

_____ 6. The <u>*I*</u> in that paper are hard to read.

_____ 7. The teacher gave five <u>D</u> on the test.

_____ 8. Her <u>*I*</u> look like *one*.

_____ 9. Tamara has a hard time pronouncing *r*.

_____10. Your first sentence contains four *so*.

Exercise B: Proofreading   On the line provided, rewrite each of the following sentences and add apostrophes as needed.

EXAMPLE: 1. My sister can write *x*s now.

<u>*My sister can write x's now.*</u>

1. Try not to overuse *and*s and *but*s in your writing.

_____

2. Your undotted *i*s look like *e*s.

_____

3. There are no *if*s about it; you're not wearing that to school!

_____

4. Do you mix up *I*s and *L*s?

_____

Chapter 14: Punctuation

WORKSHEET 6 — *Hyphens in Divided Words*

Use a hyphen to divide a word at the end of a line.

Isaac Bashevis Singer wrote novels and short stories in the Yiddish language.

When dividing a word at the end of a line, keep in mind these rules:

(1) Do not divide one-syllable words.

(2) Divide a word only between syllables.

(3) Usually divide words with double consonants between those two consonants.

(4) Usually divide a word with a prefix or a suffix between the prefix and the base
word (or root) or between the root and the suffix.

(5) Divide an already hyphenated word only at a hyphen.

(6) Do not divide a word so that one letter stands alone.

Exercise A   Write each of the following words, and use a hyphen to indicate where the
word may be divided at the end of a line. (If necessary, check a dictionary.) If a word
should not be divided, write *one-syllable word*.

EXAMPLES: 1. thoroughly *thor-ough-ly*
            2. cooked *one-syllable word*

1. original   _____   4. corporation   _____

2. unprecedented   _____   5. son-in-law   _____

3. breathe   _____

Exercise B: Proofreading   The following paragraph contains five divided words. On
the line provided, write *C* if a word is hyphenated correctly. If it is not, write the word
correctly hyphenated. If the word should not be hyphenated, write *no hyphen*. You may
consult a dictionary.

EXAMPLE: Do you enjoy reading about rulers [1] through-
          out history?

          1. ___*C*___

Mohammed Askia was once king of the Songhai Empire, in [1] western Africa. The major city, Timbuktu, was a rich and prominent [2] center of trade. Mohammed Askia made it also a leading center [3] o-
f learning. Never a self-important, all-powerful ruler, [4] Mohammed Askia funded a large university and paid high salaries to [5] a-
ttract the finest teachers and doctors.

1. _____   4. _____

2. _____   5. _____

3. _____

Chapter 14: Punctuation

WORKSHEET 7
Hyphens and Compound Words

Use a hyphen with some compound words. Consult a dictionary.

> Have you ever been to a **house-raising**?

Use a hyphen with compound numbers from *twenty-one* to *ninety-nine* and with fractions used as adjectives, as in "*one-fourth* cup of flour."

Use a hyphen with the prefixes *ex–*, *self–*, and *all–*; with the suffix *–elect*; and with all prefixes before proper nouns or proper adjectives.

> **Governor-elect** Yue, a **self-made** man, is an **ex-Canadian** tennis player.

Use a hyphen in a compound adjective when the compound adjective precedes the noun it modifies.

> a **well-directed** movie [a movie that is well directed]

Exercise A: Proofreading   Insert hyphens in the words that should be hyphenated in the following sentences.

> EXAMPLE: 1.   Until 1959, the United States flag had forty-eight stars.

1. The ex ambassador's lecture focused on the post Andean era.

2. Did the band really have seventy six trombones?

3. The police issued an all points bulletin for the suspect.

4. The brown haired girl smiled at me.

5. The biscuit recipe calls for one half cup of honey.

Exercise B: Proofreading   The following paragraph contains five words that need hyphens. Proofread the paragraph to find the words, and write them correctly on the lines provided.

> EXAMPLE: Tasty snacks are an all important part of any successful meeting.
>
>   1. *all-important*

   As president elect of the Spanish club, I hosted last month's meeting. Thirty three members came to my house for the meeting. I served a well received popcorn dish. Here is my hit recipe for the Mexican popcorn topping: Mix together one fourth cup of chili powder, one half teaspoon of salt, and one teaspoon each of garlic powder, cilantro, and cumin. (Those last two are herbs.) Sprinkle the mixture over plain popcorn.

1. _____

2. _____

3. _____

4. _____

5. _____

WORKSHEET 8 | *Using Dashes*

Many words and phrases are used *parenthetically;* that is, they break into the main thought of a sentence. Parenthetical words and expressions are usually set off by commas or by parentheses. Sometimes, such parenthetical words and phrases demand stronger emphasis.

Use a *dash* to indicate an abrupt break in thought or speech.

Mr. Gonzales—in my opinion, a talented artist—painted this mural.

Use a dash to indicate an unfinished statement or question.

"I'm sure that you—"she blurted out, but then fell silent.

Use a dash to mean *namely, that is, in other words,* and similar expressions that introduce explanations.

Dad gave his permission—I can go. [in other words]

Exercise A: Proofreading   Each of the following sentences needs at least one dash inserted. Place a caret (^) where each dash should appear.

EXAMPLE: 1.   The election ᵡI hope I win! ᵡwill be on Tuesday.

1. "You're you're not serious!" Marita exclaimed.

2. "Tomorrow I think I'll" Josh mumbled before falling asleep.

3. "Yes, I do have a pet in mind that calico cat," Juan said.

4. My great-uncle he's eighty-nine retired at sixty-two and moved to Israel.

5. Will there be time I hope so! to stop for lunch on our way to the meeting?

Exercise B: Proofreading   On the line provided, rewrite each sentence below correctly by adding dashes where necessary. If a sentence is correct, write *C.*

EXAMPLE: 1.   My favorite teacher what a shock! is moving.

My favorite teacher—what a shock!—is moving.

1. The problem and it's one I need your help on is how to motivate the team.

_____

2. Kameko just was not prepared for the test she didn't do well at all.

_____

3. "Why why are you so upset?" Winsie asked gently.

_____

4. "Ride! Come on, go as fast as" the rider yelled just before falling off the horse.

_____

5. This dress is really beautiful, and I think it would be perfect for the prom.

_____

Chapter 14: Punctuation

Using Parentheses

Use *parentheses* to enclose material that is not considered of major importance in a sentence. The material may range from a single word to a short sentence.

Mount Pelee (4,583 feet high) is a volcano on Martinique.

Address the envelope and mail it. (Don't forget the stamp!)

Last year we spent one month (June) at my aunt's house.

As in the examples above, punctuation marks are used within parentheses when the punctuation belongs with the parenthetical matter. However, a punctuation mark is not placed within parentheses if the mark belongs to the sentence as a whole.

Use parentheses if the parenthetical material may be omitted without changing the basic meaning and construction of the sentence. To show that elements are closely related to the rest of the sentence, use commas. To indicate an abrupt change in thought, use dashes. Don't overuse parenthetical material.

Exercise A: Proofreading   Insert parentheses where necessary in each of the following sentences.

EXAMPLE: 1. I reread all the *Oz* books that I own (a considerable number).

1. The nominee worked for the ex-governor for ten years 1970–1980.

2. Dean's Diner only three blocks from the office is a convenient place for lunch.

3. Aunt Luisa actually she is my great-aunt has just opened a dinner theater.

4. Booker T. Washington founded Tuskegee Institute. See Chapter 5.

5. The city of Elmwood population 64,000 is a leading manufacturing center.

Exercise B: Revising   The following paragraph contains too many parenthetical expressions. On the lines provided, rewrite the paragraph to make it clearer.

Chop the mushrooms. (Wash them first.) Rinse the pea pods. (Don't forget to snap off the tops.) Dissolve two teaspoons of cornstarch in one-half cup (hot) of water (or chicken broth). Then heat the oil (corn oil or peanut oil) in a large pan. (Use a wok if you have one.) Stir-fry the vegetables in the oil for three minutes. Add the cornstarch mixture. (Swirl to thicken slightly.) Serve (and enjoy!).

_____

_____

_____

_____

_____

_____

_____

MECHANICS

Chapter 14: Punctuation

 **WORKSHEET 10** **_Review_**

Exercise A: Proofreading   Identify and circle the ten incorrect possessive forms in the following paragraph. Then, on the line provided, write each form correctly.

> EXAMPLE: Several women welcomed us to the Shaker village of Pleasant
> Hill, Kentucky, during our history (class') field trip last spring.
> 1.   _class's_

The style of the womens dresses was quite old. The villages history goes back to 1806. That year the religious group known as the Shakers founded they're own community. We learned that the Shaker's lively way of dancing gave the group it's name. Everyones life in the Shaker village was orderly, simple, and productive. This basic harmony was true even of the childrens' routines. During the days tour of the village, we saw several people practicing Shaker crafts. One guide of our's told us that the Shakers invented the common clothespin and the flat broom and designed useful furniture and boxes. I enjoyed visiting the gardens and the Centre Family House and imagining how a Shakers' life must have been.

1. _____   6. _____

2. _____   7. _____

3. _____   8. _____

4. _____   9. _____

5. _____   10. _____

Exercise B: Proofreading   Circle the ten words in the following paragraph that require apostrophes. Then, on the line provided, write each word correctly.

> EXAMPLE: Have you ever heard of the (U.S. Patent Offices) Hall of Fame
> for inventors?
> 1.   _U.S. Patent Office's_

The Hall of Fame's members, who are both American and foreign, include many people that you've probably heard of as well as some you havent. Vladimir Kosma Zworykin's picture tube helped lead to televisions development. Willis Haviland Carrier changed peoples lives all over the world with his work on air conditioning and refrigerators. Luther Burbanks accomplishment was the development of more than eight hundred new plant varieties. Heart patients _hurrays_ go to the inventor of pacemakers, Wilson Greatbatch. You'll probably recognize such famous inventors as the Ford Motor

Companys founder, Henry Ford. Of course, Thomas Edisons and Alexander Graham Bells achievements assured their enduring fame. Its not surprising that Orville and Wilbur Wrights invention of the airplane landed them in such good company, too.

1. _____   6. _____

2. _____   7. _____

3. _____   8. _____

4. _____   9. _____

5. _____   10. _____

Exercise C: Proofreading   On the lines provided, rewrite each of the following sentences, and insert hyphens, dashes, and parentheses where they are needed. Don't add commas.

EXAMPLE: 1. Comanche chief Quanah Parker 1845–1911 was a man of strong character.

Comanche chief Quanah Parker (1845–1911) was a man of strong character.

1. Parker became famous as two types of chiefs a great war chief and a great peace chief.

   _____

2. He was the son of a Comanche tribal leader and a young woman a white settler who was captured during a raid on a Texas home stead.

   _____

   _____

3. In the 1870s, Quanah Parker led a band of Comanche war riors in the Texas Panhandle.

   _____

   _____

4. Parker's band the Kwahadis surrendered in 1875, but they were the last Indians to do so on the southern plains.

   _____

5. After surrendering, Parker became a prosperous rancher quite a change of lifestyle and even owned railroad stock.

   _____

6. In fact, he embodied the idea of the self made man.

   _____

MECHANICS

7. This thirty five page article states that Parker encouraged his children to learn the ways of the settlers.

_____

8. Parker guided the Comanches his title was principal chief during difficult times after the war ended.

_____

9. In later years, he went to Washington, D.C., and this fact may surprise you became a friend of President Theodore Roosevelt.

_____

10. *Quanah* a Comanche word meaning "sweet-smelling" became the name of a Texas city named after this well known chief.

_____

Exercise D: Proofreading   Proofread the following sentences, and insert hyphens, dashes, and parentheses where they are needed. Don't add commas.

> EXAMPLE: 1. Nancy Wing she is the ex-champion will award the golf trophies.

1. Yori will be twenty one on the twenty first of Sep tember this year.

2. "That sounds like" gasped Jeff as he dashed for the window.

3. A former all state quarterback, our coach insists that there is no such thing as a self made star.

4. A dog I think it was a poodle jumped into the lake.

5. The Historical Society the local members, that is will conduct a two hour tour of the harbor.

6. My sister Patricia she is in college now wants to be a marine biologist.

7. The recipe for winter herb bread calls for one and one half cups of whole wheat flour.

8. At the auction someone bid one thousand dollars for a pre Revolutionary desk.

9. The great Incan civilization *circa* A.D. 1000 to 1500 flourished until the arrival of Francisco Pizarro 1531.

10. Next month of course, I'll write you before then we're going on an overnight hike.

Name _____ Date _____ Class _____

 **Improving Your Spelling**

The following techniques can help you spell words correctly.

Pronounce a word, study it, and write it. Pronounce words carefully. Mispronunciation can cause misspelling. For example, the word *liable* is pronounced *li-a-ble,* not *li-ble.* As you study the word, notice especially any parts that might be hard to remember. Write the word from memory, and then check your spelling. If you missed the word, repeat these steps.

Use a dictionary. When you look up the spelling of a word, make sure that its use isn't limited by a label such as *British* or *chiefly British, obsolete,* or *archaic.*

Spell by syllables. A **syllable** is a word part that can be pronounced by itself.

    lunch [one syllable]

    region [two syllables]

    triumphant [three syllables]

Proofread for careless spelling errors. Reread your writing carefully, and correct any mistakes and unclear letters. For example, make sure your *t*'s are crossed.

Keep a spelling notebook. Divide each page into four columns.

    Column 1: Correctly spell the word you missed.

    Column 2: Write the word again, dividing it into syllables and marking the stressed syllable(s). (Use a dictionary, if necessary.)

    Column 3: Write the word once more and circle the spot(s) that give you trouble.

    Column 4: Jot down any comments that may help you remember the correct spelling.

Exercise   Look up the following words in a dictionary. On the line provided, divide each word into syllables, and place hyphens between syllables. Pronounce each syllable correctly, and learn to spell the word by syllables.

        EXAMPLE: 1. lightning *light-ning*

1. representative   _____

2. fascinate   _____

3. candidate   _____

4. temperature   _____

5. apparent   _____

6. similar   _____

7. benefit   _____

8. definition   _____

9. acquaintance   _____

10. awkward   _____

MECHANICS

Chapter 15: Spelling and Vocabulary

 **WORKSHEET 2** *Roots*

Many English words contain word parts from other languages or earlier forms of English.

The **root** is the part of the word that carries the word's core meaning. Other word parts can be added to a root to create many different words. Here are some common roots that appear in many English words.

Source	Roots	Meanings	Examples
Latin	–aud–, –audit–	hear	auditory
	–bene–	well, good	benefactor
	–duc–, –duct–	lead	product
	–magn–	large	magnificent
	–mit–, –miss–	send	mission
	–ped–	foot	pedestrian
	–port–	carry, bear	import
	–vid–, –vis–	see	visible
Greek	–anthro–	human	anthropologist
	–chron–	time	chronicle
	–cycl–	circle, wheel	tricycle
	–graph–	write, writing	biography
	–micr–	small	microphone
	–phil–	like, love	Philadelphia
	–phon–	sound	phonics

Exercise   Each of the following words contains one root. Underline each root you find. Then, on the line provided, use the meaning of the root and your own knowledge to write a definition of each word. Check your definition in a dictionary.

EXAMPLE: 1. <u>bene</u>ficial *producing benefits; advantageous; favorable*

1. magnitude _____

2. transportation _____

3. conductor _____

4. transmit _____

5. microfilm _____

6. vision _____

7. phonology _____

8. pedestal _____

9. historiographer _____

10. chronological _____

Chapter 15: Spelling and Vocabulary

WORKSHEET 3 *Prefixes*

A **prefix** is a word part that is added before a root. When a prefix is added to a root, the new word combines the meanings of the prefix and root. Here are some common prefixes that appear in many English words.

Source	Prefixes	Meanings	Examples
Old English	mis–	badly, not, wrongly	mistake
	over–	above, excessive	overdone
	un–	not, reverse of	unkind
Latin and Latin-French	bi–	two	biweekly
	co–, con–	with, together	coeducational
	de–	away, from, off, down	decrease
	non–	not	nonproductive
	pre–	before	prepare
	sub–	under, beneath	subgroup
Greek	anti–	against	antipollutant
	dia–	through, across	diagram
	hyper–	excessive, over	hypercritical
	para–	beside, beyond	paramilitary
	sym–, syn–	together, with	synthesis

Exercise Underline the prefix in each of the following words. Then use the meanings of the prefix and the root and your own knowledge to write a definition of each word. Check your definition in a dictionary.

EXAMPLE: 1. <u>hyper</u>ventilation *extremely rapid or deep breathing*

1. submarine _____

2. preview _____

3. overcharge _____

4. antisocial _____

5. coincidence _____

6. misunderstand _____

7. unimportant _____

8. nonfiction _____

9. defrost _____

10. synonym _____

Name _____ Date _____ Class _____

 **WORKSHEET 4** *Suffixes*

A **suffix** is a word part that is added after a root. Often, adding a suffix changes both a word's part of speech and its meaning.

Source	Suffixes	Meanings	Examples
	NOUN SUFFIXES		
Old English	–dom	state, condition	kingdom
	–hood	state, condition	motherhood
Latin, French, Greek	–er	doer, native of	trumpeter
	–ment	means, result	commitment
	ADJECTIVE SUFFIXES		
Old English	–ful	full of	hopeful
	–ish	like	boyish
Latin, French, Greek	–able	able, likely	manageable
	–ous	marked by, given to	poisonous
	–ant, –ent	actor, agent, showing	pleasant
	VERB SUFFIXES		
Latin, French, Greek	–ate	become, cause	hyphenate
	–fy	make, cause	rectify
	–ize	make, cause to be	Americanize

Exercise Underline the suffix in each of the following words. Then use the meanings of the suffix and the root and your own knowledge to write a definition of each word. Check your definition in a dictionary.

EXAMPLE: 1. lonel<u>iness</u> *state or condition of being lonely*

1. famous _____

2. martyrdom _____

3. neighborhood _____

4. personify _____

5. independent _____

6. mechanize _____

7. foolish _____

8. noticeable _____

9. announcement _____

10. thoughtful _____

Name _____ Date _____ Class _____

WORKSHEET 5 | ***Spelling Rules A***

MECHANICS

Write *ie* when the sound is long *e*, except after *c*.

	EXAMPLES:	**fie**ld	rece**i**ve	cei**l**ing	grief	niece
	SOME EXCEPTIONS:	**ei**ther	leisure	neither	seize	weird

Write *ei* when the sound is not long *e*.

	EXAMPLES:	for**ei**gn	heir	veil	weigh
	SOME EXCEPTIONS:	friend	mischief	view	ancient

NOTE: These rules apply only when the *i* and the *e* are in the same syllable.

Only one English word ends in *–sede: supersede*. Only three words end in *–ceed: exceed, proceed,* and *succeed*. All other words with this sound end in *–cede*.

concede   intercede   recede   secede

Exercise: Proofreading   The following paragraph contains ten spelling errors involving the use of *ie, ei, –ceed, –cede,* and *–sede*. For each sentence, write the misspelled word or words correctly on the line provided. If a sentence has no spelling error, write C.

EXAMPLE: [1] On my birthday I recieved a wonderful gift.

1. *received*

[1] My neighbor, who is a good freind of mine, went on a trip out West. [2] He sent me a Dream Catcher, used by the Sioux to sheild themselves against bad dreams. [3] Such charms once hung in each tepee, and mine hangs from the cieling near my bed. [4] According to legend, bad dreams get caught in the web and only good ones succede in reaching the sleeper. [5] I do not really believe that my Dream Catcher can interceed on my behalf, but I have not had one wierd dream since my birthday! [6] The Plains Indians moved their homes often, so their possessions could be niether bulky nor heavy. [7] Consequently, the Sioux who made the Dream Catcher had to use common, lightweight materials. [8] The twig bent into a ring is willow wood, and tiny glass beads represent nightmares siezed by the web. [9] Gracefully hanging from either side is a beautiful feather or a horsehair tassel. [10] Wonderful peices of workmanship like this ensure that the culture of the Sioux will never resede into the past.

1. _____   6. _____

2. _____   7. _____

3. _____   8. _____

4. _____   9. _____

5. _____   10. _____

Name _____ Date _____ Class _____

WORKSHEET 6 *Spelling Rules B*

When a prefix is added to a word, the spelling of the original word remains the same.

    mis + spell = **mis**spell   im + movable = **im**movable   un + able = **un**able

When the suffix *–ness* or *–ly* is added to a word, the spelling of the original word remains the same. However, *true, due,* and *whole* drop the final *e* before *–ly.*

    sad + ness = sad**ness**   solid + ly = solid**ly**   due + ly = du**ly**

Words ending in *y* usually change the *y* to *i* before *–ness* and *–ly.* However, most one-syllable adjectives ending in *y* do not change.

    silly + ly = sill**ily**   funny + ness = funn**iness**   sly + ness = sly**ness**

Drop the final silent *e* before adding a suffix that begins with a vowel.

    fire + ing = fir**ing**   tame + est = tam**est**

Keep the final silent *e* in words ending in *ce* or *ge* before a suffix beginning with *a* or *o.*

    service + able = servic**eable**   courage + ous = courag**eous**

Additionally, keep the silent *e* when adding *–ing* to the words *dye* and *singe* (*dyeing, singeing*) and when adding *–age* to the word *mile* (*mileage*).

Keep the final silent *e* before adding a suffix that begins with a consonant.

               EXAMPLES: move + ment = move**ment**   tire + some = tire**some**

        SOME EXCEPTIONS: judge + ment = judg**ment**   nine + th = nin**th**

When a word ends in *y* preceded by a consonant, change the *y* to *i* before any suffix except one beginning with *i.*

    hurry + ed = hurr**ied**   horrify + ing = horrify**ing**

When a word ends in *y* preceded by a vowel, simply add the suffix.

               EXAMPLES: play + ful = play**ful**   coy + ness = coy**ness**

        SOME EXCEPTIONS: day + ly = da**ily**   pay + ed = pa**id**

Exercise   On the lines provided, spell each of the following words with the given prefix or suffix.

               EXAMPLE: 1. loud + ness *loudness*

1. continue + ous _____

2. un + heard _____

3. gray + ness _____

4. announce + ment _____

5. codify + ing _____

6. immense + ness _____

7. dye + ing _____

8. extraordinary + ly _____

9. sub + text _____

10. trace + able _____

Name _____ Date _____ Class _____

Spelling Rules C

When a word ends in a consonant, double the final consonant before a suffix that begins with a vowel only if the word (1) has only one syllable or is accented on the last syllable, and (2) ends in a *single* consonant preceded by a *single* vowel. Otherwise, simply add the suffix.

DOUBLE FINAL CONSONANT: **spin** + **ing** = **spinning** [*Spin* has one syllable and ends in a single consonant preceded by a single vowel.]

refer + **ed** = **referred** [*Refer* has two syllables with the accent on the last one and ends in a single consonant preceded by a single vowel.]

DO NOT DOUBLE: **track** + **ing** = **tracking** [*Track* ends in two consonants.]

profit + **able** = **profitable** [*Profit* does not have the accent on the last syllable.]

NOTE: The final consonant in some words may or may not be doubled. Both spellings are equally correct.

carol + **er** = caroler *or* caroller

Exercise   On the line provided in each sentence, write the word made by adding the word parts shown in parentheses.

EXAMPLE: 1. Harlem's Apollo Theater *opened* in 1913. (open + ed)

1. The Apollo was first known as the Hurtig and Seaman Theater but was later

   _____ the Apollo Theater. (call + ed)

2. My parents remember _____ in the audience on amateur night.
   (sit + ing)

3. They recall _____ for a new singer named Aretha Franklin.
   (clap + ing)

4. People always _____ at the chance to see the great performers at
   the Apollo. (jump + ed)

5. My mom and dad _____ that they never saw Duke Ellington
   perform. (regret + ed)

Chapter 15: Spelling and Vocabulary

Plurals of Nouns A

To form the plurals of most English nouns, simply add –*s*.

game → games   book → books

To form the plurals of other nouns, follow these rules.

If the noun ends in *s, x, z, ch,* or *sh,* add –*es.* Proper nouns usually follow this rule, too.

mass → masses   wish → wishes   Kostas → the Kostases

If the noun ends in *y* preceded by a consonant, change the *y* to *i* and add –*es.* However, proper nouns do not follow this rule.

pony → ponies   country → countries   Terry → the Terrys

If the noun ends in *y* preceded by a vowel, add –*s.*

boy → boys   trolley → trolleys

For some nouns ending in *f* or *fe,* add –*s.* For other such nouns, change the *f* or *fe* to *v* and add –*es.*

tariff → tariffs   shelf → shelves

If the noun ends in *o* preceded by a vowel, add –*s.*

rodeo → rodeos   radio → radios

If the noun ends in *o* preceded by a consonant, add –*es.* However, some such common nouns, especially musical terms, and some proper nouns form the plural by adding only –*s.*

hero → heroes   alto → altos

NOTE: A number of nouns that end in *o* preceded by a consonant have two plural forms.

hobo → hobos *or* hoboes

Exercise   On the lines provided, spell the plural form of each of the following nouns.

EXAMPLE: 1. color *colors*

1. toy   _____

2. minute   _____

3. ally   _____

4. torpedo   _____

5. chef   _____

6. ax   _____

7. watch   _____

8. stereo   _____

9. cafeteria   _____

10. thief   _____

Chapter 15: Spelling and Vocabulary

 **WORKSHEET 9** *Plurals of Nouns B*

The plurals of some nouns are formed in irregular ways.

    mouse → **mice**   woman → wom**en**

Some nouns have the same form in both the singular and the plural.

    moose   sheep   species   spacecraft

If a compound noun is written as one word, form the plural by adding –*s* or –*es* to the end of the compound.

    bedspread → bedspread**s**   sandbox → sandbox**es**

If a compound noun is hyphenated or written as two words, make the main noun plural. The **main noun** is the noun that is modified.

    mother-in-law → mother**s**-in-law   attorney general → attorney**s** general

NOTE: A few compound nouns form the plural in irregular ways.

    ten-year-old → ten-year-old**s**   shake-up → shake-up**s**

Some nouns borrowed from Latin and Greek form the plural as they do in the original language.

    datum → dat**a**   parenthesis → parenthe**ses**

NOTE: A few Latin and Greek loanwords have two plural forms.

    criterion → criteri**a** *or* criterion**s**

To form the plurals of numerals, most capital letters, symbols, and words used as words, add either –*s* or an apostrophe and –*s*.

    1900**'s** (or 1900**s**)   *R***'s** (or *R***s**)   ?**s** (or ?**'s**)   *if***s** (or *if***'s**)

To prevent confusion, always use an apostrophe and an –*s* to form the plurals of lowercase letters, certain capital letters, and some words used as words.

    *e***'s**   *A***'s**   *hi***'s**

Exercise On the lines provided, spell the plural form of each of the following nouns. [Note: Italics indicate words used as words or letters used as letters.]

          EXAMPLE: 1. A *A's*

1. *9* _____

2. goose _____

3. *to* _____

4. man-of-war _____

5. fulcrum _____

6. ox _____

7. Vietnamese _____

8. armful _____

9. three-year-old _____

10. *a* _____

Chapter 15: Spelling and Vocabulary

 **WORKSHEET 10** *Using Context Clues A*

The **context** of a word includes the words that surround the word and the circumstances in which the word is used. While reading, you can often use **context clues** to help you to define an unfamiliar word. Here are three types of context clues.

1. **Definitions and restatements:** words that define the term or restate it in other words

   The king was an **omnipotent** ruler, having full power and authority over his subjects. [Clues indicate that *omnipotent* means "having full power and authority."]

2. **Examples:** words that reveal the meaning of an unfamiliar word

   Some of the **denizens** of the forest include deer, bears, rabbits, and many species of birds. [Examples suggest that *denizens* means "inhabitants" or "residents."]

3. **Synonyms:** words or phrases that are similar in meaning to an unfamiliar word

   This medicine may be **beneficial** for your cold, and a nap might be helpful, too. [Clue suggests that *beneficial* means "helpful."]

Exercise   Each of the following sentences contains an italicized word. At the bottom of the page is a list of definitions. Use context clues to determine which definition matches each italicized word. On the line before each sentence, write the letter of the correct definition.

_____ 1. The hotel's major *clientele* were tourists and traveling business people.

_____ 2. Marla's plan seemed *imprudent,* and even downright foolish, to me.

_____ 3. The store had a wide variety of *millinery,* including straw bonnets and sombreros.

_____ 4. The candidate *vacillated* on the issues, changing her mind depending on the views of the audience.

_____ 5. One of my personal *foibles,* or flaws, is my tendency to be shy.

_____ 6. Tourist *accommodations* here include motels, hotels, and campgrounds.

_____ 7. Carlo seems very *atrabilious,* or glum, over the contest results.

_____ 8. Some of the world's most *arid* areas are the Sahara Desert and the Gobi Desert.

_____ 9. The blaring radio, ringing phone, and barking dog created sheer *cacophony.*

_____10. They *refurbished* the old house by rebuilding the walls and replacing the roof.

a. hats	b. lodgings	c. harsh noise	d. faults	e. unwise
f. fixed up	g. customers	h. melancholy	i. wavered	j. dry

Chapter 15: Spelling and Vocabulary

Using Context Clues B

The **context** of a word includes the words that surround the word and the circumstances in which the word is used. While reading, you can often use **context clues** to help you to define an unfamiliar word. Here are three types of context clues.

1. **Comparisons:** clues that indicate that an unfamiliar word is compared with a familiar word

   Elia has a calm **temperament,** just like my old cat's nature. [Clue suggests that *temperament* means "nature."]

2. **Contrast:** clues that indicate that an unfamiliar word is contrasted to a familiar word or phrase

   As a kitten, the cat was quite **affectionate,** but now she is not loving at all. [The word *but* indicates a contrast between *affectionate* and "not loving," thereby suggesting that *affectionate* means "loving."]

3. **Cause and effect:** clues that indicate that an unfamiliar word is related to the cause of or is the result of an action, feeling, or idea

   The police officer **chastised** the motorist for speeding. [The motorist's speeding was the cause of the police officer's action. The result was that the police officer *chastised* ("scolded or punished") the motorist.]

Writers don't include obvious context clues in every sentence or paragraph. Sometimes, you must "read between the lines" to understand the meaning of an unfamiliar word. Often, you can draw on your own knowledge and experience to figure out the meaning of a word.

Because it is **imperative** that I do well on the test, I studied carefully. [The context of the sentence suggests that *imperative* means "absolutely necessary."]

Exercise   Each of the following sentences contains an italicized word. At the bottom of the page is a list of definitions. Use context clues to determine which definition matches each italicized word. On the line before each sentence, write the letter of the correct definition.

_____ 1. When I tripped and fell in front of all of those people, I felt *humiliated*.

_____ 2. The critics *extolled* the brilliant talents of the new young actor, but they did not like the talents of his leading lady.

_____ 3. Please *reiterate* your story slowly and clearly so that I can understand it, repeating it as you would for a young child.

_____ 4. The row of flowers *circumscribing* the young tree reminded me of a beautiful wreath around a maiden's head in a fairy tale.

_____ 5. The explorers knew that they were lost because no *vestiges* of the old trail were visible.

   a. repeat   b. praised   c. embarrassed   d. traces   e. surrounding

Chapter 15: Spelling and Vocabulary

WORKSHEET 12 *Choosing the Right Word*

English contains many **synonyms**—words that have the same general meaning but also have subtle shades of difference between them. Make sure that you understand the exact context in which the word is being used in order to choose the right synonym to fit your purpose.

The words *well-behaved, excellent,* and *delicious* are all synonyms for the word *good.* However, each word has a specific and different shade of meaning, as is shown in the following contexts.

> She was a well-behaved child. [a *good* child]
>
> Richard Wilbur is an excellent writer. [a *good* writer]
>
> We enjoyed a delicious pizza. [a *good* pizza]

Keep in mind, too, that even words that have the same **denotation,** or dictionary definition, may have different **connotations,** or feelings associated with them.

> The senator preferred to be called a **statesman** rather than a **politician.** [The word *politician* does not connote the respect and wisdom of the word *statesman.*]

Exercise A   Following is a list of synonyms for the word *bad.* Although each synonym shares the general meaning of "bad," each word has a specific and different shade of meaning. On the line provided, write the synonym from the list below that can be substituted for the word *bad* in each of the following sentences.

> **Synonyms for *bad:*** incorrect, low, grumpy, unpleasant, serious
>
> EXAMPLE: 1. News reports indicated that the fire was *bad.* serious

1. He was disappointed to receive a *bad* grade on the test.   _____

2. The skunk defends itself by spraying its attacker with a *bad* odor. _____

3. Why is LaTonya in such a *bad* mood today?   _____

4. The only flaw in Hasan's paper was *bad* spelling.   _____

Exercise B   Each of the following sentences is flat and uninteresting because it contains the overused word *nice.* On the line provided, revise each sentence, using a more interesting synonym for *nice* that fits the context of the sentence.

1. You look *nice* in that picture.

_____

2. Mrs. Sánchez is a *nice* person.

_____

3. It's not *nice* to interrupt someone who is speaking.

_____

4. Thank you for making me such a *nice* lunch.

_____

Name _____ Date _____ Class _____

 **WORKSHEET 13** *Using Word Parts*

Most English words are of two kinds: those that can be divided into smaller parts (*exceedingly, happiness*) and those that cannot (*ache, hour*). Words that are complete by themselves are called **base words**. The three types of word parts are

- **root**—the part of the word that carries the word's core meaning
- **prefix**—a word part that is added before a root
- **suffix**—a word part that is added after a root

Remember that learning the meanings of some of the most commonly used word parts can help you figure out the meanings of unfamiliar words. Follow these techniques for improving your ability to figure out the meanings of unfamiliar words.

1. Determine the meaning of each part of the word.
2. Use those meanings to make up a definition for the unfamiliar word as a whole.
3. Use a recent dictionary to check the definition of the word.

Exercise A   Identify the base words (those without prefixes or suffixes) in the following list. On the line provided, write *BW* beside each base word.

EXAMPLE: ___*BW*___ 1. scheme

_____ 1. criticism   _____ 6. vacuum

_____ 2. debtor   _____ 7. icy

_____ 3. muscle   _____ 8. chief

_____ 4. eighth   _____ 9. indispensable

_____ 5. reign   _____ 10. niece

Exercise B   Underline the prefixes and suffixes in the following words. Look up the meanings of the prefixes, suffixes, and roots in a dictionary. Then, on the line provided, write a definition of each word.

EXAMPLE: 1. use<u>ful</u> *full of service*

1. acquaintance _____

2. impersonal _____

3. publicity _____

4. overpaid _____

5. professor _____

Chapter 15: Spelling and Vocabulary

WORKSHEET 14 *Review*

Exercise A   On the line provided, write each word syllable-by-syllable. Draw a vertical line between syllables. Use a dictionary if you are unsure.

EXAMPLE: 1. furious *fu|ri|ous*

1. separate _____

2. seventy _____

3. mutual _____

4. honest _____

5. persuade _____

Exercise B   Underline the root or roots in each of the following words. Then, on the line provided, use the meaning of the root and your own knowledge to write a definition of each word. Check your definitions in a dictionary.

EXAMPLE: 1. <u>audit</u>ions *hearings*

1. portable _____

2. mission _____

3. visual _____

4. impede _____

5. audiovisual _____

Exercise C   On the line provided, give an example of a word containing each of the following prefixes. Then tell what each word means.

EXAMPLE: 1. un– *unbending—not bending; stiff or stubborn*

1. de– _____

2. pre– _____

3. non– _____

4. sub– _____

5. mis– _____

Exercise D   Underline the suffix in each of the following words. On the line provided, guess what the word means. Check your answers in a dictionary.

EXAMPLE: 1. theor<u>ize</u> *to make a theory*

1. magnify _____

2. parenthood _____

3. porous _____

4. knowable _____

5. treatment _____

Exercise E   In each group of four words, one is misspelled. On the line provided, write the word correctly. Use a dictionary if you are unsure.

EXAMPLE: 1. shoes, trays, foriegn, jumping *foreign*

1. height, believe, recieve, achieve   _____

2. sieze, neither, relief, reign   _____

3. usually, hopeing, amusement, immortal   _____

4. reccommend, truly, admiration, unnecessary   _____

5. women, tomatos, cupfuls, rodeos   _____

6. calfs, comparable, fraternity, accurate   _____

7. emergency, hindrance, consistancy, competent   _____

8. continous, fictitious, conscious, ridiculous   _____

9. comparison, conception, son-in-laws, description   _____

10. exaggerate, excercise, exciting, exist   _____

11. lovely, meanness, developement, courageous   _____

12. arguement, perspiration, occurrence, parallel   _____

13. flying, shining, ninty, safety   _____

14. proceed, pursuit, preceed, immense   _____

15. corporation, company, sopranoes, receipt   _____

16. controling, omit, picnic, professor   _____

17. often, sheriffes, hour, again   _____

18. friend, forbidden, nickel, storys   _____

19. donkeys, copies, potatos, elephant   _____

20. library, crisises, vacuum, churches   _____

Exercise F   Using context clues in each of the following sentences, choose the letter of the definition that best fits the meaning of each italicized word. Write the letter on the line provided.

a. fictional   f. noticeable

b. homes   g. flexible

c. beliefs   h. justify

d. able to float   i. determined

e. wanderers   j. ordinary

_____ 1. The lively conversations of the fascinating guests made up for the rather *mediocre* dinner.

_____ 2. Lamont draws only *mythical* creatures, like unicorns and dragons.

_____ 3. We learned in our safety class that if someone falls from a boat, you should throw the person a life vest or another *buoyant* object.

_____ 4. The doctor was pleased to see a *perceptible* improvement in her patient.

_____ 5. Carlo worked hard, *resolute* in his goal to become a great actor.

_____ 6. Early Navajos were *nomads*, moving from place to place with their herds.

_____ 7. Along the route, they used logs, dirt, and rocks to build family *hogans*.

_____ 8. One of the major *tenets* of Americans is equal rights for all men and women.

_____ 9. Kidskin is a *supple* material that is not damaged by folding or twisting.

_____ 10. I know that Elton's honesty and loyalty will *vindicate* your trust in him.

Exercise G   Following is a list of synonyms for the word *big*. Although each synonym shares the general meaning of "big," each word has a specific and different shade of meaning. On the line provided, write the synonym below that can be substituted for the word *big* in each of the following sentences.

Synonyms for *big*: oversized, ample, thundering, swollen, important

EXAMPLE: 1. The parking space is *big* enough for my car. *ample*

1. The food supply was not *big* enough to serve all the guests.   _____

2. My knee is *big* because of the injury in yesterday's game.   _____

3. Helen Hayes was a *big* star in the theater for many years.   _____

4. The audience jumped to their feet and gave the singer a *big* round of applause.   _____

5. Please check all *big* pieces of luggage.   _____

Name _____ Date _____ Class _____

Freewriting and Brainstorming

When you **freewrite,** you write whatever pops into your head. Try the steps below.

1. Set a timer for three to five minutes, and keep writing until the timer goes off.
2. Start with a word or topic that's important to you. Write whatever comes to mind without worrying about complete sentences or proper punctuation.
3. If you can't think of anything new to write, copy the same word or phrase over until something comes to mind.

Brainstorming is a way of coming up with ideas by free association done alone, with a partner, or in a group. To brainstorm, try the steps below.

1. Write any subject at the top of a sheet of paper (or on the chalkboard).
2. List every idea about the subject that comes to your mind. In a group, one person should record all of the ideas.
3. Don't stop to evaluate (judge) any of the ideas.
4. Keep going until you run out of ideas.

Exercise A   Write a favorite quotation below. Then freewrite about the quotation for three or four minutes. If you run out of room, continue writing on a blank piece of paper. You may want to use this quotation from baseball great Yogi Berra, commenting on the 1973 National League pennant race: "It ain't over till it's over."

_____

_____

_____

_____

_____

_____

Exercise B   Choose one of the following general subjects or use a topic of your own. Brainstorm about the subject by yourself or with a few classmates. On the lines below, list all the possible writing topics gathered from your brainstorming session.

Subjects: computers   advertising   inventions

Vietnam Veterans Memorial   dogs   study habits

Subject for brainstorming: _____

Possible topics gathered from brainstorming: _____

_____

_____

_____

_____

COMPOSITION

Chapter 16: The Writing Process

Clustering and Asking Questions

Clustering (also called *webbing* or *making connections*) is a technique for thinking of topics or gathering information. To cluster,

1. begin by writing a subject in the center of your paper. Circle the subject.
2. in the space around the subject, write whatever related ideas occur to you. Circle each one and draw a line from it to the original subject.
3. let your mind wander. Each idea can lead to other new ideas. Keep drawing circles and lines to show the connections.

NOTE: You can also organize ideas with a *tree diagram,* showing your main subject as the trunk and supporting details as the branches and twigs.

The *5W–How?* **questions** can help you to collect information on some subjects. Ask *Who? What? Where? When? Why?* and *How?* about your subject.

Exercise A   Choose one of the following subjects or one of your own. Write the subject in the center circle below. Then create a cluster diagram by thinking of ideas related to the subject.

Subjects: pets   Native American ways of life   fishing
               Saturdays   clothes of the future   good jobs

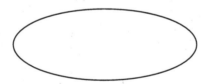

Exercise B   Choose another subject from the list given in Exercise A or come up with a subject of your own. Write the subject on the top line below. Then write six *5W-How?* questions about the subject.

Subject: _____

1. Who _____

2. What _____

3. Where _____

4. When _____

5. Why _____

6. How _____

Name _____ Date _____ Class _____

Using Your Five Senses

The five senses are sight, hearing, smell, taste, and touch. When you use details about these senses in your writing, you are using **sensory details**.

Exercise List as many sensory details as you can for one of the following subjects or for a topic of your own choice.

a CD/cassette store	an Indian (or Italian) restaurant
Chinatown	a holiday tradition in my home
a Fourth of July celebration	a party

Subject: _____

Sensory details:

Sight _____

_____

_____

_____

Hearing _____

_____

_____

_____

Smell _____

_____

_____

_____

Touch _____

_____

_____

_____

Taste _____

_____

_____

_____

COMPOSITION

Chapter 16: The Writing Process

Reading and Listening with a Focus

When you read to find information, you look for main ideas and supporting details. Keep these suggestions in mind.

1. Don't read everything. Use the index, check the table of contents, and look for chapter headings and subheadings. Skim through the material, searching only for information about your topic.

2. When you find relevant information, slow down. Read carefully for main ideas. Take notes on specific details as well as main ideas.

You can also gather ideas for writing by listening to radio programs and audiotapes, by watching television programs, and by interviewing experts. Use these suggestions to prepare in advance.

1. Write down your topic.

2. Brainstorm what you already know about the topic, or refer to your notes if you've already done some research.

3. Write down what you want to know to help guide and focus your listening.

4. With your questions in front of you, listen carefully. Take careful notes, and don't let your mind wander.

Exercise A   You are writing a paper about modern lifestyles in Indonesia, which you will compare with lifestyles in another Asian country such as China, Japan, or Korea. Find a book about Indonesia or Asia first. Using the book, list the following information.

1. key words in the index: _____

_____

2. chapters worth reading or skimming: _____

_____

Exercise B   Skim one of the chapters of the book you used in Exercise A. As you skim, list headings, charts, graphs, and illustrations that will be helpful for your report.

_____

_____

_____

Exercise C   You are about to watch a video on whale watching off the coast of Hawaii. Prepare yourself to listen by making a list of three ideas to listen for or three questions you want answered.

1. _____

2. _____

3. _____

Chapter 16: The Writing Process

"What if?" Questions and Visualizing

Asking **"What if?" questions** is a creative thinking technique that can help you gather ideas for writing. Through thinking about causes and effects, you can discover topics and details.

Visualizing means making images of something in your "mind's eye." You can use visualizing to think of details for your writing. For example, you can imagine a particular scene or you can imagine yourself doing something. You can also visualize the answer to a "What if?" question. To do so, you try to picture the situation created by the question.

Exercise A   Write one "What if?" question for each topic listed below.

1. sharks: What if _____

_____

2. the next presidential election: What if _____

_____

3. computers: What if _____

_____

4. grocery stores: What if _____

_____

5. the school year: What if _____

_____

Exercise B   Visualize the answer to one of the questions you wrote above, or visualize one of the ideas listed below. Then jot down notes that tell what you picture in your mind.

a visit to Antarctica   living in a wigwam   a forest fire
classrooms of the future   climbing Mt. Everest   a space walk

Subject: _____

Notes: _____

_____

_____

_____

_____

_____

_____

_____

COMPOSITION

Chapter 16: The Writing Process

Considering Purpose, Audience, and Tone

When you write, you always have some **purpose** (a reason for writing) in mind. You write in many different forms, but you have one or more than one basic purpose: to express yourself; to be creative; to explain, inform, or explore; or to persuade. A single piece of writing may combine two or more purposes.

As you consider your purpose, think about your **audience** (your readers) at the same time. For example: How much does the audience already know? What will be interesting to the audience? What level of language is appropriate?

Tone is the personality of your writing. You can sound casual, formal, outraged, sarcastic, serious, sad, or funny. To create tone, you pay attention to

- choice of words
- choice of details
- sentence length and structure

Exercise   Write the purpose, a possible audience, and the tone for each of the following paragraphs.

1. Although money is tight this year, it would be a shame to close Beebe High. Beebe has been around since 1947, and it has always had a reputation for excellence. Alumni of Beebe would be sad to see it disappear forever. And those of us who were hoping to graduate from Beebe would feel robbed of our chance to attend a first-rate school in our own neighborhood. On behalf of all Beebe students, past and present, we ask you to reconsider closing Beebe.

   Purpose: _____

   Audience: _____

   Tone: _____

2. The door slammed shut. Roberta was locked in the dark cellar. She could hear the footsteps of the men upstairs. Where were they going now? Would they find the hidden safe? And how would she ever get out of this cellar and get help?

   Purpose: _____

   Audience: _____

   Tone: _____

Name _____ Date _____ Class _____

WORKSHEET 7 | *Arranging Ideas A*

Before you start writing, you need to spend some time arranging your prewriting ideas. Sometimes you can arrange your ideas by using *chronological order* or *spatial order*.

Chronological order presents events as they happen in time. You use chronological order when you narrate. Stories, narrative poems, explanations of processes, history, biography, and drama often use chronological order.

Spatial order presents objects according to location. You use spatial order when you describe objects in order from near to far, left to right, top to bottom, and so on.

Exercise A Organize the information about writer Nina Otero, author of *Old Spain in Our Southwest*, in chronological order by numbering the events from 1 to 5.

_____ After college graduation, she returned to New Mexico in 1917 and became involved in the suffragist movement.

_____ Otero died in 1965.

_____ Otero was born in 1882 in Los Lunas, New Mexico.

_____ Later in 1917 she accepted the first of several important public positions, which included education director for the Works Progress Administration in Puerto Rico.

_____ Otero graduated from Maryville College in St. Louis.

Exercise B Organize the list of sentences below in spatial order by numbering the sentences from 1 to 5, from left to right.

_____ To the right of the man with the corn is a warrior.

_____ On the far right of the picture is another Pilgrim who looks less important.

_____ To the right of the center of the picture is a chief.

_____ Next to the chief, just to *his* right, is a proud Pilgrim.

_____ On the far left of the picture is a Native American with a basket of corn.

Exercise C List some signposts that a new student could look for as guides to get from one room or area of your school to another.

From _____ to _____

_____

_____

_____

_____

_____

_____

COMPOSITION

Chapter 16: The Writing Process

WORKSHEET 8 — *Arranging Ideas B*

Before you start writing, you need to spend some time arranging your prewriting ideas. You can arrange ideas by putting them in *order of importance* or *logical order*.

Using **order of importance,** you present ideas or details from least to most important or the reverse. You use order of importance when you evaluate. Persuasive writing, descriptive writing, explanatory writing, and evaluative writing often use order of importance.

Using **logical order,** you relate items and groups. You use logical order when you classify. Definitions, classifications, and comparison/contrast essays often use logical order.

Exercise A   The list below contains reasons why people should not go off trails in wilderness areas. Organize the list of ideas in order of importance by numbering the ideas from 1 (most important) to 3 (least important).

_____   You could step in poison ivy.

_____   You could get lost.

_____   Wilderness areas are ruined and animals are endangered when use is not controlled.

Exercise B   What might you say to persuade people about the value of eating the right foods in the right amounts? Think of two reasons for maintaining a healthful diet. List the more important reason last.

1. _____

   _____

2. _____

   _____

Exercise C   What are three types of cars, music, or trees that you might classify in logical order for a comparison/contrast essay? On the lines provided, list three classifications of one topic and a few details about each classification.

1. _____

   _____

2. _____

   _____

3. _____

   _____

Chapter 16: The Writing Process

Using Charts

Making a chart is a good way to arrange your prewriting notes. The most important step in creating a chart is to decide on the headings that will cover the information.

You can use a chart like the following one to help you see blocks of information and their relationships clearly.

Topic: Native American instruments used with dance and song

Peoples	Types of Instruments
Plains peoples	drums with painted horsehide heads
Northwestern peoples	wooden boxes; rattles made like masks from wood or native copper
Pueblo and other farming peoples	gourd rattles
Iroquois	turtle shell; pot or water drum

To arrange information chronologically, you can use a *time line* chart. For example, you could indicate specific events in a social or political movement beside the years they occurred.

Exercise In the space below, make a chart to organize the following information about emergency treatment of bites and stings.

    animals (dogs, etc.)—wash with clean water, soap; hold under running water for several minutes; sterile bandage; call doctor for further treatment

    snake bite (poisonous)—rush to doctor or emergency room; keep victim at rest; apply tourniquet between bite and heart (but not too tight)

    snake bite (nonpoisonous)—treat as cut; not necessary to call doctor

    bee, wasp, hornet, ant—scrape (do not pull) stinger to remove it; cold compresses or ice cube on bite; rush to doctor or emergency room if severe reaction

    spider bite—ice cube over bite to reduce pain; consult doctor for medication

Chapter 16: The Writing Process

WORKSHEET 10 *Writing a First Draft*

There's no single approach to turning prewriting notes into a first draft. Some writers work from very rough prewriting notes, while others work from a detailed outline. Some write quickly, trying just to get their ideas down on paper in sentences. Others shape each sentence slowly and connect ideas carefully. As you write your first draft, try these suggestions.

- Use your prewriting plans to guide your draft.
- Write freely, focusing on expressing your ideas clearly.
- Remember that writing is a way of discovering ideas. Include new ideas that you discover about your topic.
- Don't worry about catching or correcting errors in grammar, usage, and mechanics at this stage—you can do that later.

Exercise   Here are some prewriting notes about a great American leader, Tecumseh. Read the notes, and think about the order in which the details should be arranged. Then, on the lines below, write the first draft of a paragraph about Tecumseh.

allied himself with Britain during the War of 1812

fought under Chief Little Turtle against U.S. troops in the 1790s

a Shawnee chief, in the Ohio Valley, Northwest Territory

led Native American forces in the invasion of Ohio for the British (War of 1812)

born about 1768 in Ohio

opposed the 1809 treaty in which chiefs of several peoples sold land (three million acres) to U.S. government

called a brilliant leader, marvelous speaker

with his brother (who was called the Prophet), set out to organize all Native Americans east of the Mississippi to reject the 1809 treaty

1811, Battle of Tippecanoe in Indiana—United States defeated Native Americans in Prophet's village

defeated and killed at Battle of the Thames, 1813

_____

_____

_____

_____

_____

_____

_____

_____

_____

_____

Name _____ Date _____ Class _____

Evaluating

These techniques can help you in **evaluating** (deciding on the strengths and weaknesses of) your own writing:

1. Read your paper at least three times. First, read for *content* (what you say), then for *organization* (how you've arranged your ideas), and then for *style* (how you've used words and sentences).

2. Read your draft aloud and try to "hear" what you've written.

3. Set your draft aside for a while and come back to it later.

Professional writers almost always have someone else read and evaluate what they've written. When you participate in **peer evaluation,** remember these guidelines:

1. Tell your classmate what you think is particularly effective. Point out strengths as well as weaknesses.

2. Provide some encouragement—suggest something your classmate can do to improve the paper.

3. Look at content and organization. Don't comment on mechanical errors such as spelling or punctuation.

4. Be sensitive to the writer's feelings. When you spot a weakness, ask a question about it rather than point it out as a problem.

Exercise   Read the following paragraph. Then use the questions given below to help you write an evaluation of the paragraph.

> *You have to get nominated first, the states send some deligates to a convention. The deligates decide it all. They have the power, that's what their there for. That person goes on to be president if the person gets elected.*

1. What do you think is a good point that the paragraph makes?

_____

_____

2. What suggestion would you make about the organization in the paragraph?

_____

_____

3. What suggestion would you make about the content of the paragraph?

_____

_____

4. What question might help the writer to recognize a problem?

_____

_____

COMPOSITION

Chapter 16: The Writing Process

WORKSHEET 12 *Revising*

In **revising** your paper, you make the actual changes you decided on in evaluating. There are four main ways to revise:

1. You can *add* new information to help your audience understand your main idea. Add words, phrases, sentences, whole paragraphs.

2. You can *cut* details, examples, or words that are unrelated or distracting.

3. You can *replace* weak words or unnecessary details with more precise words or better details.

4. You can *reorder*, or move, information, details, examples, or paragraphs for variety and for an order that makes sense.

Exercise Study the revisions made to the following paragraph. Then answer the questions below.

*For example, do you want a mountain bike
or a racing bike?*

→ You need to make up your mind about the kind of bike you want. Then you

For example, what kind of seat, derailleur, and brakes do you want?

make up your mind about what you absolutely need to have on it. Also, you

exactly how much you can spend.

should decide what your limits are. ~~Maybe your parents do the same things when they~~

~~buy a car.~~ When you go to a bike store, you can end up paying a lot of money for

things you don't really need.

1. Why did the writer add the information about mountain and racing bikes, as well as the information about derailleurs, seats, and brakes?

_____

_____

2. Why did the writer cross out the sentence about buying a car?

_____

_____

3. Why did the writer move the sentence about going to a bike store?

_____

_____

4. Why did the writer replace "what your limits are" with "exactly how much you can spend"?

_____

_____

Name _____ Date _____ Class _____

Proofreading and Publishing

Proofreading is checking your paper for mistakes in grammar, usage, and mechanics (spelling, capitalization, and punctuation). To proofread, use the following guidelines.

1. Is every sentence a complete sentence, not a fragment or run-on?
2. Does every sentence end with the appropriate end mark? Are other punctuation marks used correctly?
3. Does every sentence begin with a capital letter? Are all proper nouns and proper adjectives capitalized?
4. Does every verb agree in number with its subject?
5. Are verb forms and tenses used correctly?
6. Are subject and object forms of personal pronouns used correctly?
7. Does every pronoun agree with its antecedent in number and in gender? Are pronoun references clear?
8. Are frequently confused words (such as *lie* and *lay*) used correctly?
9. Are words spelled correctly? Are the plural forms of nouns correct?
10. Is the paper neat and in correct manuscript form?

Publishing your writing means sharing it. Deciding on an audience earlier in the writing process meant you were planning to share your paper with others. When you publish, you attempt to reach that audience in a certain form. For example, your writing might appear in a school newspaper or in a class anthology, or it might be displayed on a bulletin board.

Exercise A: Proofreading   Use the guidelines above to proofread the following paragraph. Correct the errors in grammar, usage, spelling, punctuation, and capitalization. Use a dictionary and your handbook to help you.

More than a half of all the Chinese during the 19th century who came to this country, came from one province. The province of Kwangtung. The capitol city of Kwantung was Canton. For a long time, it was the only Chinese port city that was open to forreigners They were the people who learned about the world outside of the boarders of China. some of them decided to see this world. Many of them thought they were going to the U.S. for a temporary stay.

Exercise B   For each of the following writing topics and audiences, name one way that the writer could publish, or share the writing with others.

1. Topic: please recycle; Audience: people of the town of Scotia

_____

2. Topic: my favorite mystery; Audience: classmates

_____

Chapter 16: The Writing Process

WORKSHEET 14

The Aim and Process of Writing

Aim—The "Why" of Writing

WHY PEOPLE WRITE	
To express themselves	To get to know themselves, to find meaning in their own lives
To share information	To give other people information that they need or want; to share some special knowledge
To persuade	To convince other people to do something or believe something
To create literature	To be creative, to say something in a unique way

Process—The "How" of Writing

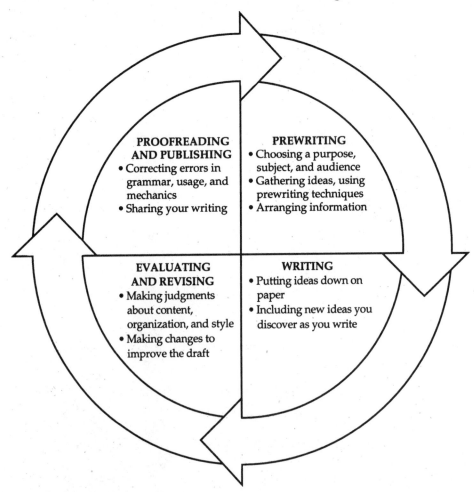

WORKSHEET 1   *The Topic Sentence*

A **paragraph** is usually defined as a group of sentences that develop a main idea. Similarly, a **composition** can be described as a group of paragraphs that develop a main idea.

A **topic sentence** is a single sentence that expresses the main idea of a paragraph. Although a topic sentence can be any place in the paragraph, it often appears as the first or second sentence.

Exercise   Underline the topic sentence of each paragraph.

1. Traditional Cherokee houses were simple and made from materials that could be gathered easily. The plaster walls were made from a mixture of clay and grass. The houses were supported by hickory, pine, or cedar poles. Their roofs were made from bark. There were holes for windows and an opening for a door.

2. Seven was an important number for the Cherokee people. The Cherokee were organized into seven towns with villages surrounding them. In each town square stood a council house with seven sides. Each town had a town chief and seven town councilmen.

3. No one's cornfield was next to a house. Families had fields, but all the men in the tribe worked in them. If someone was old or sick, his field was planted for him. If a woman had lost her husband, her field was planted for her. Everyone shared the cornfields.

4. On the night before corn planting, a special ceremony was held. In this ceremony, the people danced to the Old Woman of the Corn to protect their corn. A mortar was placed in the town square. Men and women danced around it. They made motions that suggested pouring corn or meal from a basket in one hand to a bowl in the other hand. This dance was a kind of prayer for the corn.

5. August brought another festival. This was the New Green Corn Feast, a time to repeat certain rituals and give thanks for the corn that had grown. The chief sent seven hunters into the forest to hunt deer for the feast. The chief also sent messengers to the towns to call people to the feast and to gather one ear of new green corn from each town. After six days the hunters had come out of the forest with the deer for the feast; the messengers had arrived with the corn; the people had arrived, too. On the seventh day, a fire was made at the council house and the seven ears of corn were placed there. As the ears burned, the chief gave thanks to the Old Woman of the Corn.

COMPOSITION

Chapter 17: Paragraph and Composition Structure

WORKSHEET 2 *Supporting Sentences*

Supporting sentences give details—specific bits of information—that make the main idea of a paragraph clear. Supporting sentences support your main idea with sensory details, facts or statistics, examples, or anecdotes.

Sensory details are precise bits of information that you observe, or collect, through any of your five senses—sight, hearing, smell, touch, taste.

A **fact** is something that can be proven true by concrete information. A **statistic** is a fact that is based on numbers.

There are fifty states in the United States.

Examples are specific instances, or illustrations, of a general idea.

GENERAL IDEA: Many women have fought for human rights.

EXAMPLE: Dorothy Day worked tirelessly for human rights.

An **anecdote** is an extended example, or story, usually biographical or autobiographical, used to support a main idea.

Exercise   Three general ideas you could write about are listed below. With each idea, a type of support—examples and anecdotes, facts and statistics, or sensory details—is suggested. Think up at least two details to support each main idea, and write them on the lines provided. You may have to do a little research (reading or talking to knowledgeable people) to find facts or statistics.

1. Physical education classes develop skills that you'll use throughout your life. (examples and anecdotes)

   _____

   _____

   _____

2. Ponce de León, the Spanish explorer, led an expedition to what is now Florida. (facts and statistics)

   _____

   _____

   _____

3. On a rainy, cold afternoon, nothing could be better than going to see a movie. (sensory details)

   _____

   _____

   _____

Chapter 17: Paragraph and Composition Structure

The Clincher Sentence

Sometimes, especially in long paragraphs, you may want to end with a sentence that restates or summarizes the main idea. This concluding sentence is called a **clincher sentence** because it pulls all the details together.

Exercise   Write a clincher sentence for each of the following paragraphs.

1. Although the woods are beautiful, there are things to watch out for. You need to be careful to avoid poison ivy and poison oak. You should not eat any berry you cannot identify. You also need to watch for insects that bite or sting.

   Clincher sentence: _____

2. It is autumn. From my window I can see the bright red of Mr. Woo's maple. Across the street is the vibrant yellow of the Pasquarella family's buckeye. Down the street I can see the deep wine-red of the Skowroneks' ash.

   Clincher sentence: _____

3. If you want to take a good photograph, first think about how much light you have and where you should stand in relation to the light. Then think about how close to or how far away from your subject you want to be. You should also consider the kind of film to use. In particular, you want to think about the speed of the film in relation to how much light you have.

   Clincher sentence: _____

4. Ken Burns's documentary on the Civil War is a masterpiece. It contains all kinds of interesting facts about the Civil War. It uses thousands of photographs from the time to tell the story of the famous figures of the war and of the everyday people who fought it. Several historians worked together to produce a narrative so interesting that it keeps you watching the entire series. Even the music is perfect.

   Clincher sentence: _____

5. Huntington Gardens in Pasadena, California, is a truly remarkable place. There you can see plants and flowers from all over the world. There is everything from lotus blossoms to exotic cacti. On the same grounds are a wonderful library filled with rare books and manuscripts and a great art collection with some very famous paintings.

   Clincher sentence: _____

COMPOSITION

Chapter 17: Paragraph and Composition Structure

Achieving Unity

A paragraph has **unity** when all the sentences work together as a unit to express or support one main idea. Sentences can work as a unit in one of three ways: (1) by supporting a main idea that is stated in a topic sentence, (2) by supporting a main idea that is implied (understood without being directly expressed), or (3) by expressing a related series of actions. In the following paragraph, the sentence that has been crossed out does not support the main idea, and it destroys the unity of the paragraph.

> Driver's education courses taught in high schools promote highway safety. Driver's education courses give students the opportunity to practice with a trained teacher. They help students familiarize themselves with the rules of the road. ~~Seat belts may save the lives of thousands each year.~~ The more teenagers know about cars, roads, and the laws governing both, the safer they will be in their cars.

Exercise   Each of the following paragraphs contains one sentence that destroys its unity. Find each unrelated sentence and draw a line through it.

1. American society is becoming more mobile with three out of ten families moving each year. Many families move because parents are looking for jobs. Some move because a parent has been transferred to a new job. Some move because they prefer a different town or city. Movers say that fragile items should be packed carefully and labeled clearly.

2. Modeling is usually presented as a glamorous career, but in reality it is a demanding job. For one thing, it is a job with long hours, which often begin at five o'clock in the morning. The taller you are, the more likely you'll be able to be a model. Because models work with different photographers at different studios every day, they find it difficult to sustain friendships with fellow workers. And while models wear beautiful clothes in front of the camera, they almost never get to keep them.

3. The trucks and heavy machinery are parked in the area where the big top, or huge circus tent, will be set up. Then a large number of circus workers are gathered. Although many people enjoy the clowns, the trapeze acts usually draw the biggest applause. The big top is lowered from a truck, rolled out, and set in position. With the help of elephants, heavy support poles are raised. Then, in a series of complicated steps, the big top is lifted and stretched across the many support poles. Finally, the stakes are placed around the perimeter of the tent, and many ropes are tied to hold the huge tent in place.

Chapter 17: Paragraph and Composition Structure

Coherence: Order of Ideas

A paragraph has **coherence** when all the ideas fit together. You can create coherence by paying attention to the order in which you arrange your ideas.

Chronological order is time order. It is especially useful when you are explaining a process or telling a story.

Spatial order is arrangement by ordering details according to how they are spaced—nearest to farthest, left to right, or any other reasonable arrangement by location.

Order of importance is arrangement according to how important details or ideas are. The most important idea can come first or last.

Logical order is an arrangement that makes sense because of the way the ideas are related.

Exercise   On the lines provided, tell how the ideas were arranged to create coherence.

1. Because the glaciers were melting, they moved across the earth. As the glaciers advanced, they scooped out deep valleys in the earth's crust. As the glaciers melted, these valleys filled with water. They also filled with rain water. In this way, the glaciers formed lakes.

   Order of ideas: _____

2. A visitor to Tokyo will see many similarities between that city and a large city in the United States. Tokyo, like many large American cities, has a number of tall office buildings. The city is divided into several sections, or districts, just as a large American city is. At night in the busiest parts of Tokyo, hundreds of neon signs advertise commercial products and places of entertainment. If these signs were in English, they would look like the signs in large American cities.

   Order of ideas: _____

3. As you drive into the city of Caracas from its outskirts, the city seems undeveloped. You see homes on hillsides where there is no electricity. As you get closer to the city, however, you begin to see high-rise apartment buildings as well as a tangle of modern highways. In the center of Caracas are gleaming office towers and luxury hotels, fountains, and museums.

   Order of ideas: _____

COMPOSITION

Chapter 17: Paragraph and Composition Structure

Coherence: Direct References and Transitions

A paragraph has **coherence** when all the ideas fit together. You can create coherence by connecting ideas with direct references and transitional words and phrases.

Direct references refer to a word or an idea you have used earlier. You can make a direct reference by using a noun or pronoun that refers to a word or an idea used earlier, by repeating a word used earlier, or by using a word or phrase that means the same thing as one used earlier.

Transitional words and phrases include conjunctions, prepositions, and adverbs. They are used to compare and contrast, classify, define, show cause and effect, show time, show place, and show importance.

In the following paragraph, the direct references are shown in **boldface**. The transitional words and phrases are *italicized*.

> In this photograph of Rosa Parks, **she** is sitting in the front of a bus in Montgomery, Alabama. *At one time*, **the front of the bus** had been for white people only—*until* one day *when* **Rosa Parks** sat **there**. **She** was arrested. *After* that **arrest**, a boycott took place and, *as a result*, the law was *eventually* changed. *Of course*, **this brave woman** did not **change** the **law** by **herself**, *but* **she** took the courageous *first* step.

Exercise On the lines provided, list the direct references and transitional words and phrases in the following paragraph.

> Many African Americans in Montgomery began staying off the city buses to protest the arrest of Mrs. Parks. This boycott was a hardship because it meant that some of the people had no way to get to work or other places. Rosa Parks received threatening phone calls and was fired from her job. Mr. Parks was also fired from his job. Nevertheless, the boycott continued in Montgomery until the Supreme Court ruled that segregation on the city buses was unconstitutional.

Direct References	**Transitional Words and Phrases**
_____	_____
_____	_____
_____	_____
_____	_____
_____	_____
_____	_____
_____	_____

Name _____ Date _____ Class _____

 **WORKSHEET 7** **Description**

When you want to tell what something is like or what it looks like, you use **description**. In a description, sensory details provide effective support. Often, you'll use spatial order.

Exercise   Read the following paragraph. Then complete the chart below by listing five details from the paragraph, one for each of the five senses.

My friend King Chun invited ten other friends and me to a Chinese banquet in Boston's Chinatown. As I entered the noisy, crowded restaurant, I could smell duck roasting and other delicious aromas. We had a dinner of nine courses. Each one was a feast for the mouth, nose, and eyes. Luscious green and yellow vegetables were combined with red hot peppers and black bean sauce. Pink shrimp floated in a delicate lobster sauce. There were fresh noodles, clear soups, and tender meats marinated in a variety of sauces. Everyone exclaimed in appreciation as each dish was brought out. I ate and ate until my stomach bulged over my belt. At the end of the evening, I raised my water glass and proposed a toast to my kind host. As King Chun tapped his glass against mine, we both smiled.

Sight
Hearing
Touch
Taste
Smell

COMPOSITION

Chapter 17: Paragraph and Composition Structure

WORKSHEET 8 *Narration*

If you use **narration,** which looks at events or actions in time, you'll usually arrange your ideas and information in chronological order. You may use narration to tell a story or incident, to explain a process, or to explain causes and effects.

Exercise A   Think of something you know how to do well. Write your topic on the top line below. Then list the things you would do to complete the process. Put the steps in the order in which you would do them.

Topic: _____

Steps: _____

_____

_____

_____

_____

Exercise B   Think of a story you can tell about something that happened to you or someone else. Write your topic on the top line below. Then list the things that happened in the order in which they occurred.

Topic: _____

Events: _____

_____

_____

_____

_____

Exercise C   Think of three cause-and-effect topics that you could develop through narration.

EXAMPLE: 1. *explaining in a note to a friend why you did not show up to meet her*

1. _____

_____

2. _____

_____

3. _____

_____

Name _____ Date _____ Class _____

Classification

Classification looks at a subject as it relates to other subjects in a group. When you classify, you may *divide* a subject into its parts, *define* it, or *compare and contrast* it with something else. Usually, writers use logical order—grouping related ideas together—in paragraphs that classify.

Exercise A   Choose one of the following subjects, or come up with a subject of your own. Then divide that subject into a list of parts that you could relate to one another or to the subject as a whole.

>   the seasons of the year

>   grading terms or periods in my school

Subject: _____

Parts: _____

Exercise B   Choose one of the following subjects, or come up with a subject of your own. Tell what large class it belongs to and then list at least two things that make the subject different from other members of that group.

>   my house or apartment

>   my dog or cat or other pet

Subject: _____

Class: _____

How it is unique: _____

Exercise C   Choose one of the following pairs of subjects, or come up with a pair of your own. Write at least two similarities and two differences between the two people, places, things, or ideas. You might want to research your pair of subjects to make your list.

>   science class, history class

>   George Bush, Abraham Lincoln

>   San Antonio, Texas; Seattle, Washington

Two subjects being compared: _____

Similarities	**Differences**
_____	_____
_____	_____
_____	_____
_____	_____
_____	_____

COMPOSITION

Chapter 17: Paragraph and Composition Structure

WORKSHEET 10 | *Evaluation*

Evaluation means determining the value of, or making a judgment about, something. Sometimes your purpose in evaluating a subject is to *inform* other people. At other times, your purpose may be to *persuade* them to think or act differently. An evaluation should provide reasons to support your judgment. A good way to arrange your reasons is by order of importance. You can emphasize one reason by putting it first or last in the paragraph.

The following paragraph evaluates Alfred Hitchcock's movie *North by Northwest*. The first sentence clearly states the evaluation. The next five sentences give support for the evaluation. The last sentence makes it clear that the writer's purpose is to persuade.

> *North by Northwest* is one of the most enjoyable movies you will ever see. In this movie, a man and woman become involved in a dangerous spy operation. What makes the movie so enjoyable is that it is very suspenseful, especially at the end, when the hero and heroine escape by climbing down Mount Rushmore. It is also extremely clever, because the main character must hide in many ingenious ways on a moving train as well as in other settings. The movie moves fast, but not so fast that you don't follow what is going on. In addition, to keep viewers interested, there is a touch of romance. If you have a chance, rent this movie and see it for yourself.

Exercise   Choose a television show, a play or other performance, a book, a tape, or a CD, and evaluate it. List your subject, your evaluation of it, your purpose, and at least three reasons you could use to support your judgment.

Subject: _____

Your evaluation: _____

Your purpose: _____

Reasons that support your judgment:

1. _____

   _____

2. _____

   _____

3. _____

   _____

Chapter 17: Paragraph and Composition Structure

WORKSHEET 11 | *The Thesis Statement*

A **thesis statement** is a sentence or two that announces the limited topic for your composition. It also announces your main, or unifying, idea about that topic. A thesis statement in a composition works the same way as a topic sentence works in a paragraph. Here are some guidelines for writing a thesis statement:

1. Develop your thesis statement from the information you've gathered in your prewriting.

2. Make sure that your thesis statement mentions your limited topic and states a main idea about that topic.

3. Be clear and specific. Check your thesis statement for vague words like *interesting* and *important*.

Exercise   Think about the following prewriting notes. On the lines provided, write a thesis statement that will connect the ideas in these notes.

1. Limited topic: unconventional beliefs

   Details: Charles Dickens believed that there was only one way to get a good night's sleep: to align one's bed from north to south.

   Henry Ford believed that milk should be made synthetically. He thought that dairy cows were unsanitary.

   Thomas Alva Edison believed that alternating current was very dangerous. He advocated the use of direct electrical current only.

   _____

   _____

   _____

2. Limited topic: how to control spending sprees

   Ideas and details: Set up budgets for clothes, entertainment, and so on.

   Appoint a "budget manager"—possibly a parent.

   Stay away from places of high temptation such as shopping malls, bowling alleys, video game arcades, and restaurants.

   Get a part-time job.

   _____

   _____

   _____

COMPOSITION

Chapter 17: Paragraph and Composition Structure

WORKSHEET 12 *The Early Plan*

Once you have a thesis statement, you can start to make an early plan. An **early plan** is sometimes called an **informal** or **rough outline**. In it, you simply sort your items into groups and arrange the groups in order. Here are some common ways to order ideas: chronological, or time, order (first to last or last to first); spatial order (top to bottom, bottom to top, left to right, right to left, near to far, far to near, and so on); order of importance (most important to least important or vice versa).

Exercise A   The following are some details for a composition about the writer Rudolfo Anaya. First, write what type of order you would use to organize these details. Then number the details to show that order.

Type of order to use: _____

_____ New Mexico gave him the Governor's Award for Achievement in Literature in 1980.

_____ He is currently working on his fourth novel.

_____ He was born in 1937.

_____ He wrote *Tortuga* in 1979.

Exercise B   The following list of details can be divided logically into two groups. On the lines provided, write the details for each group in order. Then write what type of order you used for each group.

Whales swim back to Alaska in late fall
The dunes inland from the beach
Whales swim south toward California in late spring
The deep, calm water of the open ocean
The rolling waves near shore
Whales give birth in summer
Whales feed in Alaska in spring
The flat, sandy beach

Group 1	Group 2
_____	_____
_____	_____
_____	_____
_____	_____
_____	_____

Type of order: _____   **Type of order:** _____

Chapter 17: Paragraph and Composition Structure

| WORKSHEET 13 | *The Formal Outline* |

A **formal outline** has a set pattern, using letters and numbers to label main headings and subheadings. The entries in a formal outline can be either topics (words and phrases) or complete sentences.

Exercise Choose one of the following thesis statements or use one of your own. On the lines provided, write at least two sections of a formal outline for a composition on that thesis statement. Use complete sentences. You may want to use an encyclopedia or another reference to develop your outline.

Many animals have complex systems for communicating with one another.

Many people have overcome physical challenges and achieved fame.

_____

_____

_____

_____

_____

_____

_____

_____

_____

_____

_____

_____

_____

_____

_____

_____

_____

_____

_____

_____

_____

COMPOSITION

Chapter 17: Paragraph and Composition Structure

WORKSHEET 14 *The Introduction*

A good **introduction** does three things: It catches the reader's attention, sets the tone of the writing, and presents the thesis statement. Here are some techniques for writing a good introduction.

1. Begin with a question.
2. Begin with an anecdote.
3. Begin by stating a startling fact or by adopting an unusual position.
4. Use an appropriate quotation.
5. Start with background information.
6. Begin with a simple statement of your thesis.

Exercise Read the following introduction, and answer the questions that follow it. Then follow the directions in item 5.

"There once was a girl who had a little curl right in the middle of her forehead. When she was good, she was very, very good. But when she was bad, she was horrid!" That old nursery rhyme describes my niece Hannah perfectly. No one ever knows what to expect from her. However, students of child development would say that Hannah is perfectly normal. Hannah is in the middle of that period of life known as "the terrible twos."

1. What is the tone of the piece of writing? _____

_____

2. What method is used in the introduction to catch the reader's interest? _____

_____

_____

3. How well do you think this method works? _____

_____

4. What is the thesis statement in this introduction? _____

_____

5. On the lines provided, write your own introduction to a paper that has the same thesis as

this one. _____

_____

_____

_____

_____

_____

_____

Chapter 17: Paragraph and Composition Structure

WORKSHEET 15   *The Body*

An effective composition consists mostly of a **body** of paragraphs. Each paragraph supports or proves a main point by developing it with supporting details. When a composition has *unity*, the separate paragraphs work together to support your thesis. When a composition has *coherence*, the ideas are easy to follow because they are arranged in an order that makes sense. Also, *transitional words and phrases* and *direct references* show how ideas are connected.

Exercise A   Underline the sentence that destroys unity in the following paragraph. Remember: To have unity, all details in a paragraph must be related to the main idea.

The women's rights movement began at the Seneca Falls Convention in New York in 1848. At that time, Elizabeth Cady Stanton introduced a resolution demanding suffrage, or the right to vote, for women. In 1869, Stanton and Susan B. Anthony formed a national organization to seek voting rights for women. By 1896, four states had given women the right to vote. In 1912, women's suffrage at last became an issue in a presidential campaign. Two years later, a suffrage petition signed by 404,000 women was presented to Congress. President Woodrow Wilson, responding to pressure by women's groups, endorsed a new amendment. Black males were granted the right to vote after the Civil War by the Fourteenth and Fifteenth Amendments. Finally, in 1919, the Nineteenth Amendment, giving women the right to vote, was passed by Congress.

Exercise B: Revising   On the lines provided, revise the following paragraph by adding transitions to connect the ideas. Feel free to rewrite or combine sentences, too.

Jason decided to hike across Glacier National Park. He decided this at a young age. He never actually did much hiking. On his eighteenth birthday, he made plans to explore Glacier National Park on foot. Jason researched the history and terrain of the park. He wrote to park headquarters. He received a package full of information and maps. He found out that much of the park, which is in the northern Rockies, is very rugged and isolated. He bought clothing and packed provisions for wilderness living. He arrived at the park and talked to the park rangers. They told Jason the best trails to follow. They gave him safety tips.

_____

_____

_____

_____

_____

_____

_____

_____

COMPOSITION

WORKSHEET 16 *The Conclusion and the Title*

A **conclusion** helps readers know that your composition is complete. Techniques for writing conclusions include restating your main idea, summarizing your major points, closing with a final idea or example, ending with a comment on the topic, calling on your readers to take action, and closing with a quotation.

The **title** of your composition should catch the reader's attention and suggest your main idea. You may think of a working title as you're writing, but be sure to evaluate it when your paper is finished. In choosing a title, keep in mind the purpose and tone of your composition.

Exercise A   Read the following first draft of a composition. Then draft a conclusion.

Among the people who explored and developed the Americas for Europe were African Americans. Estevanico, the most famous African explorer of the Americas, traveled throughout the Southwest in the 1530s. In the early seventeenth century, twenty Africans landed in the English colony of Virginia. By 1790, African Americans made up nearly one fifth of the United States' population. They helped build the foundations of this country.

Most of the African Americans came from the kingdoms of western and central Africa. Their political and social organizations were advanced. So were their art, music, and dance.

Contrary to popular belief, not all African Americans who came to the Americas were slaves. Some were indentured servants. Like indebted Europeans, they were bound to landowners in services for several years. Unfortunately, landowners began holding the indentured Africans longer than their terms.

Slavery became legal in Virginia in 1661 and in the rest of the English colonies by 1750. African Americans were skilled agricultural workers because they came from agricultural societies. They made the landowners very wealthy by cultivating their fields.

Conclusion: _____

_____

_____

_____

_____

_____

Exercise B   After reading the draft in Exercise A, write a possible title that would be suitable for the composition. Remember that a suitable title should reflect the purpose and tone of the composition.

Title: _____

Chapter 18: The Research Paper

 **WORKSHEET 1** | *Finding a Suitable Topic*

The first step in writing a research paper is choosing a suitable topic. First, identify a general subject for your report. Ideas may come from your own interests, family and neighbors, neighborhood and community; from books, magazines, and newspapers; or from movies, television, videotapes, or audiotapes. Your subject should be one that

- will inform your audience
- will interest your audience
- you can find information about
- will allow you to use a variety of outside sources

Next, limit your subject to a specific topic, one you can explore in detail in the available time and space. Here are some ways you can identify specific topics within a subject.

- Look up your subject in your library's card catalog or on-line catalog, or in the *Readers' Guide to Periodical Literature*.
- Find some books on your subject. Look through their tables of contents and indexes.
- Read an encyclopedia article about your subject.
- Talk with someone who has expert knowledge about your subject.

Exercise A   To practice finding subjects, choose two of the source areas listed below. Then, for each source, list two possible subjects for a research report.

hobbies and interests   family and neighbors   neighborhood and community
books, magazines, and newspapers   movies and television

Source 1: _____

Subject: _____

Subject: _____

Source 2: _____

Subject: _____

Subject: _____

Exercise B   To practice the process of limiting subjects to specific topics, choose two of the subjects listed below. Then list three specific topics from the subject.

the environment   the human brain   television   sports

Subject 1: _____   Subject 2: _____

Topic: _____   Topic: _____

Topic: _____   Topic: _____

Topic: _____   Topic: _____

COMPOSITION

Chapter 18: The Research Paper

WORKSHEET 2 *Purpose, Audience, and Tone*

The basic **purpose** of your research report is to inform your readers—to share the facts and details you've learned through your research. Writing a research report is also an opportunity to share any insights or conclusions that you've reached. Your **audience** should come away from your report with a better understanding of your topic. As you research and write your report, ask yourself these questions about your audience.

- Who will read my report, and what do my readers know about my topic?
- What information can I give my audience that will be surprising or new to them?
- How can I be sure to give my audience complete information, not leaving out any important area my readers want to hear about?

A research report usually has a serious, formal **tone**. Remember that a formal tone calls for

- third-person point of view—avoid using the pronoun *I*
- fairly formal language—avoid slang, colloquialisms, or contractions

Exercise   Suppose that you're writing a report on the topic "Hispanic American contributions to the American Revolution." On the lines below, answer these questions about your purpose, audience, and tone. Your audience is a ninth-grade class.

1. Which of these pieces of information might your readers know?
    a. In the 1500s, Spain established colonies in what is now the United States.
    b. Spaniards and Hispanic Americans played an important role during the American Revolution.
    c. Jorge Farragut—the father of the Civil War hero Admiral David Glasgow Farragut—was a Hispanic American who joined the Continental Army and became a major in the cavalry.

    _____

    _____

2. Junípero Serra, the founder of the Spanish missions in California, requested that each Spaniard contribute two pesos to the colonists' efforts against Britain. Why do you think you would or would not need to define the term *pesos* for your audience?

    _____

    _____

3. You believe the thirteen colonies could not have won the Revolution without Hispanic Americans. Should your report include this opinion? Why or why not?

    _____

    _____

4. Explain why the following sentence reflects an improper tone for your report. "I say there's no way the colonies could've beat the British if it hadn't been for the Hispanic Americans."

    _____

    _____

Chapter 18: The Research Paper

WORKSHEET 3

Developing Research Questions

To give yourself a sense of direction as you begin your own research, start with a list of questions. Begin with your own natural curiosity. What do *you* want to know about your topic?

Exercise   Write your topic on the line provided. Then write six questions about your topic. Begin your questions with the words *Who, What, Where, When, Why,* and *How.*

Topic: _____

Question 1: Who _____

_____ ?

Question 2: What _____

_____ ?

Question 3: Where _____

_____ ?

Question 4: When _____

_____ ?

Question 5: Why _____

_____ ?

Question 6: How _____

_____ ?

COMPOSITION

Name _____ Date _____ Class _____

Locating and Evaluating Sources

Your library and your community contain many valuable sources of information for research papers. The following chart lists some of the sources that are available.

Library Resources	Community Resources
Card catalog or on-line catalog	Local government agencies
Readers' Guide to Periodical Literature or an on-line index	Local offices of state and federal government officials
Microfilm or microfiche	Local newspaper offices
Vertical file	Museums and historical societies
General reference books	Schools and colleges
Specialized reference books	Video stores
Videotapes and audiotapes	
Librarian	

Not all information is equally helpful. Evaluate, or judge, the usefulness of a source by checking it against the following "4 R" test.

1. *Relevant.* Does the information relate directly to your topic?
2. *Reliable.* Does the information seem objective and accurate?
3. *Recent.* Does the information seem outdated?
4. *Representative.* For a controversial topic, be sure to find sources that present more than one point of view.

Exercise A Follow the directions below.

1. **Library Sources** Go to the library and find two sources of information about your topic. List the sources here.

   _____

   _____

2. **Community Sources** Find at least two community sources of information about your topic. List the sources here.

   _____

   _____

Exercise B If possible, find an article about your topic in a general reference work, such as an encyclopedia. Read the article. Then write two questions that you would like to find answers to in other sources.

1. _____

   _____

2. _____

   _____

Chapter 18: The Research Paper

WORKSHEET 5

Preparing Source Cards and Note Cards

Keeping track of your sources is essential. You'll need accurate and complete information on each source in order to prepare your *Works Cited* list, the list of sources at the end of your paper. The best system for collecting information is to put each source on a 3" × 5" index card. For each source, list the author, title, and publication information (for books, list location, publisher, and date). Then give each source card a number. If you take good notes, you'll have a record of the information you need when you draft your report. Follow these guidelines for taking notes.

- Take notes on 4" × 6" note cards or half-sheets of 8 ½" × 11" paper.
- Use a separate note card or sheet of paper for each item of information.
- Put a brief heading in the upper left-hand corner of the card.
- Write the source number (from the source card) in the upper right-hand corner and the page numbers at the bottom of the card.

Exercise A   Information for four source cards is given below. On the line provided, tell what additional information is needed to make a complete source card.

1. *Silent Spring.* Rachel Carson. Houghton.

   _____

2. Jesse Stuart. Scribner's, 1968.

   _____

3. *A Walk Through the Year.* New York: Dodd, 1978.

   _____

4. *James Herriott's Dog Stories*, James Herriott. St. Martin's, 1986.

   _____

Exercise B   You're writing a report about Chinese art. You want to take notes from page 113 of your source number 5. Fill in the note card below with the proper source information.

COMPOSITION

Chapter 18: The Research Paper

| WORKSHEET 6 | *Taking Notes*

When you take notes, you can *quote directly, summarize,* or *paraphrase.*

Direct Quotation: Use a **direct quotation** only when the author's *exact words or ideas* are an especially precise or interesting way of saying something. Be sure to copy the author's exact words, using the same capitalization, punctuation, and spelling. Put quotation marks at the beginning and end of any quoted passage.

Summary: A **summary note** includes only the main ideas and the most important supporting ideas. Shorter than the original material, it allows you to save space. Write the note in your own words and sentence structure. (Most of your notes will probably be summary notes.)

Paraphrase: A **paraphrase note** includes some of the author's details, not just the main ideas. Like the summary note, it's written in your own words and sentence structure. Begin by identifying the writer whose words you're paraphrasing.

Exercise Take notes on the following paragraph about the famous "I Have a Dream" speech by Martin Luther King, Jr. On the lines provided, write notes in which you quote directly, summarize, and paraphrase (for the paraphrase note, make up the name of the author of the paragraph).

I have a dream, too—that the literary merits of Martin Luther King's "I Have a Dream" speech will be thoroughly appreciated in every speech class in the nation. It is, quite frankly, one of the finest examples of rhetoric in this century. The speech positively rings with genuine sincerity, conviction, and purpose. King's use of repetition to stir the audience and his use of biblical allusions are masterful. The speech was given on August 28, 1963, before a quarter of a million people in Washington, D.C. It moved people then, and it continues to move us today.

1. Direct Quotation:_____

 _____

 _____

 _____

2. Summary: _____

 _____

 _____

 _____

3. Paraphrase: _____

 _____

 _____

 _____

Chapter 18: The Research Paper

Developing a Thesis Statement and an Outline

During the planning stage of your research, you should identify a preliminary **thesis statement,** or main idea, of your report. To organize the information you've collected, sort your note cards into groups according to the headings you've used while taking notes. Once you've grouped the cards, decide how best to order the ideas and which supporting details to use, in which sequence. The order of the ideas and details will give you an outline of your report. At this stage, your working outline can be in rough form. For your completed paper, however, your teacher may ask for a **formal outline** using Roman numerals and capital and lowercase letters. Such an outline serves as a table of contents.

> **Outline:** I. Major heading
> A. Subheading
> 1. Detail
> 2. Detail
> B. Subheading

Exercise A   For each subject below, write a thesis statement on the lines provided.

> EXAMPLE: 1. Topic: Community volunteerism
> Thesis statement: *Volunteerism is improving life in the inner city.*

1. Topic: Competitive school sports

   Thesis statement: _____

   _____

2. Topic: Safety programs for teenagers

   Thesis statement: _____

   _____

Exercise B   On the left is a blank outline form for a paper titled "Community Festivals Are Alive and Well." Use the information on the right to fill in the blank spaces in the outline.

> I. _____   Wood items
>
>   A. _____   German music
>
>   B. _____   Craft festivals
>
>   1. _____   Touring bands
>
>   2. _____   Pottery
>
> II. _____   Local ethnic music
>
>   A. _____   Homemade crafts
>
>   1. _____   Music festivals
>
>   2. _____   Cajun music

COMPOSITION

Chapter 18: The Research Paper

WORKSHEET 8 *Using Direct Quotations*

Working a few direct quotations into your report helps make your report livelier and more believable. Follow these guidelines for using quotations.

- Use a phrase or a clause from quoted material as part of one of your own sentences.

  Sea slugs have "fringe-like gills" covering the sides and tops of their bodies.

- Incorporate a longer quotation by identifying the writer, and follow the writer's name with the quotation itself.

  Hector Alvarez writes of sea slugs, "These little creatures have fringe-like gills that cover the tops and sides of their bodies and that wave about like tentacles."

- For a quotation longer than four lines, indent each line ten spaces from the left margin. Lead into the quotation with a few of your own words (usually followed by a colon), but do not use quotation marks—the indention takes their place.

  In *In the Wake of Cousteau*, Hector Alvarez writes of sea slugs:

  > Sea slugs are technically known as *nudibranches*. *Nudi* means 'unclothed,' and *branch* means 'gill.' These little creatures have fringe-like gills that cover the tops and sides of their bodies and that wave about like tentacles. The gills are not covered by scales or a shell but rather are exposed—hence the name.

Exercise Find a resource book about sea animals or a topic of your choice. Look through the book and find three quotations that interest you. Follow the directions below and use the lines provided to write quotations from the book.

1. Use a phrase or a clause from quoted material as part of one of your own sentences.

   _____

   _____

2. Incorporate a longer quotation by identifying the writer, and follow the writer's name with the quotation itself.

   _____

   _____

   _____

3. Use a lengthy quotation. Lead into the quotation with a few of your own words.

   _____

   _____

   _____

   _____

   _____

Chapter 18: The Research Paper

 **WORKSHEET 9** *Crediting Sources*

- If the same information can be found in several sources, it is considered common knowledge, and you don't have to give credit to a source. For example, it is common knowledge that Thurgood Marshall was a Supreme Court justice.

- To show credit in the body of a research paper, use a **parenthetical citation**. Place the source information in parentheses at the end of the sentence in which you've used someone else's words or ideas. The citation should provide just enough information to lead the reader to the full source listing on the *Works Cited* page. An author's last name and a page number are usually enough for a parenthetical citation. Follow these guidelines for print sources.

WORKS BY ONE AUTHOR:	(Hughes 14)
WORKS BY MORE THAN ONE AUTHOR:	(Hughes and Blevins 102)
WORKS BY AUTHORS WITH SAME LAST NAME:	(Randy West 32) (Blanche West 19)
WORKS WITH NO AUTHOR GIVEN:	("New Uses for Old Cars" 14)
ONE-PAGE PRINT SOURCE:	(Hughes)
MORE THAN ONE WORK BY SAME AUTHOR:	(Sawyer, *Painting Today* 17)
AUTHOR'S NAME INCLUDED IN PARAGRAPH:	(12) [number follows author's name]
STYLE FOR NONPRINT SOURCES:	(KABC News)

Exercise A   Decide which of the following statements are common knowledge—not opinions, evaluations, or unproven theories—and thus do not need to be credited in a research report. On the line provided, write *CK* for common knowledge before each statement that is common knowledge.

EXAMPLE: __CK__   1. Andrew Young was mayor of Atlanta from 1981–1989.

_____ 1. Andrew Young has been a successful, dynamic politician.

_____ 2. Young was born in New Orleans, Louisiana, on March 12, 1932.

_____ 3. He was an aide of Martin Luther King, Jr., in the Southern Christian Leadership Conference.

_____ 4. Young probably could have made more contributions to civil rights if he had remained with the Conference.

_____ 5. In 1977, Young was named U.S. ambassador to the United Nations.

Exercise B   On the line provided, write a parenthetical citation for each of the following items. (Assume an author is cited only once in the report.)

1. Page 19 of *The Greek Experience* by Cecil M. Bowra, published in 1957 by New American Library   _____

2. Page 30 of *Mutiny on the Bounty* by Charles Nordhoff and James Norman Hall, published in 1932 by Little, Brown   _____

COMPOSITION

Name _____ Date _____ Class _____

 **WORKSHEET 10** *Preparing a List of Sources*

The **Works Cited** list includes all the sources you've used in your report. Such a list may be called a **Bibliography** when it includes print sources only.

BOOKS: Hamilton, Edith. *Mythology.* Boston: Little, Brown, 1942.

ENCYCLOPEDIA ARTICLES: Namowitz, Samuel N. "Tides." *The New Book of Knowledge.* 1979 ed.

MAGAZINE ARTICLES: Grunwald, Lisa. "The Amazing Minds of Infants." *Life* July 1993: 47–60.

NEWSPAPER ARTICLES: Ansley, Leslie. "Many teens feel unsafe in school." *USA Today* 13 Aug. 1993: A2.

Use the following guidelines for preparing the list of Works Cited.

- Center the heading *Works Cited* (or *Bibliography*) on a separate sheet of paper, one inch from the top of the page.
- Begin each listing at the left margin. If the listing is longer than one line, indent the remaining lines five spaces.
- List your sources in alphabetical order by the authors' last names (or if no author is listed, by the first important word in the title of the work).
- If you use more than one source by the same author, include the author's name in only the first entry. For the same author's other entries, use three hyphens followed by a period. List the author's works alphabetically by title.

Exercise Use the following items to prepare a Works Cited list.

1. a book by David Macaulay, *The Way Things Work,* published by Houghton Mifflin, Boston, 1988

2. an article by Bruce Watson entitled "Navajo Code Talkers: A Few Good Men" in the August 1993 *Smithsonian,* pages 34–42

3. an article by Randy Lilleston entitled "White House reveals community bank plan" on page 13A of the July 16, 1993, issue of the *Arkansas Democrat-Gazette*

4. *The Truth About Unicorns,* a book by James Cross Giblin published in 1991 by HarperCollins, New York

5. "London" by Dorothy Marshall, in *The New Book of Knowledge,* 1979 edition

_____

_____

_____

_____

_____

_____

_____

_____

_____

Chapter 18: The Research Paper

WORKSHEET 11 — *Evaluating and Revising*

After you write the first draft of a research report, use the following exercise to evaluate your paper.

Exercise A Based on each of the following questions, rate the research paper **1–4**, with **1** being the lowest rating and **4** being the highest. For each rating that you give that is less than **4**, explain how the report might be revised to improve that rating.

1. Does the introduction grab the reader's attention and present a clear thesis? **1 2 3 4**

   _____

2. Are ideas and information pulled together (synthesized) and stated in the writer's own words? **1 2 3 4**

   _____

3. Are ideas supported with enough information? Will readers find the information complete? **1 2 3 4**

   _____

4. Are enough print and nonprint sources of information used? Are they recent, reliable, relevant, and representative? **1 2 3 4**

   _____

5. Does all the information relate directly to the topic? **1 2 3 4**

   _____

6. Is proper credit given for each source of information used? **1 2 3 4**

   _____

7. Is the format for giving credit to sources within a report and at the end of a report carefully followed? **1 2 3 4**

   _____

Exercise B Record at least two changes that you have made on your rough draft in response to the above evaluation.

_____

_____

_____

_____

_____

_____

COMPOSITION

Name _____ Date _____ Class _____

WORKSHEET 12 *Proofreading*

Use the following exercise to proofread the first draft of a research paper.

Exercise A Proofread the paper, and record below any problems with grammar, usage, spelling, capitalization, punctuation, and manuscript form.

	Description of Problem	Location (page and line)
Grammar and Usage		

Spelling	Misspelled Words	Correct Spellings
Capitalization	Words with Errors	Words with Errors Corrected

Punctuation	Description of Problem	Location (page and line)
Manuscript Form		

Exercise B Record two changes based on the information in the above charts that you made in your paper.

_____

_____

_____

Name _____ Date _____ Class _____

Finding Books in the Library

Libraries classify and arrange books by one of two classification systems: the *Dewey decimal system* or the *Library of Congress system*. Using one of these systems, a library can give a number and letter code—a **call number**—to each book. This number tells how the book is classified and where it is placed on the shelves. In the **Dewey decimal system,** used by most school libraries, works of nonfiction and some works of literature are grouped by subject in ten general subject areas, each assigned a range of numbers. Biographies are classified separately and are arranged in alphabetical order by the subjects' last names. Works of fiction are grouped in alphabetical order by the authors' last names.

A **card catalog** is a cabinet of drawers containing alphabetically arranged cards: *title cards, author cards,* and *subject cards*. Each book has a title card and an author card; a nonfiction book also has a subject card. Cards give the call number, author, title, and publishing information of a book, and they may give the physical description of the book and indicate cross-references. An **on-line catalog** is a computerized version of the card catalog.

Exercise   Using the card catalog or on-line catalog in your library, find the following information. Write the information on the lines provided. If the information cannot be found, write *not in our library*.

1. List the title of one book that each of the following authors has written.

   a. F. Scott Fitzgerald _____

   b. Alice Walker _____

2. Look up these title cards. If the titles are in your card catalog, list the authors' names and biographical dates.

   a. *Anne Frank: The Diary of a Young Girl* _____

   b. *Shane* _____

3. Find a book in your library on each of these subjects. List a book title, author, and call number for each.

   a. Recycling _____

   b. Sign Language _____

4. List a title, author, call number, and date of publication for a book on each of the following subjects.

   a. Careers _____

   b. Poetry _____

5. List the title, author, and call number of a book about each of the following people.

   a. Amelia Earhart _____

   b. Pancho Villa _____

Resources

| WORKSHEET 2 | *Using Reference Materials* |

Your library may contain many or all of the following sources of information.

- *Readers' Guide to Periodical Literature,* which indexes articles, poems, and stories from more than one hundred magazines
- **vertical file,** a cabinet with up-to-date materials such as pamphlets, newspaper clippings, and pictures
- **microforms,** photographically reduced articles from newspapers and magazines (including *microfilm,* a roll or reel of film, and *microfiche,* a sheet of film)
- **database,** a body of information that is stored electronically on computer for easy retrieval
- **audiovisual materials,** such as audiocassettes and videotapes
- **reference books,** such as encyclopedias, biographical references, atlases, almanacs, books of quotations, books of synonyms, and literary references

Exercise A   Go to your library and find a current volume of the *Readers' Guide.* Look up a topic, and read the information given in the listing about two articles related to that topic. Then, on the lines provided, write short summaries of the information about those two articles.

Topic: _____

1. _____

    _____

    _____

2. _____

    _____

Exercise B   The items below describe information found in various reference works. On the line provided, write the type of reference where you might find the information described.

1. the most recent figure for population of New York City _____

2. the major accomplishments of Harriet Tubman _____

3. general information about nuclear energy _____

4. location of the city of La Paz _____

5. information on film from a magazine article published last month _____

6. a Red Cross pamphlet on first aid _____

7. electronically stored information about the environment _____

8. a quotation related to the subject of team spirit _____

9. information about one of Shakespeare's plays _____

10. recent statistics on crime _____

Name _____ Date _____ Class _____

WORKSHEET 3 · *Using the Dictionary A*

Different types of dictionaries vary in the kinds of information they carry and the arrangement of their contents. An **unabridged dictionary** is very large and may contain as many as 500,000 entries. An **abridged dictionary** or **college dictionary** is shorter and contains one third to one half as many words. A **paperback dictionary** contains even fewer words.

A dictionary entry includes the following information.

- **Entry word.** The entry word shows how the word is spelled and how it is divided into syllables. The entry word may also show capitalization and alternative spellings.
- **Pronunciation.** The pronunciation, which follows the entry word, is shown by the use of accent marks and either phonetic respellings or diacritical marks. A pronunciation key explains the sounds represented by these symbols.
- **Part-of-speech labels.** These labels indicate how the entry word should be used in a sentence. Some words may be used as more than one part of speech.

Exercise A Find an unabridged and an abridged dictionary in your school or public library. Look through the dictionaries and, on the lines provided, briefly compare the two. You may want to consider size, number of pages, length of entries, and kinds of entries.

_____

_____

_____

Exercise B Look up the following words in a dictionary. Copy each entry word carefully, showing syllables, accent(s), and pronunciation.

EXAMPLE: 1. hindrance *hin′drəns*

1. appropriate (used as an adjective) _____

2. appropriate (used as a verb) _____

3. address (used as a noun) _____

4. separate (used as a verb) _____

Exercise C Look up the following words in a dictionary. Give all the parts of speech listed for each word. Then give an example of how the word is used as each part of speech.

EXAMPLE: 1. kind *noun—this kind of paper; adjective—a kind person*

1. base _____

2. plate _____

3. court _____

4. forward _____

RESOURCES

Resources

WORKSHEET 4 | *Using the Dictionary B*

Following the entry word, pronunciation, and part-of-speech labels, a dictionary entry includes the information listed below.

- **Other forms.** These spellings may show plural forms of nouns, tenses of verbs, or the comparative forms of adjectives and adverbs.
- **Etymology.** The etymology is the origin and history of a word. It tells how the word (or its parts) came into English.
- **Examples.** Phrases or sentences may demonstrate how the defined word is used.
- **Definitions.** If there is more than one meaning, definitions are numbered or lettered.
- **Special usage labels.** These labels identify words that have special meanings or that are used in special ways in certain fields.
- **Related word forms.** These various forms of the entry word are usually created by adding suffixes or prefixes.
- **Synonyms and antonyms.** Sometimes synonyms or antonyms appear at the end of an entry.

Exercise A   Look up the following words in a dictionary, and write any usage labels given for each word.

1. pep   _____

2. dude   _____

3. leader   _____

4. Plutonic   _____

5. ballyhoo   _____

Exercise B   Use a dictionary to answer the following questions. Write your answers on the lines provided.

1. What is the plural form of *tomato*? _____

2. What is the correct past tense form of *sleep*? _____

3. Where does *blacksmith* come from? _____

4. What language does *futile* come from, and what meanings do you find in the

   etymology? _____

5. How many numbered definitions are listed for *form*? _____

6. What is an example sentence for a usage of *form*? _____

7. What are some related word forms of *parent*? _____

8. What are some synonyms for *freedom*? _____

9. What are some antonyms for *loud*? _____

10. What usage label is applied to both *grannie* and *cutup*? _____

Form and Parts of a Business Letter

A business letter should be typed single-spaced (with an extra line between paragraphs) or neatly handwritten (using black or blue ink) on plain, unlined 8 ½" × 11" paper. Center the letter on the page with equal margins (usually one inch) on the sides and at the top and bottom. Use only one side of the paper. Avoid messy corrections, smudges, and erasures. Check for typing errors and misspellings.

There are six parts of a business letter. The **heading** includes your address and the date of the letter. The **inside address** contains the name and address of the person to whom you are writing. The **salutation** is the greeting. It almost always consists of *Dear* and then the person's name. The **body** is the main part of the letter. The **closing** is a polite ending, such as *Yours truly, Sincerely,* or *Sincerely yours*. The **signature** is handwritten directly below the closing. Beneath the signature, type or print your name.

The two forms of a business letter are *block form* and *modified block form*. When you use **block form**, every part of the letter begins at the left margin. When you use **modified block form**, the heading, the closing, and your signature each start to the right of the center of the page, and the first line of each paragraph is indented.

Use a polite, professional tone and standard English. Explain the purpose of your letter quickly and clearly. Also, be sure to include all necessary information.

Exercise   On a separate sheet of paper, arrange the parts of the following business letter. Use one style, either the block form or the modified block form, to place the parts of this outlined letter correctly on the page. Remember to use correct punctuation marks.

1. Heading (Use your own address and today's date.)

2. Inside Address (You are writing to Ms. Sandra Alvarez, who is the manager of the Alvarez Gallery at 14 Hartford Rd. in Austin, Texas 78703.)

3. Salutation (Use *Dear Ms. Alvarez:* as your salutation.)

4. Body (To indicate the body of your letter, draw three lines. Show indentions if appropriate to your format.)

5. Closing (Use *Yours truly,* as your closing.)

6. Signature (Use your own name.)

Resources

Types of Business Letters

In a **request letter,** you ask for something, such as information about a product. An **order letter** is a special kind of request letter that asks for something specific, such as an advertised product for which there is not a printed order form. In such letters, clearly state your request. If you are requesting information, enclose a self-addressed, stamped envelope. Include all the necessary information about your request or order, and be sure to make your request well in advance of when you need the product or service.

In a **complaint** or **adjustment letter,** you report an error or state that you have not received services or products that you have reason to expect. In such letters, be prompt about registering your complaint, be sure to mention specifics, and keep the tone of your letter calm and courteous.

In an **appreciation** or **commendation letter,** you express your appreciation for a person, a group, an organization, or a product or service. Be specific about why you are pleased.

In a **letter of application,** you provide a selection committee or a potential employer with information so that a decision can be made about whether you are qualified for a position. In letters of application, start by identifying the position you are applying for, and mention how you heard about the position. Then tell something about yourself, and offer to provide references.

Exercise A On the lines provided, briefly tell about occasions when you could have written or might want to write various types of business letters.

1. request or order letter

   _____

2. complaint or adjustment letter

   _____

3. appreciation or commendation letter

   _____

4. letter of application

   _____

Exercise B You are working on a science project or social studies report. On a separate sheet of paper, write a request letter to a scientist, a specialist, or a public figure (such as your state representative or senator) requesting information about your topic. Use your own return address and today's date. Make up any other information you need to write your letter.

Name _____ Date _____ Class _____

 **WORKSHEET 7**   *Types of Personal Letters*

Most personal letters are written to communicate personal messages. Personal letters are much less formal than business letters. Use the modified block form, but do not include an inside address. There are three main types of personal letters.

- A **thank-you letter** is an informal letter of appreciation that you send to tell someone that you appreciate his or her taking time, trouble, or expense on your behalf.
- An **invitation** is a request for someone's attendance in which you give specifics about an event you are hosting.
- A **letter of regret** should be sent when you cannot attend an event to which you've been invited. If the letters *R.S.V.P.* appear on the invitation, it's especially important to send a written reply.

Exercise A   On the lines provided, write a thank-you letter to someone you know. Express your appreciation for a specific comment, gift, or action.

_____

_____

_____

_____

_____

_____

_____

_____

Exercise B   On the lines provided, write an invitation to a theme party you are hosting. The theme can be anything you like. Some possibilities are favorite literary characters, a 1950s sock hop, or a South American festival.

_____

_____

_____

_____

_____

_____

_____

_____

RESOURCES

Resources

WORKSHEET 8

Addressing Envelopes and Completing Printed Forms

Follow these guidelines to address an envelope.

1. Place your complete return address in the top left-hand corner of the envelope.
2. On the envelope, center the name and address of the person or organization to whom you are writing. For a business letter, the addressee's name and address should exactly match the inside address.
3. Use standard two-letter postal abbreviations for state names, and use ZIP Codes.

Follow these guidelines to complete printed forms.

1. Read all of the information carefully before you begin writing.
2. Type or write neatly, using a pen or pencil as directed.
3. Proofread your completed form. Make sure you have given all requested information. Check for errors, and correct them neatly.

Exercise A   Address the envelope below to the name and address listed below. You can make up a return address or use your own.

Dr. Chloe Santiago, 444 Reynard Drive, Lancaster, PA 17601

```
┌─────────────────────────────────────────────────────────┐
│                                                         │
│                                                         │
│                                                         │
│                                                         │
│                                                         │
│                                                         │
│                                                         │
│                                                         │
│                                                         │
│                                                         │
└─────────────────────────────────────────────────────────┘
```

Exercise B   Complete the form below.

```
┌─────────────────────────────────────────────────────────┐
│  Complete each item below in ink. Print neatly.         │
│  Name _____   │
│            Last              First         Middle Initial │
│  Street Address _____    │
│  _____     │
│  City                    State           ZIP Code       │
│  Age _____    Number of brothers and sisters _____  │
│  Experience fighting dragons _____     │
└─────────────────────────────────────────────────────────┘
```

Name _____ Date _____ Class _____

Manuscript Form

A carefully prepared manuscript gives your readers a good first impression of your ideas. Use the following guidelines as you make a final copy of your paper.

Handwritten papers: Use regular 8 ½" × 11" lined paper and blue or black ink. Write legibly. Use only one side of a sheet of paper, and do not skip lines.

Typewritten papers: Use regular 8 ½" × 11" typing paper. Avoid very thin (onionskin) paper and erasable paper. Use a fresh black ribbon. Double-space between lines.

Word-processed papers: Use letter-sized sheets or continuous-feed paper that separates cleanly along the edges. Make sure that the printer you use can produce clear, dark, letter-quality type. Check with your teacher to be sure that the typeface you plan to use is acceptable. Double-space between lines.

Whether your paper is handwritten, typed, or word-processed, use the following format.

- Leave one-inch margins at the top, sides, and bottom of each page.
- Indent the first line of each paragraph five spaces from the left margin.
- Number all pages (except the first page) in the upper right-hand corner, one-half inch from the top.
- Follow your teacher's instructions for placement of your name, the date, your class, and the title of your paper.
- Make corrections neatly, using nontoxic correction fluid. To insert a word or a short phrase, use a caret mark (∧) and add the word(s) immediately above it.
- Use charts, graphs, tables, and illustrations effectively. Place such materials close to the text they illustrate. Label and number each one. The standard labels are *Table* and *Figure* or *Fig.* Give each table or figure a number and title. Whenever necessary, give the source of the material.

Exercise   On the lines following the paragraph, tell which of the above guidelines the writer failed to follow.

> *There are*
> ~~*Theres*~~ *many different kinds of salamanders. People are often interes-*
>   *can grow to be*
> *ested in the biggest ones, which ~~are~~ several feet long. The largest*
> *amphibian the*
> ~~*amfibian*~~ *on Earth is the Japanese Giant Salamander. It lives*
>   *altitudes*
> *in cold shallow streams at high ~~attitudes.~~*

_____

_____

_____

Resources

Manuscript Style A

An **abbreviation** is a shortened form of a word or phrase. In the text of a formal paper written for a general (nontechnical) audience, only a few abbreviations are appropriate. However, abbreviations are used freely to save space in tables, notes, and bibliographies.

Abbreviate given names only if the person is most commonly known that way. Leave a space between two such initials, but not between three or more.

    Alice **B.** Toklas   **W. C.** Handy   **J.R.R.** Tolkien

Abbreviate social titles such as *Mr., Ms., Sr. (Señor), Sra. (Señora),* and *Dr.* whether used before the full name or before the last name alone. Civil and military titles may be abbreviated when used before full names or before initials and last names. Spell out the titles before last names alone.

    Ms. Brodsky   **Gov.** Benito Pablo Juárez   **Governor** Juárez

Abbreviate titles and academic degrees after proper names. Do not include the titles *Mr., Mrs., Ms.,* or *Dr.* when you use a title or degree after a name.

    Mangala Singh, **M.D.** [*not* Dr. Mangala Singh, M.D.]

Spell out most company names in text. They may be abbreviated in tables, notes, and bibliographies.

    TEXT: Breed and Company   TABLES, ETC.: Breed & Co.

After spelling out the first use, abbreviate the names of agencies, organizations, and other things commonly known by their initials.

    FIRST USE: United Nations   SECOND USE: **UN**

Exercise: Proofreading On the lines provided, correct the manuscript style in the following sentences.

1. My neighbor, J. B. D. Maze, studies Mexican American author Juan Sedillo (1902–1982).

    _____

2. He intends to write to the National Broadcasting Corp., asking the National Broadcasting Corp. to consider a program about Sedillo's life.

    _____

3. Mister Maze says that Sen. Sedillo's life was most interesting.

    _____

4. I refer to him as Senator Juan Sedillo because he was a New Mexico senator.

    _____

5. Maze's wife, Dr. Julia Rodríguez, M.D., said she was surprised that Sedillo apparently wrote only one piece of fiction, "Gentleman of Río en Medio."

    _____

Resources

Manuscript Style B

In text, spell out the names of states, countries, and other political units whether they stand alone or follow any other geographical term. In tables, notes, and bibliographies, use traditional abbreviations.

    TEXT: Alabama   Mexico   TABLES, ETC.: **Ala.**   **Mex.**

In text, spell out every word in an address. Such words should be abbreviated in tables, notes, and bibliographies.

    TEXT: 1020 Park Avenue   TABLES, ETC.: 1020 Park **Ave.**

Abbreviate the two most frequently used era designations, A.D. (*anno Domini*—in the year of the Lord) and B.C. (before Christ). When used with a specific year, A.D. precedes the number. When used with the name of a century, it follows the name.

In text, spell out the names of months and days whether they appear alone or in dates. Both types of names may be abbreviated in tables, notes, and bibliographies.

Abbreviate the designations for the two halves of the day measured by clock time, A.M. (*ante meridiem*, meaning "before noon") and P.M. (*post meridiem*, meaning "after noon"). Both abbreviations follow the numerals designating the specific time. Do not use A.M. or P.M. with numbers spelled out as words or as substitutes for the words *morning, afternoon,* or *evening.* Also, do not use the words *morning, afternoon,* or *evening* with numerals followed by A.M. or P.M.

In text, spell out the names of school subjects and the words *volume, part, unit, chapter,* and *page.*

Exercise: Proofreading   On the lines provided, correct the manuscript style in the following sentences.

1. Most of the information about humpback whales off the coast of Haw. comes from Chap. 3 of the new book about whale behavior.

    _____

2. Before becoming a successful author, she taught Chem. I and other sciences to high school students.

    _____

3. *European Journal,* which is on television at two P.M., frequently focuses on Berlin and other Ger. cities.

    _____

4. The castle, which is located at 1112 Naples Boul., dates from 650 A.D.

    _____

5. Do more people get married in June or Aug.?

    _____

RESOURCES

Resources

WORKSHEET 12

Manuscript Style C

In text, spell out the names of units of measurement whether they stand alone or follow a spelled-out number or a numeral. Such names may be abbreviated in tables and notes when the names follow a numeral.

TEXT: miles

TABLES, ETC.: **mi**

In text, spell out the words for the symbols % (percent), + (plus), – (minus), = (equals), and ¢ (cents). The dollar sign ($) may be used whenever it precedes numerals. Do not substitute the symbol for the word *money* or *dollars*.

Spell out a **cardinal number**—a number that states how many—if it can be expressed in one or two words. Otherwise, use numerals. Compound cardinal numbers, such as *twenty-one*, are hyphenated.

    seven miles   **two thousand** students   **5,981** beans   **thirty-four** pencils

Do not spell out some numbers and use numerals for others in the same context. If any of the numbers require numerals, use numerals for all of them. However, to distinguish between numbers appearing beside each other, spell out one number and use numerals for the other. Also, you may use words or a combination of words and numerals for large round numbers.

    We drove **3,058** miles and saw only **5** deer.

    The club members ordered **three 5**-pound bags of short-grain rice.

    She inherited **five million** dollars!   *or*   She inherited **$5 million**!

Exercise: Proofreading   On the line provided, correct the manuscript style in each of the following sentences.

1. Paul Lee, who weighed four lbs at birth, now weighs 180 lbs.

    _____

2. About 20% of the students—a significant number—were vegetarians.

    _____

3. The Novaks received 62 pieces of junk mail last week alone!

    _____

4. The company made a million $ in its first year.

    _____

5. The 12 dogs barked almost exactly at the same time.

    _____

Name _____ Date _____ Class _____

 **Manuscript Style D**

Spell out any number that begins a sentence.

Seventy-eight people signed up for the gymnastics class.

If a number appears awkward when spelled out, revise the sentence so that it does not begin with the number.

AWKWARD: Five hundred fifty-three thousand eight hundred seventy consumers unknowingly bought the faulty machine.

IMPROVED: Unknowingly, **553,870** consumers bought the faulty machine.

Spell out an **ordinal number**—a number that expresses order.

The **third** (*not* 3rd) time really was the charm.

Use numerals to express numbers in conventional situations. Spell out a number used with *o'clock*.

Elizabeth II	Room 317	pages 81–85	County Road 48
33 degrees	10.4 ounces	June 15, 1960	in 1800
2801 Ave. G	ID# 123-40-098	8:30 A.M.	two o'clock

Exercise: Proofreading   On the line provided, correct the manuscript style in each of the following sentences.

1. What is the 2nd largest country in Asia?

   _____

2. The volunteers did not have to work past 5 o'clock most days.

   _____

3. The coldest temperature this year so far is thirty-five degrees.

   _____

4. Two hundred fifteen thousand eight hundred twenty-nine vacationers have visited the attraction.

   _____

5. Philip the Second ruled during the period under study.

   _____

Resources

Manuscript Style E

In your writing, use **nonsexist language**. Nonsexist language is language that applies to people in general, both male and female.

When you are referring to humanity as a whole, use nonsexist expressions rather than gender-specific ones. For example, the nonsexist terms *humanity, human beings,* and *people* can substitute for the gender-specific term *mankind*. Most jobs are now held by both men and women. Therefore, when referring to skills and occupations, use nonsexist expressions rather than gender-specific ones.

SEXIST: mailman, stewardess

NONSEXIST: mail carrier, flight attendant

If the antecedent of a pronoun may be either masculine or feminine, use both masculine and feminine pronouns to refer to it.

Each club member was asked to bring **his** or **her** dues to the meeting.

Often, you can avoid the awkward *his or her* construction (or the alternative *his/her*) by substituting an article (*a, an,* or *the*) for the construction. Or you can rephrase the sentence, using the plural forms of both the pronoun and its antecedent.

Club members were asked to bring **their** dues to the meeting.

Exercise: Revising   On the line provided, correct the manuscript style in each of the following sentences.

1. Mankind is increasingly becoming environmentally conscious.

   _____

2. The couple's immediate reaction was to call a policeman.

   _____

3. Anyone who wants to participate in the marathon should bring his entry form to the school by Tuesday.

   _____

4. A good stewardess prides herself on being attentive to passengers.

   _____

5. The sidewalk artist worked at night and was never seen, but he left beautiful paintings for pedestrians to admire.

   _____

Resources

WORKSHEET 15   *Review*

Exercise A   Use the card catalog in your library to find the following information. If the information cannot be found, write *not in our library*.

1. Give the titles of two books that John Steinbeck has written.

   _____

2. Find a title card for the following book: *The Call of the Wild*. List the author and the subject of the book from the information given on the card.

   _____

3. In the library find two books on Mexican history. List a title and an author for each book.

   _____

4. List the title, the author, the call number, and the date of publication for a book about consumer protection.

   _____

Exercise B   You are writing a paper about a subject related to space exploration. Go to the *Readers' Guide*, and find the listings for two articles related to this subject. On the lines provided, write the title, the author, and a brief summary of the information about each article.

1. _____

   _____

2. _____

   _____

Exercise C   You are looking for information about each of the following items. On the line provided, write the type of reference you would use for each item.

1. something that someone famous said about friendship   _____

2. the title of a poem by Maya Angelou   _____

3. the capital of Mozambique   _____

4. information from a pamphlet about bicycle safety   _____

5. an article stored on film about Mother Teresa   _____

Exercise D   On the lines provided, answer the following questions about types of dictionaries.

1. What is another name for an abridged dictionary? _____

RESOURCES

Resources, Worksheet 15, continued

2. When would you use an unabridged dictionary? Name two reasons or purposes.

_____

_____

Exercise E Use a dictionary to answer the following questions. Use the lines provided.

1. What is a part-of-speech label for the compound word *terra cotta*?

_____

2. What language does the word *shampoo* come from?

_____

3. What is the special usage label given for the word *queue*?

_____

4. Should the word *Jacuzzi* be capitalized?

_____

5. What is an example sentence for a usage of the word *model*? If there is not one, make up an example.

_____

6. How many numbered definitions are listed for the word *spell*?

_____

7. What are some related word forms of the word *exhaust*?

_____

8. What are some synonyms for the word *collect*?

_____

9. What are some antonyms for the word *peace*?

_____

10. How many syllables does the word *impose* have, and how is it pronounced?

_____

Exercise F On the lines below, write the six parts of a business letter and the information each part contains.

1. _____

_____

2. _____

_____

3. _____

_____

Resources, Worksheet 15, continued

4. _____

_____

5. _____

_____

6. _____

_____

Exercise G   On the lines provided, write the body of an order letter. Request a product or a service either from a catalog or from a company. Make up the information you need.

_____

_____

_____

_____

_____

_____

_____

_____

_____

_____

_____

_____

Exercise H   On the lines provided, write the body of a thank-you letter for a gift you have received.

_____

_____

_____

_____

_____

_____

_____

_____

_____

_____

_____

RESOURCES

Resources, Worksheet 15, continued

Exercise I Address the envelope below, using the following inside address from a business letter. You can make up a return address or use your own.

Surya Balinger
14 Clement Terrace
Milwaukee, WI 53202

Exercise J Complete the following form.

Don't answer the question about music if your last name begins with a letter from A–M. Don't answer the question about sports if your last name begins with a letter from N–Z.

Name _____
         Last   First   Middle Initial

English
Teacher's
Name _____
         Last   First   Middle Initial

Favorite Kind of Music _____

Favorite Sport _____

Exercise K On the line provided, write *T* for true or *F* for false next to each statement about the preparation of a manuscript.

_____ 1. Typewritten papers should be single-spaced.

_____ 2. The first line of each paragraph should be indented five spaces from the left margin.

_____ 3. Use both sides of a sheet of paper if your paper is handwritten.

_____ 4. Number tables, but do not number figures.

_____ 5. Leave side margins of one inch on word-processed papers.

Resources, Worksheet 15, continued

Exercise L: Proofreading   On the line provided, correct the manuscript style in each of the following sentences. If a sentence is correct, write *C*.

1. D.H. Lawrence wrote novels, short stories, and poems.

   _____

2. Mister Gonzales will discuss the field trip after his last class, which is Bio. I.

   _____

3. Superintendent Lillian Siggins will retire after forty years in the Wash. public schools.

   _____

4. Sen. Perkins has moved his office to 211B Mavis Ave.

   _____

5. My father's favorite performer was Sammy Davis, Junior.

   _____

6. The Teague Bros. Construction Co. had a good reputation.

   _____

7. William's brother wants to work for the Associated Press in Germany, but the AP is not hiring right now.

   _____

8. The coin probably dates from A.D. fourth century.

   _____

9. The merger took effect on Fri., Jan. 15, 1993, at 2:30 P.M.

   _____

10. The amusing story of the coughing dragon is on pg. 193 of Chap. 7.

    _____

11. 3 guests alone drank a gal. of the famous Dairy Hollow House tea.

    _____

12. Thirty % of the voters said the election was their 1st time to vote.

    _____

13. Will the students split the $3500 reward?

    _____

14. The principal announced that twenty five students will graduate with academic honors.

    _____

RESOURCES

Resources, Worksheet 15, continued

15. The fifteen-day journey covered 4,500 miles.

_____

16. The senator made three 50-mile trips throughout her district last weekend.

_____

17. By 2 o'clock the solar heat usually sends the thermometer up to ninety-nine degrees.

_____

18. Logan's room in Japan is barely 10 feet by fifteen feet.

_____

19. The company's address is Eleven Millard Drive.

_____

20. His ancestors came to Rhode Island during the eighteen hundreds.

_____

Exercise M: Revising   On the line provided, rewrite the following sentences to eliminate sexist language and awkward constructions.

1. A fireman's job has always seemed exciting and rewarding to me.

_____

2. The news may not reflect it, but there is much good in mankind.

_____

3. Anyone who doesn't agree can write a letter to his congressman.

_____

4. "We should find a salesman immediately," Clara said.

_____

5. How much manpower do you need to get the job done?

_____